The Pope's Children

Ireland's New Elite

The Pope's Children

Ireland's New Elite

David McWilliams

Pan Books

First published 2005 by Gill & Macmillan Ltd

First published in Great Britain in paperback 2007 by Pan Books
an imprint of Pan Macmillan Ltd
Pan Macmillan, 20 New Wharf Road, London N1 9RR
Basingstoke and Oxford
Associated companies throughout the world
www.panmacmillan.com

ISBN 978-0-330-45049-2

9 8 7 6 5 4 3 2 1

A CIP catalogue record for this book is available from
the British Library.

Printed and bound in Great Britain by
Mackays of Chatham plc, Chatham, Kent

For my parents, Alice and Des

Contents

Part 2

Two Tribes: The Decklanders and the HiCos

Acknowledgements

Three special Pope's Children — Grainne Faller, Hugh Kennedy and Andrew Sheridan — helped me research this book. Not an easy task, they dug, unearthed, checked and re-checked, always with a sense of humour, indeed a sense of the absurd. They were gentle but firm in their criticisms. Like myself, they are fascinated by the changes going on in the country and their enthusiasm carried me along. Each one brought something unique to the analysis. Grainne's attention to detail, knowledge of Gaelscoileanna, rural Ireland and Whelans of Wexford Street dragged me out of my own Dún Laoghaire ghetto; Andrew's critical faculties were always well-honed in the face of my usual sweeping statements; Hugh's prescience meant he knew which way to go when I had run up a typical *cul de sac* for the umpteenth time.

Along the way I have met and written about real people in real places, all of whom have provided me with a different insight into how we are living today. Thanks to Will the bouncy castle man, Terry the *Star* van driver, the lads at Ratoath Celtic and Boyne Rovers for opening my eyes and ears to Dulchies while trying to break my legs, to Mick Gavigan for his intimate knowledge of the Kells Angels, to the producers and researchers on 'The Big Bite' for unwittingly introducing many of the book's characters, to Patrick, Pete and Gerry for putting up with 'another of Maccer's theories' and who were there back in 1979 when all this started, to Gary Coyle for tips on New York's dive-bars, to Billy Smyth for insights into Woodies and DIY in general. To every estate agent in the country for making me laugh. Thanks also to Lios na nÓg, Gerard O'Neill, Professor Jim Walsh, the National Institute for Regional and Statistical Analysis, and Tony Fahey. Thanks to all at Gill & Macmillan, in particular Deirdre Rennison Kunz for her commitment, professionalism and last-minute cool, and also to the Publishing Director, Fergal Tobin, who suggested I write a book in the first place.

The greatest thanks go to Sian for reading everything I wrote, for drafting and redrafting patiently, for gently nudging me back on track when I lost my way. This book is the product of many chats with Sian — in the kitchen when the kids finally went to sleep, on walks up Killiney Hill and over pints in Finnegans.

October 2005

Foreword to the UK Edition

Irish Blood,
English Heart

The stereotypical image of the English and the Irish as mortal enemies can be misleading.

We all ham it up when we need to. The alleged animosity is the ethnographic pantomime of these islands. It is easier to play to the crowd than to delve more deeply into our complexities. For example, when talking to a Frenchman, it is demanded that the true Irishman dislike the Englishman. This voxpop diplomacy is both endearing and reassuring. But it's not true. Ask any Irishman on a two-week summer holiday abroad who he'd rather go out with for a few drinks, and the Englishman wins hands down every time.

That is not to say that we don't applaud the dexterity of continental goalkeepers at penalty shootouts. History reserves us that right but proximity and familiarity breed not so much contempt, as resignation. We are stuck together by history, popular culture, language and geography. When we are repelled, it is by our similarities as much as our differences.

Seen from the Irish side, the cultural scoreboard reads game, set and match to England. Linguistically, we have taken your language and given you the Tory Party — from Irish *tóraighe* which means outlaw. Hardly a fair trade!

English culture has predominated to such an extent that in everyday life from the language we speak to the Soaps we watch, the magazines we read and the football clubs we support, there is little between us. The crucial difference is that we, the Irish, know everything about you, but you know very little about us. This is, at the very least, discourteous.

Most of the intelligentsia lament the dominance of all things English in Irish popular culture, but that's the way it is. Thousands of Irish people have chosen freely to have a view on Jade Goody, support Manchester United and buy *Heat* magazine. In contrast, English water-cooler moments do not involve discussions about who won the Irish *You're a Star*, nor do the English buy the *Irish Independent* or support Shamrock Rovers.

The easy conclusion is that English culture, particularly popular culture, has, in a straight line from Victorian music halls to *Celebrity Big Brother*, steamrollered indigenous Irish culture. The drivers of this cultural wrecking ball have always been economics and demographics. Ireland, the perennial economic basket case, could never stand up to English financial and commercial prowess. Size also matters in the nation game and four and a half million people don't get much change out of fifty million.

Unless you are an unreconstructed revisionist, this is more or less the way it happened. Your lot grabbed our land, slapped us around for a few hundred years and we lived off scraps. During these great sweeps of history, ordinary people made the best of a bad hand, resulting in huge emigration from Ireland to England, particularly in the past century.

Who were these people, many of whom could not speak English when they docked in Liverpool, Holyhead or Bristol? What impact did they have, where was it felt, and what is their legacy? The Irish, England's largest ethnic minority, couldn't simply have disappeared without a trace. What happened to the children and grandchildren of the great Hibernian Exodus and what did they contribute to England?

What if, contrary to conventional wisdom, the cultural story is not a one-way street? Consider for a moment the idea that the Irish immigrants, although beaten politically and economically, got their revenge by first infiltrating, then influencing and ultimately hijacking English popular culture? What if their offspring came to dominate that one area where England excels — youth culture?

HIBERNIAN ECHOES

An interesting place to start disentangling the relationship between the native English and the Irish in England and assessing their impact is to look at people's names. When two tribes physically look so similar, only your name reveals your provenance. Let's scour the names of some of the leading players in English popular culture to see where the players are from.

Do you recognise the following names?

Séan Ó Leannáin agus Pól Mac Carthainn

Yes, they do look quite foreign, very un-English. Are they minor opera singers? The accents over the vowels are off-putting, if you haven't seen them before. But on closer inspection the endings *áin* and *ainn* appear as if they come from some common root. They do: this is the Irish language — the language spoken by the ancestors, possibly great-grandparents, of these two rather influential characters of English popular culture. These names translate as:

John Lennon and Paul Mc Cartney.

Both were the grandchildren of Irish immigrants to Liverpool, as was George Harrison, whose people came from Wexford.

It probably comes as little surprise to anyone that teenagers from Liverpool in the 1960s might be first- or second-generation Irish, given that Liverpool was home to the biggest Irish community in England for years. But the issue is whether the hybrid background of these lads influenced them or not. Was the Irish origin of the Beatles a coincidence?

Before we examine that question, let's examine other players. Check out this pair of similarly foreign-looking names:

Stiofán Ó Muirgheasa agus Seán Ó Meachair.

Again they look indecipherable with the odd 'gh' spelling in the middle. The names are unrecognisable until you Anglicise them and they become Stephen Morrissey and Johnny Marr, both sons of Irish immigrants to Manchester. The Smiths, the band that defined Englishness in the 1980s and created the very English Indie scene, hadn't actually any English blood in them at all.

And what about the following pair?

Nollaig agus Liam Ó Gallchóir.

Translate these names from the Irish original to the English and you get Noel and Liam Gallagher — the crown princes of Britpop, a term coined by the music press to describe an apparently uniquely English phenomenon in the 1990s. Yet again, the Gallaghers, like the Smiths, have no English blood in them either. They are also sons of Irish immigrants to Manchester.

Another one of these hybrids in the music scene is *Sean Ó Loideáin*. Translate this into English and you get Johnny Lydon aka Johnny Rotten, a son of Irish immigrants to London. Yet again, the face that at the time epitomised the snarling, out-of-control side of English punk adolescence was also a hybrid — genetically Irish, environmentally English.

These cultural icons, all of whom have been described as quintessentially English, were actually something else. Something quite different. When today's pop-theorists are asked what England excels at, many cite music, youth rebellion and pop-culture. There is little doubt that this is where England has been at her most creative over the past forty years. The same theorists appear on arty late-night chat shows, citing pivotal names to back up their impressive-sounding arguments. In the course of this serious sociological discussion they are highly likely to trace what they might describe as an 'uninterrupted rebellious arc', from John Lennon to Johnny Rotten, to Morrissey, Liam Gallagher and Pete Doherty.

It's hard to argue against these lads being critical influences on English pop-culture, but one link stands out more than any. Examine all their original surnames, *Ó Leannáin, Ó Loideáin, Ó Muirgheasa, Ó Gallchóir and Ó Dochartaigh*. These path-breaking rebels all have anglicised versions of Irish, originally, Gaelic clan names. These radicals are not native English, but dissenting hybrids. They are part of a hugely influential tribe — English people of Irish descent.

Might this Hibernian inheritance be the defining common thread? For example, take the men the *NME* said were the most influential people over British rock culture in the past fifty years, John Lennon, Johnny Rotten and Morrissey; is it a coincidence that they were the sons or grandsons of Irish immigrants?

They themselves don't/didn't think so. All three of them have spoken fondly of their Irish roots and suggested that this was one of the factors which drove them creatively.

John Lennon in his 1974 album *Walls and Bridges* included a booklet with a history of the Lennon name taken from the rather academic-sounding *Irish Families, their Names, Arms and Origins*. Lennon is the anglicised version of the Irish original *Ó Leannáin*, which originated in Galway. Under 'Lennon', the official entry concluded that no person with the name Lennon has ever distinguished himself in the field of culture or politics, beside which Lennon wrote, in his own handwriting, '*Oh yeah? John Lennon!*'

Morrissey's 2005 single 'Irish blood, English heart' speaks for itself and, when introducing him at a home-coming gig in Manchester last year, he described himself as 'ten parts Crumlin [the Dublin suburb his parents emigrated from], ten parts Old Trafford'.

Johnny Rotten's autobiography, *No Dogs, No Blacks, No Irish*, sums up his sense of being an outsider growing up in Islington in the 1970s. The Gallaghers, who won this year's Outstanding Contribution to British Music at the Grammys, articulated their Irishness early on in their careers. In 1995, on the eve of England's hosting Euro '96 and at the height of the Britpop movement, Noel Gallagher was asked to pen the official England Three Lions football anthem, to which he responded: 'Over my dead body, mate, we're Irish.'

Gallagher's attachment to Ireland is stronger than that of many people of Irish descent in England. For most, the attachment is emotionally ambiguous; they can be English and Irish. One identity need not dominate the other. When Kevin Keegan captained England, no one thought him less English because he was eligible to play for Ireland. The relationship is fluid, open to interpretation and revision.

The issue is not that any of these musicians or sportsmen is Irish in the way Bono, Roy Keane, Des Lynam or even Terry Wogan and Graham Norton are Irish. Nor are we talking about the likes of Elvis Costello and Shane McGowan who wear their Irishness on their sleeves. The fascinating phenomenon is that Lennon, Morrissey, Lydon, Gallagher and a whole host of others (including David Bowie, whose mother, with a name like Peggy Mary Burns, couldn't have been from anywhere else) stem from that strange hybrid: the Irish in England.

They are a specific tribe, which is rarely studied yet is prominent in all walks of English life. These people are a fusion. British people with strong Irish ancestry. They are the Hiberno-British. Let's call them HiBrits for short.

Their influence on English popular culture has been enormous. The story of how this tribe influenced English culture, particularly popular culture, has never been told. However, like Jewish influence in Hollywood, the HiBrits' impact on music, TV, football and comedy — the organs of English popular culture — has been no less impressive.

THE HiBrit

The HiBrits are Ireland's demographic echo. They are the direct product of Ireland's perennial economic underperformance, which seemed to be a defining national characteristic until about ten years ago. But our loss was England's gain. England made them and reaped the rewards.

Unlike the Irish-Americans, the HiBrits' history is a silent one. Yet Tony Blair is actually more Irish than John Fitzgerald Kennedy. Blair's mother was born in Donegal whereas Kennedy's parents were both born in the US of Irish stock.

Although rarely classed as such explicitly, they are by far the largest ethnic minority in England. A recent study suggests that one in four English people are HiBrits, claiming to have some Irish background. If this is true, that is some fourteen million people. This means that today there are close to three times as many HiBrits as real Irish. This affinity with Irish roots is particularly marked amongst younger people, 42% of whom claim to be part Irish. This implausible figure may reflect the recent phenomenon whereby all things Irish are considered hip in England. Young Londoners, never slow to spot the trend, are committed. Close to 80% claim to have Irish ancestry!

I blame this figure on uber-HiBrit Dermot O Leary! (Believe me, as an Irishman, this metamorphosis is bizarre and uncomfortable for many of us Paddies. We had got used to the caricature. We're not used to being thought of as cool. We are the ones who panic at the sight of a red velvet rope outside a nightclub.)

Quite apart from the surveys, the Irish echo in England shows up dramatically in official figures. In the last census of 2001, there were six million HiBrits in England. Over one in ten of the English population have either an Irish parent or grandparent. Given that there are less than six million Irish people in Ireland today, that's quite a statistic.

When looked at from the Irish side of the channel, however, figures on the HiBrits make sense. Close to three-quarters of the Irish who emigrated over the past seventy years now live in England. By 1971, over 900,000 Irish people lived in England, while the population of the Republic of Ireland itself was under three million. The vast majority of Irish people in England came over in the 1950s when over 500,000 emigrated to England, mainly moving to Manchester, the Midlands and London. This was the period of the disappearing Ireland when three out of every four children born in the State in the 1930s and 1940s emigrated! Their children make up the lion's share of today's HiBrit population.

There was a later but much smaller bulge in the 1980s ensuring that HiBrits are continuing to be born in maternity wards all over England. But as Ireland is transforming itself and absorbing more immigrants per head than any other country in the world, emigration to England has practically dried up. But the existing Irish population in England is still significant. So while 1971 constituted the peak, thirty years later there are still over 650,000 people born in Ireland living in England.

THE IMPACT OF THE HiBrit HYBRID

What drove this tribe to make such a contribution to youth culture? Many suggest that the creative spurt can be explained by the fact that the HiBrits were outsiders — as much outsiders, according to Dermot O Leary, as second-generation Asians. While they knew they were different, the rest of society saw people of the same colour, speaking the same language and supporting the same football clubs. More than other outsiders, they were the silent ethnics. They minded their own business and tried to get on. Their parents met in newly established Hibernian clubs and the children were sent home to the Granny in Ireland for the summer. This mongrel clan, whose parents stayed silent, found its voice in English popular culture in a variety of ways. The psychology of being in the place but not quite being of it has had a huge creative impact. This is evident in every area where the English (rightly) pride themselves as having an edge. The HiBrit knew the true Brit but also knew that he was not from the same tribe, causing him to look at his neighbour slightly differently and vice versa.

Such distance or detachment is invaluable to comedians, which might explain why so many of England's top comedians, like musicians, are HiBrits. Could anyone, except Steve Coogan (both of whose parents are Irish), have had the perspicacity to create the horribly, toe-curlingly and monstrously middle-English Alan Partridge?

Partridge's antics when dealing with Irish people — for example, patronising the Irish writers of Father Ted — are so accurate (for those of us who have experienced the gaucheness of middle England) that it must come from somewhere deep in Coogan. In terms of comedy, the influence of other HiBrits such as Peter Kay, Dave Allen, Spike Milligan, Jimmy Carr, Paul Merton, Neil Morrissey, Caroline Aherne and, of course, Billy Connolly is, again, notable.

Their fingerprints are not just in edgy comedy or rebels with guitars. Smack in the centre of mainstream broadcasting we have Judy Finnigan, Dec Donnelly (of Ant and Dec), Ann Robinson, Sharon Osbourne, Dermot O Leary, Dermot Murnighan and Martha Kearney.

Arguably it's hardly surprising that the Irish make good showmen. After all, most English people, when asked, will describe the Irish as good storytellers, good partyers who tend to be better chatterers and more sociable than the average English punter. They are, like the Hollywood Jews, instinctively well suited to the stage and the limelight.

The HiBrits have been well accepted and are part of the furniture. Many argue that they are now as English as the English themselves. Well, yes and no — there is a difference. The HiBrits knew the 'otherness' as kids when they closed their front doors and entered a very un-English, Irish world of sacred hearts, domestic service, labourers, nurses, spinster Auntie Mary and hairy bacon. But this distinction was never black and white and the lines between both tribes — the immigrants and the hosts — were often blurred. Yet there was a difference and this difference was the catalyst to a creative surge.

Today, given England's multi-cultural complexion, it is hard to imagine a time, not that long ago, when the Irish were a) the only large foreign population in England and b) when they lived huddled together in Irish areas which they rarely left. Today, these Irish ghettos are gone from urban England. But if you want to get a sense of what it might have been like a few decades ago and how it felt to be white outsiders in white England, take a stroll down to one of the Irish pubs on the Harrow Road in London or the Stockport Road in Manchester. (Hurry up before the blight of the 'Gastropub' engulfs them too.)

There you'll see the twilight world of the Irish in England. Think of what it must have been like fifty or sixty years ago when these old men at the bar first arrived. Consider how this 1950s influx of off-the-boat Paddies affected the gentrified Irish who had come over the generation before and who were already moving out to the suburbs. Contrary to popular belief, immigrants of different generations did not always stick together. Plenty of their more settled, more anglicised compatriots were hardly pleased to be reminded publicly about where they had come from and what they looked like before they acquired the habits of their English hosts.

The following story illustrates the blurred nature of HiBrit identity.

In the mid 1990s, I lived in London and played soccer with a bunch of wide East End foreign exchange traders. We were pretty awful, but that wasn't the point. The thing was to get out, put yourself about and have a laugh, followed by the obligatory rake of pints in an East End pub which (inexplicably for the middle of a sunny day) had some well-endowed local stripper going through the motions up and down a rickety pole. This wasn't a lap-dancing club. It was a standard, 'Dog and Duck' Charringtons boozer. Strange, but there you go.

We were playing a game in Mile End and being hockeyed by an outfit from some telesales company or other. There were a few young Asian players, one in particular had a full bag of tricks — a sort of Indian Ronaldo with an IT qualification. Our lads couldn't get near him and no amount of knee strapping could conceal the fact that we were over-the-hill and getting a hiding.

At full time, mercifully only two down, one of the barrow-boys, bedecked in full barrow-boy mufti — sovereign rings, chunky gold chains and Torremolinos tan — proffered the following sociological observation.

'*When I was born 'ere, it was all white*', he pronounced in that cocky City way, ego bolstered by a few large bonuses.

He looked out over Mile End.

'*Now it's full of Packies! The only whites left 'ere are fuckin' Micks.*'

'But I'm a Mick don't forget!' I blurted.

'*Nah David, not your type of Mick, you're alright, I mean our type of Micks.*'

'But Jimmy Regan, with a name like that, you're a Mick too.'

'*I know way back I'm a Mick, but I'm an English Mick — if you know what I mean. I'm Free Lions fru and fru. Don't get me wrong; I'll support the Paddies — after all my people are from Cork. I'm as much of a Mick as Andy Townsend and more than Tony Cascarino, but I'm kissing the Lions not the Shamrock.*'

It's clear then from my deracinated friend that there are various different levels of Irishness. When you're real Irish born and bred, you're all right, even possibly looked up to as having something different to offer. If you're first- or second-generation London Irish and ghettoised in an Irish area like Mile End or Cricklewood or Kilburn, you're still a thick Mick and classed as such. And if you're fourth-generation Irish or even more distant and living south of the water with a clipped front and back garden, a Vauxhall Vectra and decking, you're possibly not a Mick at all.

The HiBrits are a varied bunch. The Croxteth, Levenshulme or Kilburn HiBrit is more Hiberno than British, while the Fulham HiBrit might be more Brit than Hiberno. Yet they are all part of the same tribe.

Equally over the past few years, many HiBrits have outed themselves, possibly because the sense of Irishness and what it is to be Irish has strengthened, at the expense of the sense of what it is to be English, which has weakened. There has been much written about the vacuum in English identity and possibly, because Irishness is seen as more coherent, many HiBrits have rediscovered and flaunted their Hibernian roots. Good examples of this are Morrissey, Rotten and Kate Bush (who recorded in Gaelic). In a sea of bland, being a HiBrit makes you distinctive.

In recent years, HiBrits who might have hidden their Irishness in the past, as it put them a bit too close for comfort to the mad drunk who howls at strangers in Piccadilly Tube Station, have begun to revisit their Hibernian side. This metamorphosis mirrors the changing image of Ireland in England. Where once we were feckless, lazy and drunken, the same characteristics are now seen as carefree, liberated and spontaneous — all the things that modern English corporate values squash. This change occurred sometime in the mid 1990s and has created a new vision of Ireland that is very attractive to the discerning HiBrit.

As a bizarre result, many young HiBrits develop a romantic notion of Ireland. They employ this to suggest that in the arts, having Irish blood automatically puts you in a race who, when compared with the English, are by nature more artistic less commercial, more romantic less pragmatic, more dreamy less realistic and as such more artistic/dramatic/creative. A HiBrit like Daniel Day Lewis is the poster boy for this sub-group.

The relationship among all of us is still fluid. Irishmen like me who arrived over in the early 1990s, with education and a certain amount of self-confidence, are regarded on a par. (I say self-confidence because my mother is of that generation of Irish person who thinks that people who speak with a middle-class English accent must be classier and, thus, more intelligent. She and thousands of Irish pensioners like her defer to some of the most vacuous bores known to man simply because they can pronounce 'th'.)

However, those who arrived a generation ago or two or even three, who stuck together in Irish ghettos whether they were Scotland Road in Liverpool, Levenshulme in Manchester or Mile End or Kilburn in London, these and their offspring were looked down on even by their own who had managed to embrace Englishness usually by moving to the new 1950s suburbs.

Yet the creative wave has come from this more raw second-generation HiBrit. The numbers, individuals and trends are startling. From Dusty Springfield (whose real name was Mary Catherine O Brien) and John Lennon to Pete Docherty and Cat Deely. They are everywhere.

Yet they needed England as much as England needed them. It is clear to anyone brought up in the stuffy Ireland of the 1970s or 1980s or listening to older people talking about the 1950s and 1960s, that these hybrid products of mass immigration could never have made it in Ireland. The HiBrit is a unique fusion that could neither be fully Irish nor fully English. Can you imagine Boy George (George O Dowd), Julian Clary or Paul O Grady — all HiBrits — getting away with cross-dressing in Ireland back then? They still risked being lynched in rural Ireland, where their people came from, as late as the early 1990s.

Tolerant England gave them the chance to breathe, maybe the opportunity to be outsiders and, most definitely, the commercial backdrop to express themselves in a way that Ireland, up until recently, could never have done. In a way, they have drawn from the well of both cultures and forged something special. They — the HiBrit pop aristocracy — have contributed enormously to English popular culture, creating a generational echo of millions of Irish immigrants who wanted to speak but felt that they had to keep their heads down. Today, through their children and grandchildren, they are being heard.

Today we are at a crossroads because the single most important factor in creating the HiBrit is demographics. The economic renaissance of the New Ireland means that the relationship between the two peoples has changed. It is like an ageing marriage. Power is shifting. The once virile, overbearing and dominant husband is getting doddery and the formerly pliant wife, who is still sprightly, is getting bolshy. As Ireland's economic performance surges ahead of England for the first time ever (the Irish are now on average 20% richer than the English) the flow of people and money between the two countries is reversing.

The affair has come full circle. For the past two hundred years, the poorer Irish emigrated to England and the richer English invested their money in Ireland, today, the opposite is the case.

Now the poorer English are emigrating to Ireland seeking opportunity and the richer Irish are investing in England seeking capital gain. According to the last Irish census, the English are the largest ethnic minority in Ireland. Half of our 400,000 new immigrants come from England. Not so long ago, Irishmen were blowing up London's trophy buildings; today they are buying them up. From Wentworth Golf Club to the Savoy and the Gherkin, Irish investors are the biggest foreign players in the UK property market. The Micks have gone from put-upon tenants to absentee landlords in one generation.

What will happen to the HiBrit tribe and their place in English popular culture? Where will the next Morrisseys, Lennons, Lydons and Gallaghers come from? And equally, from the Irish perspective, will tortured second-generation English immigrants in Ireland be the font of a new type of Irish creativity?

The economic miracle in Ireland is not only of interest to English people in the narrow financial or political sense of how was it achieved and whether England can learn anything or even copy it. (As the possible next Chancellor George Osborne was suggesting in *the Times* recently.)

Arguably a more interesting question is what will happen to the relationship between these two great tribes of this part of the world. To get a handle on this, let's take a trip to the oldest Irish community in England which has produced that newest and most explosive HiBrit: Wayne Rooney.

WAYNE ROONEY — PORTRAIT OF A HiBrit

The 7.55 am Ryanair FR442 — one of the hundreds of jets Mick O'Leary bought in the post 9/11 Boeing fire-sale — takes off on time, bound for Liverpool. Out past the suburbs — over the giant steel and chrome motorway slug of commuting morning traffic and straight across the Irish Sea. It is only thirty-five minutes to John Lennon International which is not enough time for even Ryanair to sell you something.

As you come through security the first sign welcoming you to England tells you that 'Blackpool is Brilliant'.

Surely neither John Lennon's grandad, the Dublin seaman Jack

Lennon, nor his grandmother, Mary Maguire, ever thought anything would be named after one of their own when they both, like millions of other Irish, made the same trip, never to return home.

The Croxteth orchestra of sirens, shouting kids and screaming mothers is momentarily drowned out by the traffic on the East Lancs. This place is home to the longest continuous Catholic congregation in the North of England. The Blood of the Martyrs Catholic Church — named according to the local priest, Father Inch, because Catholicism in this part of England was maintained by the blood of the martyrs — is where Wayne Rooney was baptised and confirmed a Catholic — an Irish Catholic.

Father Inch is a Toffee true and true. Everton Football Club is the Irish team in Liverpool and it's no surprise, therefore, that Rooney is a Blue.

Bob Pendleton, the Evertonian who scouted Rooney, remembers seeing young Wayne for the first time aged nine. Jeanette, his mother, would take him and his two brothers on the bus down to Fazakerly to play for Copplehouse in the Walton and Kirkdale Junior League. Wayne was a different class to the rest. Other HiBrit kids, Jamie Carragher, Danny Murphy and Steve Mc Manaman, came from the same schoolboy league in the years before Rooney, but talented as they were, none had the scouts whispering the way Rooney did. Bob remembers that Rooney was so keen to play and get on with the game that when the ball was kicked over the walls into Everton Cemetery it was always Wayne who hurtled over amongst the headstones to get the ball.

The Cemetery itself tells the story of Liverpool's immigrants — not just the Irish. You can see that Liverpool was multicultural way before most other English cities. There is a huge Jewish part, host to Ringo Starr's people, who arrived in the great Jewish migrations from Eastern Europe of the late 19th century, while today, enormous Chinese mausoleums testify to the changing immigrant aristocracy in modern Liverpool. Quite apart from the other immigrant tribes, the names on the headstones evidence the presence and passing of the biggest minority: O' Briens, Forans, O' Haras, Mc Cabes and Kellys.

Given the joy Wayne brought even as a child playing here, it saddens Bob that the roof of the dressing rooms at Fazakerly was daubed for weeks on end with 'Rooney You Scab' when he signed for United.

Down the road, past East Derby, is the Western Approaches, the Rooney family's local. There's something about the smashed car windscreen glass, which fragments into thousands of particles, that tells you you'd better walk in here with a local. It's early afternoon, school's just finished and skinny young lads on bikes are doing wheelies, trying to avoid the teenage mothers whose top-of-the-range strollers suggest that, despite the recent Revenue assessment, the Giro isn't the only income in the house.

There's a small lad with no neck, poured into an Everton strip, swearing at a William Hill betting slip, while a few women in pink pyjamas are hanging around Cost Cutters, having a smoke and a natter. No-neck steals up behind one of the grans and takes her from behind. Everyone pisses themselves and no-neck makes off bright red from the laughing.

A Citroën Sax weighed down by an enormous subwoofer blasts rap out at the traffic lights. 'Slapper' shouts one of the young lads, as he grabs his crotch and thrusts in her direction. The girl in the passenger seat, in pristine white Juicy Couture, hoop de hoop earrings and full Croydon facelift, gives him the licked finger as she pulls off. Older ladies with tartan trolleys wait patiently at the bus stop, oblivious to the pubescent girls from Saint Swithin's Primary scratching their fellas' names on the shelter.

Bob, the local Everton scout, who met his missus in the Western, points me up to the bar. Gerard Houllier was amazed, he said, when looking for talent that there were no black kids in Croxteth.

This is a HiBrit neck of the woods. Most people here are straight from Scotland Road — the traditional home of the Liverpool Irish. In fact, Scottie Road was so Irish that, in the late 19th century, it returned an Irish Home Rule MP for years. The Western is simply Costigans on Scottie Road forty years on: the same people, the same names and the same culture.

The door opens grudgingly. We are in familiar surroundings: red carpets, screwed-down barstools, flock wallpaper, posters advertising bingo and tired men and women. Skinny old men with hollow cheeks scan their betting stubs, while local brazzers reveal a bit too much on top, as they shout across the bar for their fourth Smirnoff Ice. We get stuck in, chatting with a few punters on the Irish theme.

'*Alright Bob.*'

'*Couple of lagers please.*'

'*Rooney's never,*' says a visiting Geordie whose two loves are Newcastle and Everton.

'He is, you know, just look at the name. No Longshanks were ever called Rooney.'

'Not one English ounce?'

'Not a drop.'

'He's pure Scottie Road Irish.'

'On both sides?'

'Yep, Holy Cross parish.'

'On the Murray side too?'

'Sure Jeanette's ma's name's Patricia Fitzsimons.'

'Good job Jack Charlton didn't see him when he was a nipper.'

'Too right.'

'How far back?'

'Four generations.'

'No fucking way.'

'He's hardly English at all.'

'Just look at him — he looks like a Mick!'

'Two more pints of lager please, a whiskey chaser, a pack of Lamberts and one for yourself.'

Just as the racing was about to start there was a newsflash announcing that North Korea had just successfully tested a crude nuclear bomb. BBC News 24 went all serious. The weirdest state on earth has just stuck its jaw out, bared its teeth and challenged the world to, 'C'mon have a go if you think you're hard enough.'

John Reid, the Home Secretary, is put out to bat and is prattling on about Britain's international duty to react to this threat to world security. He is joined by Tony Blair at a hastily convened conference and they are both interviewed by Martha Kearney. If you thought HiBrits were limited to music, comedy or football, think again. Here are three of them making and dissecting Britain's foreign policy. When you scratch the surface, the HiBrits are everywhere from top to bottom.

At a small table, close to the loo, is Patricia Fitzsimons — Wayne Rooney's Nan. Even before Wayne exploded onto the scene, Patricia Fitzsimons, whose lot are from Derry, was famous locally for being born on 17 March, St Patrick's Day — hence the name Patricia. The first thing you notice is the crucifix and her clear, strong blue eyes. Straight off she starts referring to herself as Irish and to me as 'one of our own'. Within seconds she's back in 1960s Liverpool sharing memories of running away from the King Billys (as she calls them) on 12 July, reiterating just how sectarian the city was until recently.

The Western is rocking now. A few winners, a few pints and the place is alive. It's Monday afternoon, late October, and Patricia is talking about some German professor who claims to be Wayne's half-brother. Billy Murray, Wayne's grandad, pulls up a stool and starts reminiscing about sectarian scraps in the 1960s. The Orangies were always causing trouble and throwing bricks at his Patricia when she was looking beautiful in her finest Hibs Irish dancing costume at the top of the St Patrick's Day Parade.

The Western is the type of pub that works. Located at the end of the street where young Rooney first went to school at Our Lady of St Swithin's Catholic Primary, it might not be pretty, but it and the adjacent Our Lady of the Martyrs Church, where Father Inch baptised Wayne, are at the heart of this community.

Across the road is St John Bosco Catholic School for Girls where one Miss Colleen McCullough graduated three years ago, and within 100 yards is De La Salle Brothers Catholic Secondary School for Boys, where the man-child Rooney honed his footballing skills.

This is an Irish part of town. All the older people, like Patricia Fitzsimons, were moved here in the slum clearances of the late 1940s and 1950s. They, like thousands of Irish before them, lived in Scottie Road, as they call it. Scottie was the first port of call for desperate Irish emigrants who flooded Liverpool for over 100 years after the Famine.

Like its black community, Liverpool hosts the oldest Irish community in Britain and Irish immigrants and their descendants have been central to the development of the city. As Liverpool's economic strength declined, so too did new arrivals from Ireland. Yet, even today, when only 10% of the population of England is Catholic, 60% of Croxteth's children are baptised Catholic. They are Irish, Catholic, Evertonians and proud of it.

'*Could Wayne have played for Ireland?*' I whispered, thinking of all those HiBrits who'd worn the Green. From Steve Heighway to Ray Houghton, who headed England out of the 1988 Euro Championship, and Kevin Sheedy, who equalised against England in the 1990 World Cup. There was John Aldridge, Andy Townsend and John Sheridan. The list goes on and on.

And what about the HiBrits who played the other way — four recent English captains: Kevin Keegan, Steve McMahon, Martin Keown and Tony Adams?

'*Nah,*' replied Patricia, '*he's English on the outside.*'

She looked up, '*But, pure Irish on the inside.*' She checked her betting slip, looked up again. '*He's a half-breed.*'

TABLES TURNED — THE END OF THE HiBRIT?

On 8 June 1999 something monumental occurred in the relations between Ireland and England. On that day, Ireland officially became richer than England. Since then a yawning gap has opened up with average Irish incomes today almost 20% higher than those across the water.

This has created a new type of Paddy in England, it has prompted the biggest movement of people from England to Ireland since the Tudor Plantations and it has also probably sounded the death knell for the HiBrit.

London City Airport

Beep, beep. Is there any peace? And what do they think is so urgent that they are punching in their passwords before we actually land? Mobiles are on; the corporate world is ready for battle. The suits check their messages frantically while the air hostess tut-tuts through her armour of Mac foundation trying to signal that we haven't landed yet. Ignoring her, the battalion of Armani horn-rimmed glasses furiously search for a local network. They've been in the air from Dublin for all of fifty minutes. Who knows what financial tsunami could have struck in the meantime? The lawyer (there's always a lawyer who thinks the deal is his and speaks of it in proprietorial terms) is trotting behind his masters, worried sick about the terms in one of the financing tranches. Hopefully, he'll be able to sort it out with his opposite number at Linklaters.

These are changed Paddies in changed times.

The deal they are closing is the largest leveraged property deal any of them have been involved in. The debt/equity split is 95% and the syndicated notes further down the food chain are practically junk. If anything goes wrong in the London commercial market, those holders are toast. But they don't care. Back in Dublin bragging rights are afforded to those who are 'part' of these deals. Boomtime Dublin, particularly at the top table, is a nose-tapping fest. Those in the know tap their prominent noses, suggesting that they are in on some deal from which the others are excluded. Being part of a syndicate is now the Holy Grail and being involved in the biggest deal thus far confers balls on the person. In a town of wannabes, you are a player.

The past few years have been a roller coaster as the Irish have gone from the lads who built, to the lads who buy. They are now the largest foreign investors in the UK property market. Last year, 53% of all deals done with foreigners in the London market were done with Irish investors. Landmark buildings like Battersea Power Station, Harvey Nichols and Bishopsgate have also recently been snapped up by Irish oligarchs.

The black cab moves quickly from City Airport (owned by the same Irish oligarch who owns Celtic FC). It pulls up at 100 Liverpool Street, home of UBS, one of Europe's largest banks. As always the 'power foyers' of these places are full of the same types. Power women race for the door, clutching their yoga mats for the lunch-time alignment of their chakras. They brush past the preening French financial analyst, head to toe in his 'le look anglais', who reverentially brandishes his sushi. Upstairs on the dealing floor, American gym-bunny salesmen with their ties swept over their shoulders tuck into alfalfa and beansprout salad, eyes glued to screen, bloomberging early-bird college friends in Wall Street. The cosmopolitan elite like to stay in touch.

Back downstairs, to the faint synchronised chimes of lifts ascending and descending, the twin-setted and pearled Sloaney fund manager, all expensive blonde highlights and pencil skirt, rabbits into her top-of-the-range Motorola camera phone, while two identically turned-out Japanese businessmen in neat-fitting navy suits and twin-like side partings get their shoes shined by the automatic 'buff-stop shoeshine'. Even the new Irish property oligarchs on their way out this morning to buy half the West End haven't the chutzpah to get their brogues polished in public.

The Irish oligarchs — unlike many other multi-millionaires — haven't much time for the obsequiousness of investment bankers. They realise there's more to business than a signet ring on the little finger, a pink shirt and bespoke suit. They also understand that behind all the bluster, the bankers are simply employees; well paid, well-heeled, but employees nonetheless. Bankers are salarymen who believe in insurance, market signals and respectability. The oligarchs, in contrast, believe in risk and have bungee-jumped into the property market — many pleasantly surprised that the elastic rope hasn't broken yet.

But this deal is mega. It involves a mix of residential and commercial buildings all over the West End, from Piccadilly, to St James's and down to Knightsbridge. The one-billion-pound transaction will be financed by various different tranches of debt. The ultimate owners will be the four men around the table, but at least fifty smaller investors will be needed to get it over the line and they will use the smarmy Sandhurst bankers to find them.

Times have changed, Ireland has been transformed and its relationship with England is undergoing an enormous makeover. Ireland's people used to be England's poor cousins, providing cheap labour for the English economy and turning run-down areas into Irish ghettos.

In turn, England saved millions of Irish from destitution in their homeland, a country that seemed incapable of getting its economic act together. These migrants formed the Irish community and in turn spawned the HiBrits who have affected English popular culture and profoundly added to the mix that makes the English who they are. Their presence over the coming generations will be missed by both tribes.

This book is about that demographic, economic and social change in Ireland. This book is about why the conveyor belt that served England so well and generated the HiBrits has stopped. It is about why there'll be no more Morrisseys, McCartneys, Lennons, Gallaghers, Lydons, Keegans and Rooneys.

This is about the last of the HiBrits.

Part I

Where are we now and how did we get here?

Chapter 1
Full-On Nation

Ireland has arrived.

We are richer than any of us imagined possible ten years ago. No Irish person has to emigrate, none of us need pay for education and even our universities are free. Unemployment is the lowest in our history. We have more choice than ever, the place is more tolerant and no-one can be legally discriminated against. We have more cash in our back pockets than almost anyone in Europe. We are better off than 99% of humanity. We are top of foreigners' lists as places to live. Unlike many of our rich neighbours, in survey after survey we claim to be very happy.[1] We no longer need to beg from others in the EU; in fact, we are giving them cash. We are a success. We have money and time. We can now afford to kick back and take stock, reflect and relax a bit. Why not go for a walk, be frivolous or just stop the clock and slow down? The hard part is over. Or at least that's what you might think. If economists ruled the world they would say that Irish people will react to their new-found elevation by behaving rationally. We would take more days off, spend time with our families and chill out.

But instead of winding down and luxuriating in our new-found wealth, we are accelerating as never before. We have to be there first, have the best, the brightest, the newest and the biggest. We must also be the ones who are most fun, loudest, best *craic* and most off our head. We are borrowing, spending, shopping, shagging, eating, drinking and taking more drugs than any other nation. We are

Europe's hedonists and the most decadent Irish generation ever. Interestingly, this carry-on is ubiquitous. At one end of the scale, Irish teenagers are losing their virginity and taking drugs earlier, while at the other end of the scale, our forty and fifty-somethings are binge drinking, swinging and hoovering cocaine to allow them to stick the pace and have one last drink. We are the full-on nation.

We are eating more than ever, obsessing about food, writing about it, talking about it and savouring it. We are in ingestion heaven. We are getting fatter, quicker. Not so long ago, we were skinny and all our hard men were wiry little fellas who wouldn't have been out of place on the set of *Trainspotting*. Of all the characters in Irving Welsh's novel about four young Edinburgh skangers, Begbie was the most realistic and the scariest, the quintessential psychopath, the hardest hard chaw on the estate, a man who would glass you as soon as he'd shake your hand. In the follow-up film, Robert Carlyle expertly played Begbie. And Carlyle's Begbie 'hadn't a pick on him'. When I read *Trainspotting*, my Begbie was scrawny, wiry, contorted, unstable and extremely violent. Most of all, he was skinny.

Growing up in Dún Laoghaire in the 1980s, I remember all the hard men were sinewy, scrawny lads, hence the local description 'more meat on a seagull'. The reason was simple: they were undernourished. Perched on the church wall in the town were skinny, arseless lads, spitting and smoking Majors. The young wans, despite a couple of babies, were more or less the same, pinched, flat-chested and drawn. Today, Dún Laoghaire's hard men are fat. Rolls of flab strain the Liverpool away strip. Double chins are *de rigueur* and little piggy eyes are squeezed into sockets among the flab. Gravity has also got the better of the young wans, as their corpulent bums, like two puppies in a bag, make unsightly bids for freedom over their entirely ill-advised ultra low-rise jeans.

According to the national task force on obesity, 30% of Irish women are overweight and a further 12% are obese, while nearly half of Irish adult males are overweight and 14% are obese.[2] We are gorging ourselves into an almost certain diabetes epidemic. Even our babies are coming out bigger. We are turning into a race of Sumo wrestlers with 20% of our infants weighing more than ten pounds when they are delivered — up 400% from the same figure in 1990.[3] Is this any surprise when we spend more on crisps than on pharmaceutical drugs? According to the latest household budget survey,[4] our spending on chip shops and takeaways went up by over 70% in the past seven years. We also increased spending on sweets by just over 50%, while we spent 42% more on sugary soft drinks. We spent €721 million on teeth-rotting fizzy drinks last year, almost twice as much as we do on calcium-rich milk. Is it any wonder that diabetes is the fastest growing disease in the country when our Kit Kat and Snickers bill alone per year dwarfs our total spending on organic food? And it is the poor who are becoming fatter quickest. Only 8% of university graduates are obese, whereas close to one in five of those who left school before the Junior Cert are waddling around in sports wear, getting sores between the thighs as their blubber legs rub up against each other. In the past, fatness was a sign of wealth, education and privilege. In contrast, the poor were skinny. These days, the rich and smart are thin.

But just in case you believed the spin of *Loaded* and *Cosmo* and thought that only thin people have vigorous, varied and interesting sex lives, think again. The blubbery Paddies are going at it like rabbits. We are having sex on average 105 times a year — that puts us way above the abstemious Japanese who only cop-off 47 times a year, but far below the amorous French and Greeks who get it 137 and 133 times respectively.[5] Irish women love talking about sex and in a recent survey Irish women said that they were happiest when they were talking about sex to each other. Carrie, Miranda and the other two, please step forward. When it comes to talk, however, in typical Irish fashion we are saying one thing and doing something completely different. For example, according to a Durex worldwide survey,[6] just over half of us claimed, responsibly, that we were worried about contracting HIV, yet 52% of Irish people have had unprotected sex. We are also having lots of sex younger; typically we start at seventeen and have on average eleven sexual partners. Irish teen mags are getting much more explicit. One I just picked up in Eason's which was stuffed with sex tips, adult chat lines and phone sex numbers came with a free — wait for it — packet of children's sweets! I wonder what age group is its target market.

Meanwhile back in bed, in a break with our full-on hectic lifestyle, Irish men take their time. We are the third most generous, thoughtful and slow lovers in the world, spending on average 21.8 minutes on foreplay, but this seems to be wasted time because only an underwhelming 17% of Irish women orgasm during sex. Clearly lots of spade-work but not much technique from the Paddies. But not to worry, you'd never know it because four in ten Irish women have faked orgasms in the past twelve months. So the lads can avoid the wet patch and roll over happy. This may also go some way to explaining why 36% of Irish women claim to own a vibrator.

We are also becoming more adventurous. Nearly half of us use blindfolds or handcuffs, while close to one in three like to dress up. 48% of Irish lovers watch porn together, while the camcorder is quite busy, with 23% liking to video each other. This voyeurism is exceptional and much more evident here than in other countries. And a kinky 31% of Irish lovers are into spanking — way above the global average of 19%. So the suburbs are considerably more interesting places than the pebble dash would suggest, and behind our lace curtains, anything goes. We are considerably more expressive in the scratcher than we'd like to admit openly. We suggest innocently that the two sexiest attributes in our partners are eyes and a sense of humour — God bless the patent leather obsessed nuns, you did a good job. This innocent response contrasts with the up-front Brazilians who put boobs and ass as the two sexiest features. But spare a thought for all those new millionaires knocking around thinking they are big swingers: we rank wealth as being entirely immaterial when it comes to sexiness. So put your Kompressor away, it doesn't do it for her. Just to prove that democracy is alive and well, in the full-on nation you can be poor and very sexy.

MAD-FOR-IT NATION

If there is one thing that the full-on nation is not demure about it is our boozing which is now off the scales. We are heroic drinkers and Ireland is the only place on earth where mature family men boast like students about necking ten pints the night before. Drinking is an Irish badge of honour. It knows no class barriers. Rich and poor — we are all guzzlers. In fact it is fair to say that many of us are suspicious of non-drinkers, particularly if they are *not* recovering alcoholics. Immigrants, many of whom now work behind our bars, are shocked by the sight of teenagers vomiting in the loos, wiping themselves, putting on a bit of lippy, marching back to the bar and ordering another double Vodka and Red Bull. Twenty-five years ago we spent €3.4 billion on booze but that figure has almost doubled and now the nation is spending an astonishing €6.5 billion annually on the demon drink. And it is not just stout and whiskey, although the stout figures are startling. We spent €1.6 billion on stout which not only is 20% of the entire global market, but is some €400 million more than the total Department of Education budget for all primary school education in this country. Wine drinking has sky-rocketed. We now drink more beer than the Germans, far more alcohol than the supposedly alcoholic Russians. We are on a national bender; we spend more in restaurants, more in off-licences and at the bar than anyone else.

When it comes to drink and drugs we are Keith Richards, Axl Rose and Brendan Behan all rolled into one explosive mix. Young Irish women drink not twice or three times but ten times more than their Italian equivalents. Four out of five of our young men are regular drinkers compared to 34% of the EU average. We drink more pure alcohol than anyone else in the world at 25.3 pints on average per person per year. That is three times more pure distilled alcohol than we have blood in our veins. It's a wonder we are still alive. Contrary to popular myth, we have not always been the mad-out-of-it nation. Back in the early 1960s, Ireland's boozing was the fifth lowest in the OECD with eight countries guzzling more than us. Now we are on a national binge, buying rounds, shorts, bottles of wine, snakebites, pints, glasses, naggins, small ones and quick sharpeners, with the result that we are the drinking champions of the world. We drink more than any other nation. Interestingly, there was a spike in boozing in the mid-1990s and we have been drinking copiously since then. So the correlation between drinking and money is quite marked — as we have got wealthier, we have got drunker.

We admit to drinking on average 262 pints of beer each a year which is the second highest in the world after the Czechs. We are the world's number one cider drinkers. We spend more on booze than anyone else, forking out €1,584 per head on drink every year[7] — that's more than we do on health insurance. Lucozade, a proven hangover healer which does not sell well at all in the UK, is the biggest selling pharmaceutical product on the market, while Solpadeine, a strong headache relief tablet, is also a huge seller every morning of the week. This is interesting because there are many people addicted to soluble Solpadeine and the high incidence of Solpadeine sold here reflects both hung-over drunkards and over-the-counter addicts.

The expression a 'water cooler moment' means something quite different in Ireland to anywhere else in the world. Everywhere else it is used to describe the office event that takes place when employees natter away beside the water cooler. It is associated with the buzz of gossip. In Ireland, water coolers are silent. They are essential, life-saving rehydration stations for hungover employees, twenty-somethings experiencing menopausal hot-flushes that can only be banished by buckets of water. No-one speaks at Irish water coolers.

And one of the most significant developments is that we drink considerably more than anyone else despite alcohol being very expensive here and, as prices have gone up, we have drunk more! So not for the first time, the laws of economics are turned on their heads in Ireland. Our sociability gets the better of us always. We love going out. Four drinks out of five are sunk in the pub and, remarkably, when we don't go out we don't tend to drink heavily at home. This contrasts with the rest of the world where people drink mainly in the privacy of their own home. We are exhibitionists. We like getting locked in public. In beer-guzzling Germany, for example, only one third of all booze is drunk in bars. The Irish are desperately addicted to company as well as alcohol. We can't stand being on our own.

When it comes to Irish teenagers, the full-on nation becomes even more apparent. This will not surprise anyone; I have yet to meet someone who did not start drinking early in bus shelters, fields, half-built estates, on the streets or in back gardens. That is what we do. In another study[8] of 35 nations, the Irish came out top of the delinquent league for underage boozing. We have the highest level of teen binge drinking. One in three of our sixteen-year-old girls has been drunk more than ten times in the past year. Along with the Danes, Irish boys binge drink, get plastered and then typically lose their virginity to people as hammered as they are. While Danish boys might be up there with our boys, Irish girls are peerless when it comes to boozing. But they seem to be just about able to get the rubbers on because we are not having any more teenage mums than we had ten years ago, so we are slightly more responsible than you'd expect after five Alco pops.

But just in case you thought we weren't messy enough, we are necking Es like Smarties. The UN claims that the Irish are the second biggest users of ecstasy in the world after the Aussies.[9] The price of ecstasy has dropped dramatically and it is the drug of choice for the new generation. When ecstasy first arrived on the scene it cost £20 a tab. It now costs €5 (or a dozen for €50), which is considerably cheaper than a gin and tonic in most bars. But it's not limited to teenagers. The middle youth generation, who simply won't grow up, are at it big time. Many 40th birthday parties have been kept rocking due to liberal amounts of ecstasy being munched by respectable professionals. Biology suggests that forty year olds rarely last till dawn unless of course they are powdering their noses. Again the price of cocaine has dropped precipitously and a recent RTÉ 'Prime Time' documentary indicated that 80% of suburban loos had traces of chopped lines on their surfaces.

Drug use in Ireland knows neither class nor region. Provincial Ireland rather than Dublin is the E epicentre of Europe and back in Dublin 4, crisp €50 notes are being rolled perfectly every night as society hostesses hoover up cocaine just before the canapés are served by Filipino radiographers in dinner jackets. The Irish drug scene is a recreational affair mainly. Fuelling this are parties. We are having more parties than ever before: 18ths, 21sts, 30ths, 40ths, 50ths, weddings, 2nd weddings. We are engaging professional party organisers and keeping an entire industry of garden marquee sellers in business. And we want more. In a recent survey,[10] when asked what we would do with more money 57% of us said that we 'would enjoy ourselves more' as opposed to only 25% who said they would support a good cause. Similarly, when asked what we'd do with more time, 50% said we'd enjoy ourselves more.

We eat more chips than the British. We eat more chocolate than the Belgians — in fact we are third in Europe for chocolate munching. And, remarkably, we spend more on snacks than prescribed medicines. And for a nation that proudly claims to read more newspapers than any other, we actually spend more in the bookies than we do on newspapers. The punter nation is now gambling 24/7. Horseracing is the fastest growing sport in the country and its hand-maiden, gambling, is booming. We are betting, squaring, laying, accumulating, forecasting, spread betting, calculating, winning and losing fortunes every day. Shares in Paddy Power the bookmaker are trading at twenty times earnings which implies that even the stock market sees massive growth in this business over the coming years.

Any objective chronicler would deduce that if we are being so hedonistic we must also be indolent, lazy and work-shy. Nothing could be further from the truth. Miraculously, the Irish are the most productive workforce in the world.

So when we are not betting, drinking, snorting, eating and generally good-timing, we are working, commuting, taking work home, working weekends or changing jobs. We aspire to have full diaries. No more hanging about for the Irish; we have rejected the stereotype of good partyers, bad workers. As Mick Wallace might say, the full-on nation plays hard and works even harder. We want to be busy, hard-working and sorted. Have you noticed that 'how are you?' has been usurped by 'are you … busy?' This suggests a subliminal preoccupation. In China, the expression used most often is 'hello, how are you, have you eaten?' which describes the fact that in a country with so many famines, being hungry is a state of being. In Ireland that condition is busy. To be busy is now regarded as a state of grace and to be not busy is to admit failure.

A recent survey[11] by O2 of the Irish self-employed found that we are workaholics: 60% of bosses are working more than 40 hours a week and 13% of them work more than 63 hours a week. Just under half miss special family occasions such as weddings, anniversaries, birthdays or communions because of work. Four out of five work weekends and 43% do not take their full annual leave entitlement. Half of Irish bosses claim that their way of relaxing is the healthy activity of vegging in front of the TV, while one in three go drinking in the pub and a quarter go shopping. Irish workers are also slaving. The average worker puts in more hours per week than any other Europeans apart from the Brits. One in twelve has at least two jobs, which is well above the EU average, and because we spend twice as long commuting, the work experience, particularly for commuters, is typically eating up about ten to twelve hours of our day. Many workers leave before seven and get home after seven.

When we are not working, we are changing jobs. Over 100,000 of us will sell ourselves, doctor our CVs, inflate our past experience and lie about our achievements next year. This is because one in every twenty of us will change job and practically all of us will be moving upwards. Our papers bulge with ads luring us to other challenges that always offer breadth, depth, complexity, always demand high performance and always promise substantial rewards for the right candidate who is always accomplished, a good team player and flexible. These recruitment ads sound more like a lonely hearts column than a job spec. Interestingly, after property ads, they generate more money for newspapers than any other category.

Although we are all working harder in the full-on nation, it is Irish women who are working much harder than ever. Since the late 1980s the number of women working has more than doubled (116%), while the number of men has gone up but only by 43%. Women are obsessively front-loading their careers which means they are working extremely hard in their twenties to try and scurry up the corporate ladder and are postponing having children until much later. The average age of an Irish mother giving birth this year is thirty and seven months — the oldest in the EU.[12] Even before the kids arrive, we are sleeping less and drinking more Red Bull — last year, we spent over €100 million on energy drinks[13] — to keep us awake.

OVER-HYPED, OVER-SPENT AND OVER-DRAWN

According to one *Irish Times* report, the arrival of the Hermes handbag store in Brown Thomas was welcomed by someone enthusing that 'it was a great day for the country'! It is clear that Ireland is a shopaholic nation with an insatiable appetite for newness. This year we will spend €70 billion consuming.[14] That is over €20,000 or close to three quarters of the average industrial wage for every man, woman and child in the country! And when we are not actually out elbowing competitors aside in superstores or boutiques, we are talking about shopping, reading about shopping and thinking about shopping. The range of what tickles our fancy is quite astonishing. For example, we must have some very pampered dogs out there as we spent €125 million on pet food last year. We forked out €50 million on Chinese savoury sauces, €18 million on hair dye and €23 million on Mars bars. We spend five times more on Hula Hoops than we do purchasing textbooks for children from needy backgrounds and we splash out more on Coca Cola (€115 million) than we do on the entire school transport bill which carried 130,000 children to and from school every day. (And this year we have seen the tragic result of this perverted priority.) We spent more on our mobile phones in the first three months of the year than the entire annual budget for overseas development aid. We spend more on the rather adolescently pungent Lynx than we donate to Trócaire!

And we are spending when we are travelling. As recently as 2000, Ireland had a healthy surplus when it came to tourist spending. Tourists here spent much more than we did when we went on our holliers. By 2003, that had reversed. We now spend €4.2 billion on our holliers, while tourists here in this, the most expensive country in Europe, are spending €4.1 billion. We are spending more in total, even though we are travelling to countries that are much cheaper than Ireland — some achievement!

And how are we financing this? Through debt, of course. This year Ireland's total personal debt surpassed our income for the first time ever. And it is rising rapidly. By the end of 2005, it will be in the region of 130%. In the ten years to 2004, credit card use doubled to 33% and cash card use has increased from 40% to 60% of the population.[15] And as a recent central bank report noted, using credit cards allows us to juggle bills, paying a bit off here and a bit off there. Bill juggling is a new development. When you think that the older population will not be using credit cards as much, you can see that our most productive generation — those between 20 and 40 — are moving rapidly into levels of debt that would concern outsiders looking in. But us, we don't care, because we believe our own propaganda that this time it's different. So borrowing continues apace. We borrowed 25% more in 2005 than we did in 2004. And we are spending this cash on flashy items. In the past four years, the market share of BMWs and Mercs has doubled, from 3.6% to 6.2%. We are Europe's bling nation. Per head, there now are more Mercs sold here than in Germany. The two big banks — our principal moneylenders — are, as a result of our splurge, the most profitable in Europe, making around €350 profit per customer.

If we are not being full-on, we are doing more yoga to relax. This is one of the delicious paradoxes of modern Ireland. While we seem intent on obliterating our livers, kidneys and hearts by drinking and carousing, we are also in the grip of a health kick. We are fussier about what we eat, flocking to nutritionists and homeopathic practitioners, taking more echinacea, devouring advice on healthy options, taking more Prozac and spending €21 million on L'Oreal skin cream. The same people who are snorting coke and drinking a couple of bottles of Chablis each on Friday nights are fretting about food additives and won't take an Anadin for their headaches. We will drink seven gins but won't touch tap water. We will feed our hangovers with carbohydrates but then, when fully rehydrated and sober, regard mashed potatoes as the Devil's spawn. We sit in our cars from early morning, eating an amazing 17% of all our food at the dashboard[16] — most new cars now come with pull-out dining trays. We then slouch at our desks all day, order in lunch, careful to avoid any physical activity at all. We leave work, catch our reflection in the tinted windows of our BMW X series SUV and then fret about being overweight, unhealthy or not beautiful. So we drive to the gym or the health club. Instead of going for a regular stroll every evening, we get a personal trainer at the appropriately named 'Curves' gym for one manic morning a week. The Golden Pages has over 2,000 entries under health clubs and centres.

The full-on nation is burning the candle at both ends.

Chapter 2

The Great Blurring

HELLO BOYS! WONDERBRA ECONOMICS

Yuri quite likes the job. He had divided the strawberries, as he would back home, into three batches of €2, €3 and €5 a piece. He couldn't get rid of the €2 or €3 punnets, but the €5 simply flew off the rickety table which doubled as his makeshift shop-front on the Navan side of the N3 just outside Kells.

Every June the roads of Ireland are dotted with little stalls selling strawberries. This is a typical Irish scene, particularly on all the main routes back into Dublin on long weekends. In fact, so typical is it that it is regularly used by Leaving Cert economics teachers as an example of what is known as 'perfect competition'. This is a term used to describe a market with many small sellers, where no-one has advantage over anyone else and no-one can raise his price without the punter copping on and going to the next seller. It is the polar opposite of a monopoly. In other words, you won't make a fortune out of selling strawberries on the side of the road. However, the fact that such an Irish tradition attracts a twenty-one-year-old from Kazakhstan, doing the job that used to be reserved for local small farmers, indicates that some of our old descriptions, divisions and assumptions are blurring. Yuri, the Asiatic-looking Kazakh strawberry seller, is but one of thousands of new images that Irish people have had to take on board over the past five years in what can be described as part of a great blurring.

So many aspects of our society are blurring. The classes are blurring, the distinction between old and middle aged is evaporating, as are the traditional splits between urban and rural, natives and foreigners, left and right, rich and poor, educated and uneducated. What was once distinctive is now common, the nation is blurring and the most significant aspect of this is in class. In fact, Ireland is becoming the most middle-class, suburban nation in Europe and the most startling development in the past six years has been the rapid social mobility that the country is experiencing. The vast majority of us are climbing the social ladder at a rate not seen anywhere in Europe in forty years. We are now a middle-class nation.

Look around the country at the cars, the houses, the holidays, the clothes, the aspirations and the full restaurants. What is happening? Yes, we are spending, but something much more interesting is going on. Ireland is compressing into the middle. One of the most fascinating, and massively underreported developments of the past five years is the great compression. We have been condensed into the middle class at a rapid rate, as if a great designer has squashed the Irish population into the centre.

But not only have we been squeezed together, we have experienced the social equivalent of the Wonderbra effect. We have been pressed together in the middle and lifted up, allowing us to display our impressive material cleavage.

The uplift has been remarkable given the goods we had to work with in the past. Let's look at the country, the society and the different social classes via the census, which is the most definitive statistical snapshot of a country at a point in time. Every five years it asks people what they do for a living. It breaks these jobs down into seven classes. The first six are a traditional top-to-bottom list from highest paying jobs to lowest. The seventh category is a catch-all category which collates all non-traditional jobs — new professions like web designers and tele-workers. The latest figures published last year show that the middle and upper middle classes have grown dramatically, while the lower, working or small farmer class has shrunk considerably. So times are good, not just for a tiny minority at the top but for the vast majority. Joe Soap has experienced the Wonderbra effect — considerable social uplift.

Most of us can see this in our everyday life. The figures from the census are startling nonetheless. So all the Thai cooking, Bordeaux, cabriolets, lattes and Pilates don't lie — we are now wealthy, aspirant and materialistic. Contrary to much of the reportage, the middle and upper middle classes are the fastest growing classes in the country. The hard numbers reflect the new cars, foreign holidays and organic carrot sales. Close to half the nation is in the top three social classes as defined by the census. And if you were to add the 18% per cent who are working in new jobs not defined by the traditional census question, that middle-class figure rises to nearly 65% of us. Arguably, this may be overstating the case, but there is no doubt that a significant proportion of this change mirrors developments picked up elsewhere in the census which indicate a structural shift into white collar 'middle-class' jobs. It is interesting to note that a substantial amount of this change has come in the western seaboard where the recent migrations of people seeking an alternative lifestyle has led to a conspicuous blurring of classes. More importantly, the middle class has grown by 25% in the short time since 1996. This type of social mobility is unheard of in most developed countries.

By contrast, since 1996 every poor class has shrunk and the poorest class has shrunk most, by an enormous 29%. The next poorest class contracted by 8% and the lower middle class by 9%. All these people have moved up the social ladder. In the past ten years, 200,000 people have moved out of the poorest classes into the middle class.

Think about the extremes: the number of people in the very top social class has increased by 22.34% in the five years to 2002, while the number at the very bottom, as noted, fell by 29%. This constitutes extraordinary compression into the middle. This is the great blurring. Wonderbra economics works. The number of people in the second richest social class — which is now the biggest class with over one million in total — rose by a staggering 25.6% or just over 200,000 people, while the number of people in the second lowest class fell by 8%. The figure reveals very strong upward social mobility both in absolute terms and relative to any period in the past. There are now more people in the second richest class than in the four poorer strata below it. This explains the huge increase in demand for private education and grind schools as well as BMWs, slate wet-rooms and patio heaters. If we examine the figures for the greater Dublin area where the population is growing quickest, the great blurring is even more definitive. In the Dublin area, the numbers in the top two classes have increased by 44% while the amount of people in the lowest two classes has fallen by 51%. Between the canals, the Wonderbra effect has been more dramatic. The numbers in the top two social classes grew by 63% while those in the bottom two classes fell by 21%.[1] Far from the picture painted by the media of a more polarised society where the rich live in gated communities and the poor in hopeless ghettos, the census reveals that we are all living much closer together — rich and poor — and that the traditional distinctions between rich and poor areas (in both rural and urban Ireland) are blurring as well. Close to one million people are on the move — and they are moving upwards.

Wonderbra economics has also supported an extraordinary educational uplift. Traditionally, educational achievement equates to upward social mobility. If you are going to college, you are climbing up the ladder. In this case, the new generation of Irish hod-carriers is clambering up.

Again the figures are quite remarkable. The number of Irish people with third-level qualifications rose by 39.9% in the period from 1996 to 2002. This is unprecedented. During the same period, and again here we see the great compression, those of us with only basic education fell by 5.6%. At the extremes, not only did the amount of poorly educated people fall, but the numbers of very educated rose dramatically. The last census reveals that the number of PhDs in Ireland rose by 65.8%. Again, Dublin between the canals reveals an extreme transformation. There has been an enormous 80% jump in those people in inner-city Dublin with university degrees and a 115% increase in inner-city Dubs with PhDs![2] This obviously reflects the rapid gentrification of the inner city — comprised of suburban-born students, young workers and immigrants moving into the centre of the city for the first time ever. But that said, these are also largely the children of people who never did their Leaving Cert and they are now going to college in huge numbers.

The full-on nation is swotting like never before and rapidly becoming the most overqualified nation in the world. Even taking into account a little bit of grade inflation and the demographic explosion that drove them into the universities in the first place, the educational achievement of an entire generation is startling.

This is not bad for people who spent most of their Sunday afternoons in a Ford Cortina waiting outside the pub with a few packets of Tayto, a bottle of Fanta and the window rolled down so that they and the dog wouldn't suffocate.

This educational uplift will have a permanent effect on the nature of the class system here. It has already led to the emergence of a new creative class. International economics is now becoming more and more focused on the educational level of nations, because in the future that is all that matters. The only scarce resource is smart people and the country with the smartest people should be the one that wins out. As a result of the Wonderbra effect, according to a recent study,[3] Ireland now tops the world in the amount of us who are regarded as being in the creative class — 34% of the workforce. For a country that was exporting people and cattle not too long ago, the transformation, the great blurring and class compression has been startling.

NEVER LET THE FACTS GET IN THE WAY OF A GOOD STORY
So why has this most important societal development been largely ignored in the media? Sometimes reading the papers or listening to the radio or television, one could be forgiven for thinking that Ireland was the most unequal and desperate place in the world. For example, in the summer of 2005 *The Irish Times* ran an article with the headline, '*Ireland — simply the worst*'. Why is this? What drives our most credible newspaper to write this type of stuff?

We are sometimes depicted as a Latin American style country with a tiny minority of oligarchs owning everything, and a huge, seething and disenfranchised underclass, without anyone in the middle. The truth is the opposite. Yes, there is a very small amount of immensely rich individuals at one extreme and an all-too-big, but by international standards modest, underclass at the other, but the real action is where 70% of us are — in the middle.

Maybe the reason that the positive social effects of the great compression have been under-reported is that the 'Commentariat' is ideologically jaundiced and can't see beyond its own ideological ghetto. The Commentariat (by which I mean the aristocracy of commentators, opinion makers and editorial writers) seems to have wilfully ignored the facts regarding Irish society and the economy. Perhaps they prefer to fight old battles which are more appropriate to the 1970s than the 21st century. Or, possibly, the Commentariat is experiencing a form of status neurosis. Those members of the Commentariat drawn from the traditional professional middle classes have seen their status eroded by all this upward social mobility and perhaps they do not like it.

A combination of ideology and old-fashioned snobbery might explain why so much of the media coverage has focused on the slight negatives rather than the overwhelming positives.

The last decade has been kind to car salesmen, commercial travellers, and those who service the property industry like sub-contractors, bricklayers, private gardeners. Borrowers of any kind have seen their risk-taking rewarded. Self-employed tradesmen and anyone who got their hands on property of any sort, anywhere, before 1996 are now wealthy. In contrast, some professions, such as journalists, university lecturers and teachers, have seen their status fall. The unwillingness of savers to roll the dice and take a risk has seen them punished materially. Into this broad group we can also lump guards, middle-ranking civil servants, doctors, politicians, senior trade union members and the chattering classes.

As they fall down the social pecking order, they naturally do not like it. Some can't stand getting out-bought whether at auction or in Brown Thomas by people they always thought of as their lessers. They do not like the embarrassment. Others don't like the fact that the old system has been, to a large extent, overthrown and golf club membership alone cannot guarantee success. Some don't like the essentially democratic nature of easy credit, where anyone with initiative can get on these days. There are also those old-fashioned snobs who are threatened by social mobility and believe in the old class system.

So instead of objective reporting, arguably we have received an incessant barrage of opinion, editorialising and propaganda which has missed the big story — the Wonderbra effect — the biggest social compression experienced in a developed country in the past forty years. Instead, the gap between the very rich and very poor is reported again and again. Of course, anyone who gets left behind is indeed a tragedy — both from the narrow economic perspective and from a broad societal viewpoint. However, focusing on individual tragedies, while laudable and understandable, overlooks the great opportunities seized by the majority. In Ireland, there appears to be a very 1970s fascination with the very rich (tax exiles) and the very poor (the underclass), when in fact it is the seven out of ten of us in the middle who are driving everything.

It is not uncommon to hear commentators blithely claim that

Ireland is one of the most unequal countries in the world. This is not true. Ireland is smack in the middle of the European average when it comes to income distribution. The latest comparative figures on this are from the European Union in its excellent Eurostat publication entitled *The Social Situation in Europe*.[4] According to this definitive account which divides the income of the richest 20% by the poorest 20% in each country, the European average is 4.4 times. So the richest 20% earns 4.4 times the poorest 20% across the EU. And what is the figure for the so-called bastion of inequality, Ireland? It must surely be way above this: 6 times, 8 times or even 10 times? Wrong. The actual figure is 4.5 times. We are fractionally above the EU average and considerably more equal than Italy, Spain, Portugal, the UK, Estonia, Latvia or Greece. So as well as being richer than the 200 odd million people living in these countries, we spread our wealth around more!

The international standard tool used to measure inequality is the Gini co-efficient.[5] Eurostat also uses this. It is a measurement which runs from zero to 100. Perfect equality is zero, perfect inequality is 100. On this measurement Ireland again lies in the middle. Hyper-equal Denmark has a score of 22; we have a score of 29. France is slightly more equal at 27 and Britain at 31 is more unequal. Spain is yet more unequal at 35 and Portugal more unequal again with a figure of 39. The US has a score of 40. This implies that far from being the most unequal society in Europe, we are actually closer to nice Denmark than to the nasty US in terms of spreading our wealth.

The figures speak for themselves. The last census confirms what we already knew. All the foreign holidays and new kitchens, DVDs and PhDs, new cars, restaurants and outside decking are telling us something definitive — we are all lumped together in the middle now. The hard numbers reflect the mood that can be sensed on the streets. Irish people are moving up the social ladder quicker than ever and very few are falling backwards. The Irish make extremely good capitalists.

A recent report called *Social Mobility and Meritocracy: Reflections on the Irish Experience* by Christopher T. Whelan and Richard Layte backed up these findings. They observed a 'significant upgrading of the class structure' during the period as the number of 'higher-level occupations increased'. In terms of 'absolute mobility, the general pattern was one of increased opportunity for upward mobility. One of the striking consequences of such changes was increased access to the professional and managerial class.'

Just to recap. Close to half of us are in the top three social classes as defined by the census, based on what we do for a living. And if you add the almost 20% who are working in 'new' jobs, which are not defined by the traditional census questions but suggest teleworking, working from home and sole traders, that middle-class figure rises to nearly 65% of us. More importantly, the middle class has grown by 25% in the short time since 1996. In contrast, the poorest class shrunk by almost 30%. There is clear shunting up the social ladder. This is extraordinary social change.

If Ireland was 'simply the worst' as *The Irish Times* contends, why would we be experiencing net immigration? Immigration is probably the most accurate and clearest barometer of positive social change in a country. People vote with their feet. If people are leaving a country in droves, there is something badly wrong. If they are banging down the door to get into a country, there is something right going on. The host country is by definition an attractive place to live. Immigrants see in the host country a place that they can get on, move up and achieve their potential. It is the country where their children will have a better chance than they had. They are giving it the thumbs up. Hundreds of thousands of foreign people have given Ireland the thumbs up in the past ten years. Indeed, as a percentage of the population there are eight times more immigrants choosing so-called inegalitarian Ireland over egalitarian France at the moment.

These days, the immigrant's assessment of a country is instantaneous. Take our eastern European, new EU immigrants as an example. They are texting, emailing and phoning home every minute. They can hop on a cheap flight and be here in a matter of two or three hours. They are choosing Ireland over other countries because they have made a rational adult choice that this is where they will prosper. This is where they will blur into the background, where they will be able to join a rapidly expanding middle class, where they can have a good life and their children have better opportunities. In a recent survey,[6] over half the immigrants interviewed said that their standard of living had improved since coming here, while for 22% it remained the same. Again this flies in the face of the Commentariat's assertion that they are miserable and are being exploited. On the contrary, they feel liberated. The social message is very clear. The great blurring is benefiting the vast majority and we are more equal than ever.

This blurring does not suit traditional political rhetoric. Take for example the two political parties that speak out most strongly about the need to raise taxes and redistribute income, the Greens and the Labour Party. One would expect their supporters to be drawn from those who have lost out in the great blurring and yet they are in fact the richest voters in the country. Green Party supporters are the richest in Ireland.[7] The Labour Party, bizarrely for a left-wing party, has the second richest supporters, while Fianna Fáil, the tax-cutting, supposedly right-wing, government party, gets the lion's share of the poorest vote.

We are a centrist country with centrist foibles and idiosyncrasies. We are all riding the wave. All those suvs, second holidays, new kitchens and decks in back gardens are not an illusion. We feel, smell, act and increasingly look — thanks to expensive orthodontics — middle class. Ireland is turning into one large Ralph Lauren ad, all New England smiles, Cape Cod clothes and Boston Brahmin bank accounts.

Manufacturing is on the way out. Only 16% of us make anything anymore. Less than one in twenty works the land. One in ten works in construction, building, amongst other things, holiday homes — over 40,000 of them this year. The rest of us, which is just under three out of every five, toil away at the water cooler in office jobs with well manicured nails, lunch on O'Brien's sandwiches and spend long weekends on the tear. We are all white-collar, service-sector commuters now. It's not romantic, but nor is it bitter.

What is more, we appear to be happy and isn't happiness what it is all about? If we are happy, it should not matter how we got here, even if it was by tax-cutting, freewheeling, full-on capitalism. Again, many in the Commentariat seem to be more concerned with equality, inequality and the inequities of the tax system or the shallowness of an afternoon spent in Liffey Valley, the Curragh or drinking with friends. Maybe all these things make people happy and we should be asking people whether they are *actually* happy with their lot rather than spelling out to them what *should* make them content.

A few years ago I had the pleasure of working with a kind and smart Serb whose life had been turned upside down by the war in the Balkans. How did he deal with this? How can you forgive your neighbours? How can you come to terms with eviction, brutalisation and terrorism? He seemed to be quite relaxed about everything and it struck me as almost superhuman to have such a deep well of humanity, forgiveness and tolerance, to be able to see the world through someone else's eyes.

I met him recently in the Clarion Hotel in Dublin. He was in shock. This formerly implacably calm individual, who had come through the horrors of ethnic cleansing both performed in and against his name, was agitated, hurt and perplexed. What could have got at him, here in Ireland? The reason it transpired was quite straightforward. He was the author of a late-2004 study by the *Economist*[8] which reported that Irish people had claimed that Ireland was the best place to live in in the world. We came out top in the world quality of life index. This conclusion was arrived at by collating all the EU surveys asking people how they felt about the world, their lives, the family, the future and the country. In addition to asking us how we felt, the *Economist* took health indicators, political stability and security indicators and combined these with a variety of other benchmarks like family and community life, to arrive at a sophisticated index that aimed, correctly, to move the debate away from the normal narrow economic calculations. Crucially, much of the data was simply the reflection of what we, the Irish people, had said about how we thought our lives were going. We were happy, content and optimistic about the future and we felt that Ireland, warts and all, was a good place to live.

What effrontery, cried the Commentariat. What audacity, cried others. Bogus, shouted the editorials. This international report was met with derision in Ireland. 'An assault on the truth proportionate to the US bombardment of Fallujah' was how the *Irish Examiner* reacted, while the *Sunday Independent* simply dismissed it as 'drivel'.

As we all know, sometimes reports can get it wrong, and basic common sense can be more instructive than some statistics, but this report was a simple input/output matrix used by the *Economist* whereby they put recorded data into a model and Ireland came out top of their quality of life indicator. The subsequent report was published without opinion, qualification or editorialising. My friend could not believe the Irish media's reaction. How could the Commentariat be so out of step with the people, he asked? How could the Commentariat be so enraged by the optimism of their fellow countrymen?

However, for those of us who live here, the Commentariat's

reaction is not too difficult to comprehend. Possibly, this is just the reaction of opinion makers in a society that is going through a short period of rapid change following a prolonged period of utter stagnation. History tells us that this is not unusual. When societies are faced with what appear to be monumental changes, the people who are paid to comment, agitate and point out, get going like never before.

But whatever way you look at it, the change, its pace and the direction in which it is taking us is making us happy — 42% of us describe ourselves as being 'very happy'. This is the highest in the world. According to the World Values Survey,[9] the *Economist* is right. Ireland scores second highest in the wvs life satisfaction index. With 77% of us saying we are very proud of the place, we are the most patriotic country in the world. Despite all the scandals, we are second in the world when it comes to trusting the police, while we are top of the oecd league when it comes to trusting our civil service (with six out of ten of us believing that the civil service is trustworthy).[10] And despite all the rhetoric about the nation becoming more and more selfish, we are smack in the middle of the eu league for social and civic involvement.[11] 86% of us in another survey said we were either quite happy[12] or very happy and 71% claimed that our lives had improved over the past five years.[13] Yet this is rarely reported.

Survey after survey indicates that we are very content. Compared to the responses given by more equal countries, many of whom verge on the depressed, maybe we are better where we are. So, for example, according to the eu, we are less equal than Germany and Hungary,[14] but considerably happier[15] than these people. In the same way that having more money after a basic income level does not incrementally lead to happiness, having more equality beyond a certain civilised level — the eu average — doesn't make the society any happier either. Just to see this in operation, take a country like Bulgaria which is a candidate for eu membership. It is considerably more equal than Ireland with the richest 20% earning only 3.8 times that of the poorest 20%. It scores 26 on its Gini coefficient score,[16] better than Ireland, yet the people are the most miserable in Europe[17] and close to 60% are having difficulty making ends meet.[18] Only 4%[19] of Irish households said that they were having difficulty making ends meet and we are the third most satisfied race in Europe with our lot. What's better, being poverty-stricken but equal and miserable or being rich, very happy and smack in the middle of the EU when it comes to equality?

So, taking a bit of altitude, the full-on nation is reasonably at ease with itself, compared to the rest of the world. We seem to be happy with the blurring that has occurred across the old distinctive lines. We are one big, aspiring, white-collar suburb, diffusing into the countryside. Ireland is a land of Spars and Centras, of hot food counters and off-licences all on hand to serve the commuter. Yes the costs of housing, the creaking infrastructure and the health service concern us greatly, but the majority put this down to the country catching up and there is a sense that we will catch up. The traditional urban/rural divide appears to be blurring. Go to a GAA match between Dublin and Meath and hear the number of Dubs with children in Meath kit to get a flavour of just how much the old lines are blurring. Every now and then we get battles between An Taisce whose big-house, theme-park view of the country rightly annoys the inter-county, one-off housing, GAA set. However, the set-piece, stylised Ireland where farmers and an industrial working class had inimical interests and a middle class lived in fear of either tax hikes or a worker revolt is gone.

In June 2005, Amárach consultants carried out a survey about what class people believed they were in.[20] Just over 50% of those who responded with a view on this believed that they belonged to the broad middle classes, while fewer than 30% believed that they were working class, 10% felt they had no particular class and a small 2% claimed to be upper class. When you break this down into various different groups, we see that of those working, again 50% say that they are middle class, reflecting the massive switch to white-collar jobs over a relatively short period. This result tallies with the census finding.

So if the country has blurred into a classless nation where the middle classes have grown by 25% in the past seven years and the poorest class has shrunk by 29%, what is the most sensitive class indicator and where are we likely to see the most conspicuous blurring?

Typically you would expect the area where individuals live or what they do for a crust or some other material sign to signal class. But interestingly, in early 21st-century Ireland, the Amárach survey reveals that accent is regarded as the most significant indicator of class — more than house, job, clothes, car or schooling. This is particularly interesting because this is where we are seeing the most notable outward evidence of a blurring. The Irish accent is changing rapidly and young Irish teenagers are now speaking a strange mid-Atlantic dialect, conforming to the age-old rule that the way you speak says more about you than anything else. The middle class, urban/rural blurring is driving us to sound the same. This is not new. This is a hybrid, globalised version of *Pygmalion*. Shaw's Eliza Doolittle wanted to sound like an Edwardian aristocrat; our aspirants today want to sound like Buffy.

I first heard it amongst teenagers in Malahide — Ireland's richest town — a few years ago. It is a customised Irish version of the language of American sitcoms like 'Friends', 'Buffy', 'Will and Grace' and a liberal sprinkling of earlier Aussie soaps like 'Neighbours'. Let's call this new Irish dialect, Malahidealect. (In contrast, Estuary English, the accent of choice of English teenagers — named after the Thames estuary — is much more down-market and is more Mike Skinner than Margaret Thatcher.)

Versions of Malahidealect are used all over the world. It is the language of supermodels, rock stars, Hollywood stars and celebrities of all sorts and it has permeated Ireland. Young girls and grown men say things like '*Hello*' (three syllables, with an o fada) rather than 'wise up', 'come on' or the quintessentially Irish 'cop yourself on'. The intonation has to be that Australian half-question rising inflection at the end.

'*I was like, so totally not right.*' '*He was, like, wasted.*' '*We were like so, laughing out loud.*' '*It was like so fun.*' '*Totally*' '*Whatever*' '*Don't go there!*' '*I'm so not going there.*' This is our teenagers speaking, not just in Dartland Dublin but in Loughrea, Clonakilty and Nenagh. Notice the rising intonation towards the end of a sentence making all sentences sound like questions. This is Malahidealect, 21st-century Estuary Irish — the language of 'Buffy the Vampire Slayer'.

Together with highlights, expensive orthodontics, silicone, lip-gloss, credit cards, sling backs and the 'Friends' DVD back catalogue, this is the look, feel and, more importantly sound, of modern middle-class Ireland.

For many years Irish scholars tried to downplay the loss of our native language by the elevation of what was called Hiberno-English. This was the English spoken here — a type of hybrid English which was the result of our dropping our native language for English in the

19th century. This language is evident in the over-the-top plays of Synge. It can still be heard amongst older people in the country:

> *'Hello John, I didn't salute you at all'; 'The heart went out of me'; 'I lost my life'; 'He put a plaque in the graveyard for somebody who belonged to him'; 'I do not believe any of that ould blather about seeing a horse with white socks on a fair day, pass it by without looking'; 'Lord, but they were the impudent divils'; 'He didn't half make shite of my car'; 'There's been a fierce gathering'; 'He scored a point that wasn't a point at all'; 'We are still doing it yet'; 'If it's timber you want, it's timber you'll get.'*

However, it is gradually disappearing and being replaced by Malahidealect which is now so ubiquitous amongst the teenagers there is little doubt that it will be the lingua franca of the next generation. A good acid test is the word for our mothers. Over the past ten years, the Irish mammy, or the Hibernian mam, became the British mum and increasingly now is the American mom.

In the past, accents used to start in Dublin and disseminate out. Dublin was the 'resonance chamber' for the rest of the country. This is no longer the case. Globalisation, TV, the explosion of American cinema and DVDs have ensured that the accent goes straight from the HBO studios in New York to New Delhi and New Ross simultaneously.

The blurring and the accent change are complementary developments and the accent change is as old as history itself. People change accent in the same way as animals change colour; it is social camouflage. We do it when we want to blend in to obscure our differences and blur the canvas. The Wonderbra effect has pushed us together and lifted us all. And why is the Commentariat still fighting old battles and not acknowledging the change? Your guess is as good as mine, but what is happening in the great middle-class nation is as fascinating, outrageous and convoluted as anything we Irish have seen before. Hold on to your seat for a full-speed drive through the full-on nation. Let's examine the full-on nation, to see who it is, where it lives, what it looks like, what it wants and where it is heading. To those who believe that it is all bland, uninteresting and terribly inegalitarian, I say open your eyes to the Wonderbra effect, or as Eva Herzigova might question in her best Malahidealect — Hello Boys!

Chapter 3
The Pope's Children

WHO IS THE FULL-ON NATION?

In September 1979, 26 years ago this year, a friend of my older sister lost her virginity. Obviously it was a significant day for her but maybe not for you. Yet the way she lost it is important for all of us. She was deflowered in a tent in Galway. No big deal you might say. But she was attending the Pope's Mass for the pious and chaste 'young people of Ireland' at the time. Now that is important. As an elderly, clerical gentleman from Poland lectured about pre-marital sex, Ireland's teenagers were fornicating within earshot.

This scandalous news went around our area like wildfire and caused consternation. Not only because she had popped her cherry whilst that other great Lothario Bishop Eamonn Casey was leading the Papal choir, but because her mother had been the sanctimonious moral conscience of the parish, one of the leading Holy Joes and a self-aggrandising minister of the Eucharist, no less. And to cap it all, her daughter lost it to a howaya from Ballybrack after a few flagons. This caused class, as well as moral, outrage. It was the south Dublin social equivalent of a black man having his way with a southern belle. The only thing lace curtain Ireland feared more than the Church, was the working class and this young girl had aimed her high-heels right up the rump of both sleeping dogs.

But she wasn't alone, because 1979 was also the year when Irish people went at it like rabbits; maybe in response to the Pope, who knows? The American baby boom peaked in the early 1960s, the British one in the late 1960s and when do you think the Irish baby boom peaked? In June of 1980 — nine months to the day after the Pope kissed the tarmac in Dublin.

Seventy-four thousand little John Pauls and Marys emerged, screaming and kicking from maternity wards around the country in 1980. This was the high point of our baby boom that had begun in the early 1970s. This was the first generation since the Famine to witness an increase in the population, which took off in the seventies and peaked in 1980. Let's call this generation, the demographic bulge that peaked nine months after the Pope preached his gospel, the Pope's Children.

Their baby boom — the kids born in the 1970s — is Ireland's crucial generation. Today, the youngest Pope's Children are 25, the oldest are 35. There are close to 620,000[1] of them and they constitute the key generation in this country for their effect on our economy, attitudes, politics, art and literature. They are the creative dynamo of Ireland and will shape this country's destiny in the 21st century. If you want to understand modern Ireland, it will be helpful to understand the mind of the Pope's Children. However, the country they find themselves in today is markedly different to that which existed in 1979.

1979 was the year everything changed in Ireland. Until then, Ireland had closed herself off to many of the cosmopolitan influences that were shaping the globe. This was explicit. Ireland was seen as Hibernian, unique in its culture, religion and history. So instead of taking ideas from the outside and moulding them to suit ourselves, there existed a view that outside influences could only dilute what made the Irish special and were to be repelled at all costs.

But 1979 was the tipping point, when the old Hibernian regime which had been stitched together since Independence began to fray at the seams. Yet 1979 seems a fairly insignificant date at first. Obviously, Chippy Brady won the FA cup final for Arsenal all on his own, Hill 16 lamented the passing of the great Dubs side of the era, the Clash played the Top Hat and apparently 70,000 people saw a teenage U2 in the Dandelion Market (which was the GPO for that generation) but there was no revolution, no outward sign of regime change. Indeed, the big event was the Pope's visit which surely could be seen as the triumphal procession of Hibernian Ireland. After all, one million people in the Phoenix Park and a couple of hundred thousand around the country had turned up to celebrate. Almost one in three of the population went to see him.

Yet it was all cosmetic. Not only were the young people of Ireland fornicating, but underneath the pomp, ceremony and synchronised Ave Marias, a new cosmopolitan Ireland was oozing out, ready to challenge the Hibernian orthodoxy at every turn. The tipping point was not signalled by a moment, an event or a revolution, it was just a quiet demographic and social tide that carried cosmopolitan ideas relentlessly towards the Hibernian shore.

This quiet demographic tide was unprecedented. It is important to examine the figures to assess just how unique are the Pope's Children. Ireland has probably the oddest population dynamics in Europe. Our family structure and birth trends all go against international norms.[2] One of the strangest things to appreciate is just how many adult virgins there were in Ireland because if we go back a bit, the figures are startling. In the 1930s, half of Ireland's 30–34 year olds were single and sexless. Even by 1960, 30% of Irish women between the ages of 30–34 were single and most were virgins.[3] Those women who were having sex were, by international standards, having enormous families late in life. An amazing statistic is that one-third of all births in Dublin's maternity hospitals in 1960 were the fifth birth or higher. There were one and a half times as many fifth births in that year as first births.[4]

In the 1970s, this started to change and we had a marriage boom with fewer and fewer Irish women and men being what used to be termed 'left on the shelf'. In 1974 the Irish marriage boom peaked at 22,800 and it was these marriages that spawned the Pope's Children.[5]

The Pope's Children were young during the 1980s. Most of them were barely out of nappies when the great conservative versus liberal battle raged. The emigration of that decade passed them by. Their experience of being Irish is quite different from the generations who went before. During the 1980s, the recession had a strong impact on Irish birth rates which fell dramatically from close to four children per mother to two children per mother, which is near enough to the average in the developed world. In the 1980s we also saw the Catholic church being kicked out of the bedroom as the number of babies born outside marriage rocketed from less than 5% to one in four by 1990. The figure today is one in three.[6]

So the Pope's Children were the young adults of the 1990s. They are the product of full employment, wealth and a new Ireland. They are the beneficiaries of a dramatic blurring in the country which can be described in demographic terms. Up until their birth, Ireland had all the costs of high fertility but none of the benefits because when the children were fed, watered and educated, they emigrated, leaving the country with a large overdraft and no-one to pay for it. In contrast, because the Pope's Children stuck around, we now have all the benefits of low fertility with none of the costs. We have the added bonus of immigration, meaning that we are acquiring other countries' talent for free as well as our own. In fact, with our new east European immigrants, Ireland is benefiting from the last great 'Fire Sale' of white Christian immigrants the world is likely to see. This is a positive double-whammy. But back then in 1979 none of this was expected. The 620,000 Pope's Children were born to the sick man of Europe. The idea of perennial economic under-achievement was becoming ingrained. Yet economic events were occurring that would lay the foundation for the future economic boom and the era of the Pope's Children.

In the 1970s, one of the local schools in my area used to send a football team touring to England. These 'big lads', as they were known on our road, came back every Easter with three commodities that were banned in Ireland: porn mags, condoms and, believe it or not, illicit sweets.

Now at a stretch, I can understand the religious aversion to condoms and porn mags, but a fatwa on Curlywurlys is perplexing. Until, that is, you understand that the country not only tried to protect itself from outside influences that might pollute our minds, dilate our pupils and hijack our sperm: the state was protectionist to its core. The dominant philosophy at the time constructed by the state, articulated by the Church and upheld by the people was that outside was bad, inside was pure. All things Irish or Hibernian were good for us. In contrast, foreign or cosmopolitan influences were degenerate.

To an economic evangelist, banning filthy, decadent, cosmopolitan Curlywurlys was a way of preserving virtuous, wholesome, Hibernian Macaroon bars. The battle lines between the Hibernian and the Cosmopolitan were everywhere, crucially governing what you could and could not put in your mouth. Granted now I am going to mix my religious metaphors, but the ban on Curlywurlys was economic kosherism and, like any orthodoxy, economic kosherism was applied strictly. Certain things were kosher and others were strictly forbidden. And, like the basis of kosher diets, the objective was to keep us apart from the others, the outsiders and financial goyim who might threaten our Hibernian bloodlines. Hibernian Ireland kept a kosher economy.

Like the 1940s' and 1950s' lists of banned books, lists of banned sweets in Ireland included Curlywurlys, Twixes, Toblerones and (my own favourite at the time for some bizarre reason) Opal Fruits. Those of us living on the east coast had to endure the torture of ads on HTV — that strange Welsh-language version of UTV — which beamed blonde British kids into our living-rooms, their mouths stuffed with banned goodies such as 'Opal Fruits, made to make your mouth water'. In the real Hibernian twilight outside, we had to make do with gammy Irish Macaroon bars made only by patriotic hands in Inchicore. In 1979, the fatwa on Curlywurlys was lifted, leading to an explosion of choice, E numbers and subsequently a marked rise in diabetes. (I know this because Curlywurlys appeared in shops for the first time ever on St Patrick's Day of 1979. With typical Irish expedience, you were allowed to break your Lenten fast on the day of the Great Saint.)

On a different but related economic issue, when the fatwa lifted, it signalled the beginning of a move, from a country with no competition in the 1970s, to a country with some competition in the 1980s, on to free competition in the 1990s and finally, to an era of hyper-competition in the 21st century. Today, you can buy what you want, when you want, wherever and whenever you want.

But to avail of all these goodies, you have to have the cash or the credit to pay for them. History is replete with examples of countries that opened up to free competition (usually as a result of listening to too many economists whose idea of risk is a post office savings account and a semi-D in Deansgrange) without having the wealth or at least credit in the hands of the punters. When this happens, as it did in Russia in the early 1990s, a Mafia comes in, grabs all the goodies and leaves only a handful of rich who can enjoy the Diesels, Jimmy Choos or Fendis and the rest are left outside the gate.

In 1979, we took a great leap forward to ensure that Russification did not happen. It was the year that Irish politicians inadvertently signed their own redundancy cheques. They did this by linking the Irish Punt to the German Mark in an exchange rate arrangement called the European Monetary System. Now we won't get too technical here but let's just say that this was the first step on our road to robbing Germany's savings. They did not realise it at the time, but Germans were giving the Paddies the PIN code to their Banklinks. We kept schtumm about this until we had suckered them into the Euro — the Frankenstein child of the EMS. Now with the rich, old Germans safely and irrevocably in the Euro, we can plunder their savings whenever we want and at interest rates that suit *us*, not *them*.

Without young people spending, the economy falters, and when the German economy faltered in the 1990s, interest rates fell too. So Germany today is a country with lots of money stashed away and not enough young people to spend it.

And this is where we come in. Ireland, with the 620,000 Pope's Children, was the polar opposite of Germany. We had loads of young people and not enough money. So we were glad to take the Germans' savings from them. Because our population is so small, no matter how much we borrow, we will not really make a dent in the savings of eighty million Germans. So we get a free lunch. We can have all the German money we want, via the Euro, to feed our overblown boom, at low interest rates which are really only appropriate for Germany's recession.

But back in dear old fornicating 1979 none of this was clear, when, in the climax of initial European enthusiasm, we offered our economic sovereignty up on the Teutonic altar of fiscal rectitude. On that day, we also ensured that the Dáil reduced itself to a rubber-stamping administrative body. The reason is simple. If you can't print your own money, you have no real power: just ask Eva Peron. So instead of dealing with the big issues of the day, our politicians overnight became in essence superannuated county councillors. And with no power, you typically get a gradual hollowing out of talent, leaving a rump parliament, which over time loses respect. People realise that without power, there is no magic wand and without the magic wand there is no gold dust and no point believing in the political Fairy Godmother. What's the point of a Fairy Godmother who can't, with a flick of her wand, turn mice into princes?

So joining the EMS in 1979 and subsequent deeper involvement in

Europe, in economic, political and social affairs, was the beginning of the end for credible Irish politics. The Irish people understand the diminishing powers of the Fairy Godmother and have stayed away from the polls in increasing numbers. For example, in 1979, Ireland held its first European election. The turnout was 76%. In 2004, 25 years on, the turnout for the European elections fell under 50%.[7] General election turnout peaked in 1979 and has been falling ever since as well. The Haughey *putsch* in Fianna Fáil in the same year kicked off a cycle that led directly to the Dublin Castle tribunals and, more than anything else, this malarkey eroded trust in politics and politicians. Survey after survey reveals that politicians are now the least trusted people in society; they were amongst the most respected in 1979.[8]

So 1979 was the year of the Pope's Children, when monumental developments occurred which were to change the course of Irish history and dictate the agenda for the 21st century. First and by far the most important, the Pope's visit coincided with a final fornicating fling which signalled the peak of the largest baby boom Ireland has experienced since before the Famine. The birth rate has not reached these heights since. There are 620,000 of these boomers. The second crucial factor was that with the lifting of the Curlywurly fatwa, Ireland opened itself up to competition and we went from a country with no competition to a country with hyper-competition. To avail of all these goodies we needed the cash or at least the credit. In 1979 the third change came which allowed us to begin this process of national liberation by credit. By hitching our financial wagon to the Germans in 1979, we gradually availed of Germany's credit and, ultimately, paved the way for EMU. The significance of this is that for the first time in Irish history, credit, or the lack of it, would not be an impediment to the ambitions of the ordinary man on the street. Finally, by getting deeper into Europe, we signalled the beginning of the end for independent economic policies, and in so doing, signalled the gradual irrelevance of the Dáil. Not surprisingly, voter turnout has fallen progressively since then; national politicians who were once local chieftains become little more than glorified county councillors.

But let's talk about the real heroes. The Pope's Children are the special generation. They are today's twenty and thirty somethings; they are the future of the country. This book is about them — the Pope's Children, their kids and their parents.

Where do they live, what do they do for a crust, how will they mould the place and what will Ireland look like when they finally take up the reins of power? Let's go out there. Let's have a look at the Pope's Children.

Chapter 4
The Kells Angels

DELIVERY
- *Wake me up if anything happens.*
- *Is everything packed?*
- *Yes.*
- *What time is the alarm set for?*
- *Half six. Grand. Night.*
- *What?*
- *It's starting.*
- *Are you sure?*
- *I don't usually wet the bed, do I?*
- *Ok, let's go.*
- *What time is it?*
- *Ten past six.*
- *Four hours sleep only.*
- *Careful, careful.*
- *Do we have everything?*
- *Yes, peejays and all the other stuff?*
- *Yes, yes. Let's go or I'll have it here in the kitchen.*

Be the first one off the tee. Impress your friends. Cúlfada, 3 bed detached homes of distinction. Only an hour from Dublin. €299K and no stamps.

– *Slow down.*
– *How do you mean slow down?*
– *Ooh they're coming in waves now.*
– *Are you ok?*
– *Just drive. Can this bloody seat go back any further?*
– *Yes, just pull the handle under there.*
– *I can't see my toes — how do you expect me to reach under the fucking seat. And turn off the fucking radio.*

Tara, Home of the Kings. No Motorway here. Sick of commuting? Check out www.workinmeath.ie.

– *They're coming quicker now. Will we make it?*
– *Should do, we're past Dunshaughlin and there's shag all around us.*
– *Ok just move.*
– *Do you want anything?*
– *No. I'm scared.*

Fairyhouse Race Week — Be a winner with Paddy Power.

– *It'll be all right.*
– *And how the fuck would you know?*
– *I dunno, but the book said if we get there on time, all will go well.*
– *You just remember the magic word — epidural. Straight away, no messing around.*
– *Don't worry, I'll be there. But what about your one, the natural childbirth hippy and all the stuff about what she said they'd do to you?*
– *Screw her. She'd have me in a bath in the hall, surrounded by aromatherapy candles and fucking Enya* CDs.
– *Turn on the radio for the traffic.*

Ian Dempsey, bring on the day with Nescafé.
Morning. It's a sunny Thursday Morning May 27th.

– *He's always so fucking chirpy Dempsey.*
– *Yeah but he's good, and Gift Grub is always spot on.*

Morning Carol from AA: What's it like out there?
Moving well on all routes in, no serious delays but reports coming in of a truck overturned on the Blanchardstown exit, so expect serious delays.

- *Oh Jesus, I can't believe there's a tailback at Liffey Valley.*
- *What if it comes in the car?*
- *Shut up and drive up the hard shoulder. They're coming much quicker now, oh God.*

Liffey Valley — A great day out for all the family.

- *I think it's coming. Oh fuck.*
- *Will I call your Ma?*
- *And what could she do?*

The Irish Times — 'You live life, we look at it.'

- *Are you ok, love?*
- *Yes, I mean no.*

Go Harvey go. Go Harvey Norman at the Airside Retail Park and Dundalk.

- *Are they long or short?*
- *Long, Mum.*
- *That's a good sign. Are you going to Holles Street?*
- *Yes, yes, I was down for a section tomorrow. Five days late.*
- *Just take deep breaths.*
- *Jesus, JP, keep your eyes on the road.*
- *I'm leaving right now, love, keep breathing and I'll see you there.*
- *Keep your phone on.*

It's just gone 7.20, and here's Des with all the latest sports news.

— Forget it, just use the bus lane.

— Fuck off you taxiprick. You ok?

— Yeah, yeah, I haven't had one for a few minutes. God I feel so big. Look at the size of me. How am I going to get it out? I hope it'll be all right.

— It'll be grand. The scans said so.

— Yeah but they can miss all sorts and what if it's breach and the cord gets caught.

— Don't worry, the doctors will be there.

— Don't let them use forceps, love.

— I won't let them touch you.

Iarnród Éireann — We're not there yet but we're getting there.

— Jesus, it's like Mozambique in here.

— Shush.

— When did the waters break, love?

— About three hours ago.

— Ok. Hop up there till we check you.

— Right, four centimetres dilated. That's good.

Assaults or abusive behaviour towards members of staff will result in arrest.

— Just breathe in the gas and air.

— Nice and slow.

— Deeply, deeply.

— Oh man, it's like being off my tits, really tingly the gas and air.

— Shush Emms, 'nough of the yoke stuff now.

— Ok, ok.

— The anaesthetist will be up in a few minutes. Just a few more minutes, dear.

— It's only working down one side.

— Nearly there, nine centimetres. Ten. Big push now.

— And again, good girl, good girl.

— Head's just there.

– One more now, big push.
– I can't.
– Good girl, that's the girl.
– Jeeeeesus Chrriiiiiist!

Free Maternity Pack contains vouchers for Pampers and Johnson's Baby Lotion — sponsored by Mothercare.

Seven pounds two ounces, JP kept saying over and over, like a mantra in his head. Bizarre how people always ask the bloke what weight the baby is — as if he knows (a) the difference between six and seven pounds and (b) the significance. But it's always the first question. Not can the baby see, hear, has it two arms and legs but oh no — nothing as trivial as that. The question on everyone's lips is, 'What weight?' And then when seven pounds is mentioned they all nod sagaciously, as if there were an informal club of obstetrician weight watchers that met every Tuesday night to calculate ideal infant body mass indices and give out prizes accordingly. As the comedian Ardal O'Hanlon has wittily observed, it's just the birth weight and never the corpse weight. You never hear people asking the weight of a corpse, do you? Rarely at a country funeral do you hear people saying, 'Ah yes, poor old Dinny only weighed twelve stone eight when the Lord called him, poor soul, God rest him.'

But maybe there is some logic in obstetric weight watchers because Irish babies are coming out heavier and heavier. We are the birthing pool Billy Bunters of Europe. In the past thirty years, little Celtic sumo wrestlers are emerging and those over ten pounds at birth have risen from 12% to 20% of the total delivered. The traditional seven pound baby is now a waif of a thing — the Kate Moss of infants.[1]

In my mother's day, the heavier a child was the healthier. This may well have been a hangover from days when there wasn't enough food to go around but the 'lick your plate' generation certainly subscribed to the view that children could not be heavy enough. The more the child looked like an overfed medieval Pope the better. Recent research suggests that not only is this misguided but it is dangerous and that a marked increase in birth weight implies that mother and child are not healthy. The mother is ingesting far too much sugar and the child may well develop problems such as type 2 diabetes — the fastest growing disease in the country — in early teens.[2]

Faced with the ordeal of pushing out enormous infants, it's probably not surprising that we are fast becoming the Caesarean queens of Europe. The 'too posh to push' brigade has asserted itself and today over one in five mums book themselves in for elective Caesareans (corresponding nicely to the one in five babies that are now over ten pounds) — double the figure of their mothers' generation.[3]

As you read this, over one hundred and eighty bemused new Irish fathers (whose babies were born in the past 24 hours) are knowingly spoofing about the weight of their just born infants. They have perfected the fabrication of looking troubled if the child is either too small or too big — the former concern for the infant, the latter for the mother. It is all part of the great metamorphosis in the suburbs where previously laddish football supporters — typical Pope's Children — are turning into walking versions of Mothercare dad, *au fait* with prams, cots, Pampers and wipes. Irishmen now compare slings and car seats, yawn a lot and complain about sleep deprivation. It's a group thing, the knowing nods, the resigned roll of the eyes and the incessant role-playing.

Just in case you hadn't noticed or haven't been mowed off the path by a super-sized articulated stroller, we are in the grips of a baby boom. The Pope's Children are settling down. In the past eight years, the birth rate has gone up by a quarter — without precedent in modern Europe. The demand for out-sized maternity bras has also gone through the roof, not just because the average Irish cup-size has expanded from 32B to a 34C since 1990 but because the breastfeeding Inquisition has taken charge. Lactating Torqemadas scour our pre-natal clinics bearing their puckered Yeti proportioned breasts, encouraging Irish mothers to breastfeed for up to two years. The propaganda is extreme, forecasting every ailment from asthma to eczema to the poor infant whose errant mother does not breastfeed. I know mothers who have been discovered with contraband Cow & Gate stuffed down the side of their maternity beds and have not yet recovered from the emotional mauling doled out by these serial lactators. It is impossible to walk into any antenatal clinic these days without seeing posters and government-driven health campaigns urging mothers to go through the nipple pain barrier.

Today, over one in four Irish mothers breastfeed, up 30% since the day Mary Robinson won the presidential election. The Pope's Children, very few of whom ever went near their mother's chest, are breastfeeding, leading to probably healthier children but definitely more post-natal boob jobs to rectify the damage.

So why are we having a second baby boom? Well, obviously the Pope's Children are coming of age. This is John Paul's legacy. An urban myth links it to drunken groping following Ray Houghton putting the ball in the Italian net on that balmy New York night back in 1994. In terms of timing, it is undeniable that the baby boom did start in 1994, but football can't be blamed for every domestic ill. Since then one thing is clear, evenings in the suburbs have never been the same. The quietness of a falling birth rate has been replaced by noisy nights of teething children and frustrated parents.

We are seeing now what demographers would call Pope John Paul's echo. The Pope's Children have grown up and their children are the spawn of Ireland's first commuter generation — the Kells Angels.

AT HOME IN THE BABYBELT WITH THE KELLS ANGELS

Cúlfada — a development of three hundred distinctive houses — is the home of some of the *Kells Angels*, Ireland's first long-distance commuters. The Kells Angels are the oldest, richest, best-educated and most-travelled Irish parents ever. Yet they live in the outer suburbs, clustered around former market towns. For example Kells, Drogheda, Tullamore, Kildare, Naas or Gorey on the east coast, places like Watergrass Hill, Midleton, Carrigaline and Ballincollig around Cork, and towns such as Loughrea, Claregalway, Tuam and Barna in Galway. These are Ireland's new suburbs and they will be the most vibrant part of the country by 2020, but today they are dormitories which empty out in the morning and fill up again in the evening. The great Irish suburban movie — Irish Beauty — when it is eventually made, will be based here starring an ageing Colin Farrell as a lecherous bank official going through a mid-life crisis.

Take a helicopter from Leinster House to the Galway races and fly over the subjects of the realm with the rest of the Cabinet and you will see the future. Stretching out from east to west, a two-storey creeper of low-rise, semi-D estates, without footpaths, enveloping, like a concrete strangler, the throats of former provincial market towns.

Look at three towns in the Midlands of Ireland: Mullingar, Tullamore and Athlone. Each town has seen massive development over the past six years. But something very strange has happened. In the past, these towns were their own places, with their own local histories, rivalries, local dynasties and economies. Now they are dormitory towns for commuters. Nearly six out of ten people who live in Athlone (the dead centre of the country) commute; the corresponding figure for Mullingar is 51% and 47% for Tullamore.[4] Dublin is the sun and the moon for all these towns. Their occupants orbit around Dublin, depending on it for heat and light, and the ebb and flow of commuters is dictated by Dublin's gravitational pull.

You are now in Ireland's *BabyBelt*. These towns and regions have seen the most rapid population growth in the past six years. Meath, Kildare and Laois are Ireland's most fertile counties where the birth rate increased by close to 20% in the six years to 2002. This is an extraordinary increase in babies. Up until the early 1990s, there were as many old people dying as babies born in these counties. From Dublin, the BabyBelt spreads in a great tarmac arc out north to Louth, south Cavan and Westmeath and south to Wicklow and Wexford. It also surrounds Galway, Limerick and Cork. This is where the action is, yet the BabyBelt is less than ten years old. It is still unsure of itself. It is the world of Westmeath-born children wearing Dublin GAA jerseys in the summer.

Over the years one of the great Irish put-downs is to be accused of being a blow-in. The blow-in is less than a real person in the eyes of the natives. He has just rocked up and has no real idea of the culture of the place. The blow-in is exactly what it sounds like: someone who has just blown in via a gust of wind. There is nothing permanent, solid or grounded about him. He is in the place, but is not of the place.

Ireland had better get used to blow-ins because the BabyBelt is full of them. Chapters of Kells Angels are filling up formerly rural townlands with young couples, most of whom have absolutely no connection with the place. For example, over 60% of the increase in people in Carlow from 1996 to 2002 were migrants, largely from Dublin with no roots in the county. The figure for blow-ins into Meath was higher at 73%, and 66% for Wicklow. For Westmeath, the corresponding figure was 69%, while the same figure for Kildare was 61%. This is not just a greater Dublin phenomenon. In Clare, 66% of the increase in the population since 1996 is a result of non-Clare people moving in, reflecting the spread of the Limerick conurbation in the south and exploding Galway in the north.[5]

Ireland is being turned inside out. No longer are the Dubs being swamped by the Culchies but the Culchies are being overrun with Dubs. We are seeing reverse migration out of Dublin. In the 1960s and 1970s country people flocked into Dublin and actually displayed quite tribal homing patterns, with people from Mayo and Galway settling in west and north-west Dublin to ease the way home at weekends. Likewise, people from Cork and Kerry tended to settle in south-west Dublin. All this has now changed. The Kells Angels are 'Dulchies' — Dubs living in former culchie fiefdoms. They are displaying the same homing instincts as their country cousins years ago. Southsiders are moving to Wicklow and Wexford. Northsiders are heading to Louth and Meath, and original Westies are moving out to Kildare and beyond.

And of course, guess what county has had the least migration into it since 1996? Dublin. Silly house prices, as well as killing the art of conversation, are driving Dublin's Pope's Children out into the BabyBelt and turning them into Kells Angels. Dublin is getting older faster, while the BabyBelt is getting younger quicker. In the course of the next decades, the BabyBelt will be the creative hub of the country. Movies and books will be inspired by the new suburbs. If you are looking for the next U2, don't hang around Temple Bar, the Village or Whelans. Head to Naas, Ireland's great intersection — the *buckle* of the *BabyBelt*. Ireland's youth culture of the future will spring from a place like this.

At the moment, Dublin's truly Galilean dominance means that commuting begins in the womb. The commuting foetus is uniquely Irish. In the same way as maternity books advise mothers to play classical music to their unborn children, the fact that expectant mothers have to commute in the traffic to Dublin for scans and proper antenatal care can be seen as perfect pre-birth training for life on the outside. The new-born child will be able to tell his Mozart from his Bach, his hard shoulder from his road works, his unleaded from his diesel, his M50 from his N11 and his Abbeyleix jam from his Monasterevin bypass. A perfect traffic symphony for the traffic people — a sort of fanfare for the common commuter.

And when it is time for the waters to break, the Kells Angels have to commute from their dormitory towns to give birth before driving back again. *Dublin delivers while the BabyBelt bawls.* Reflecting this commuter crush, there were more babies delivered in Dublin than in the entire province of Munster last year — an area 20 times bigger.

There were three times more babies delivered in Dublin than in the entire province of Connacht.[6]

These developments are being mirrored all over the country. An agonising way to see it all is from behind the wheel of a Nissan Primera going at four miles an hour. Every morning and every evening, traffic snakes around the arteries of this country, bumper to bumper, snarling, fuming, crashing and maiming.

A survey published in January 2005[7] revealed that respondents who are commuting more than one and a half hours per day, live in a sinister crescent enveloping the BabyBelt which stretches a full thirty-mile radius around Cork, Galway and Limerick. One in three of those living in estates outside autonomous market towns like Fermoy and Macroom and ports like Youghal, are commuting for ninety minutes or more. Likewise, Galway's Kells Angels are living in Ballinasloe and Loughrea. That's a lot of wine, TV dinners and arguments when they finally get home.

Back in Dublin things are worse. A few years ago I worked on a breakfast radio show. This is probably the only job that benefits from the early morning traffic chaos. Every morning, we asked listeners to alert fellow travellers to traffic black spots. In 2002, the frustrated texts about traffic chaos typically came flooding in after a quarter to eight. The usual places would be jammed on the main arteries from the west, north and south. As time progressed, each month these traffic texts arrived earlier and earlier, so by the time I left the job in 2004, we were inundated before the show at 7 am with texts from commuters in Wicklow, Meath and Louth fulminating about pre-dawn traffic snarl-ups. The traffic textometer was probably the finest gauge of the worsening of Dublin's traffic, the increasing car dependency of the culture and the deteriorating quality of life for hundreds of thousands of BabyBelt commuters.

The Kells Angels are a strange hybrid because, out in the BabyBelt, the more qualified you are, the more commuting you do. There is a direct correlation between education in Ireland and quality of life. It is negative. The more degrees you have, the more likely you are to be a Kells Angel. You might belong to the Carrigaline Chapter, the Gorey Chapter or the Loughrea Chapter, but you are still a Kells Angel living in Ireland's BabyBelt. The educational alphas live like epsilons.

The better your internet access giving you instant communication with the rest of the world, the more likely you are to spend over one and a half hours in traffic per day. The better your career, the less likely you are to vote and the more you spend on crèches. In fact, many spend more on childcare than on their substantial mortgage. The more you climb up the greasy pole, the less time you have to spend with your family. The fewer kids you have, the less likely you are to see them at all and when you do see them, you are likely to be tired and half way into your first bottle of red — so yes, Drunk Dad.

These days, there are rumours of motorists going missing for days on the infamous Red Cow Roundabout — the Bermuda triangle of the M50. There could be some silver linings. For example, traffic must be handy if you are having an affair. It's only a matter of time before some entrepreneur opens a highly profitable 'hot sheet' hotel, a glorified knocking shop where rooms rent by the hour. Commuters could blame the cute girl from AA Roadwatch rather than the cute girl from Accounts.

MISS KELLS ANGEL

Back at Holles Street, the Kells Angel is about to leave with her firstborn swaddled in a Bart Simpson blanket. She is thirty-two, highlighted, GHDed and intent on shedding her pregnancy pounds. She has had at least eight previous sexual partners (but tells even anonymous surveys she has had four) — two of which were one-night stands. In college, she was an expert joint roller but has given up. She smokes Silk Cut purple. Kelly Angel still binge drinks at least twice a month with her mates. Our Kells Angel will probably be unfaithful at least once and entertains having a bit of nip/tuck to keep in shape. Up until two weeks before her baby, she was still working in the marketing department of one of the mobile phone companies and commuting full time. She has one third-level degree and a diploma. When she puts her recent experience to one side, she will have a second baby and be done by the time she is thirty-four.[8]

If she were not married — as, this year, 35% of mums weren't — she would typically be twenty-seven and, like Kelly Angel, be well-educated and travelled. The rise in unmarried mothers is the biggest change in maternity Ireland since the Papa preached against sex before marriage. However, we are seeing a significant change in the age and therefore social status of unmarried mums. Every year, Irish unmarried mothers are getting older which means that women are simply taking control of their bodies and the old 'wisdom' about unmarried meaning unwanted is no longer true. But the contrast between the Pope's Children and their parents is stark. In 1979, 6% of children were born outside marriage; this year it is more than one in three.[9]

Another striking difference between the Kells Angels and their mothers is that very few now are choosing to have big families. Back in the 1970s a quarter of the women giving birth at any one time in Holles Street were having their fifth child or more. This figure has collapsed to only one in a hundred.[10] Kelly Angel is planning her pregnancy to fit in with her career — as they say in the investment world, it's all about timing.

As well as having more unmarried mums than ever before, we are also having more weddings. We are in the grip of wedding mania — complete with Bridezillas — the perfectly normal young women who turn into napkin-obsessed monsters the minute the countdown to the big day starts. There were more weddings in Ireland last year than at any time since 1974. Weddings are in and the more outlandish the better.

Today in the era of the great blurring, we are a country of professional, better-educated women having fewer children as opposed to the Ireland of Inter-Cert educated, full-time mums with lots of kids. So the picture is lots of separate, small families rather than a few, large families. These kids are the most precious Irish children ever. Because they are quite likely to be only children, with parents who have more money than time, they are the most pampered generation ever. The only child of the Kells Angels will be Destiny's Child, over-indulged, over-praised and mollycoddled like no Irish child ever.

DESTINY'S CHILD

When mother and baby emerge — usually within twelve hours of giving birth to free-up the precious beds — from the United Nations of Holles Street, they will be whisked off to a warm suburban house, with new clothes (no hand-me-downs because (a) there are no older siblings and (b) that's not done).

All you can hear above a crying child is the constant whir of the camcorder, there to document, record and assess every hand movement, blink and utterance. You can't test and assess them early enough.

If our Kells Angel has managed to avoid being press-ganged by the serial lactators, her giant chrome and granite kitchen, with matching Velux windows, double-doors to the outside deck, will sport an industrial-sized, state-of-the-art steriliser. The Kells Angels are obsessive compulsives. They are obsessed with germs that could attack Destiny's Child. Everything has to be sterilised. 87 Cúlfada Downs is like Howard Hughes' bedroom in Las Vegas, scrubbed clean, washed down and all items disposed of immediately after use. It is more like a clinic than a kitchen. The steriliser is the 21st-century equivalent of the Guardian Angel — there to ward off all evil airborne pathogens and spirits and to keep baby safe and well in the night. In the dead of night, when the suburb is asleep, all that can be seen is a red light blinking in the corner of the kitchen. In the old days this used to be the Sacred Heart gazing down as you glanced up guiltily. Today the constant red light is the quadraphonic Bose, surround sound, home-entertainment/baby-monitor which umbilically links the special one, Destiny's Child, to Kells Angel no matter where she is.

The enormous double-doored fridge will be stuffed with Cow & Gate formula, and the softest wipes that money can buy will be on hand. The background music will be gentle and comforting — the new Coldplay CD — and the new cot spotless and expensive. Dad will be flustering around awkwardly in his combats that are pulled up too high — the way thirty-something suburban men do — somewhere around his diaphragm rather than his hips.

The room will be a temple to the pink goddess of fertility. This ancient goddess dates back to 1950s American suburbia and was invented by those weird people at Hallmark Cards. All is pink — pillows, cards, blankets and Babygros. Unlike the Pope's children, Destiny's Child will always have a room of her own. No sharing with older sisters. Everything is soft, saccharine and safe — a secure shrine to the special one.

Destiny's Children will be like no other generation: they will be staunchly middle class. The Pope's Children have fallen into an increasingly classless society where, like our dear leader Bertie Ahern, anyone can make it.

WHERE HAVE ALL THE JOHNS AND MARYS GONE?

How many times have you heard a young mother roll her eyes up to heaven at the sound of another mum calling out the name of her child, only to realise that the name she picked is now common as muck? They thought when they chose the name that it was lovely sounding, old fashioned, a bit classy and most importantly, reasonably unusual. Everyone else had the same idea and there are now Sophies everywhere.

What's the big deal, you might ask? Well there is none really until you examine the psychology behind names. The name you choose for your child is supposed to mark the child out and, more interestingly, say something about the type of person you think you are. So the Pope's Children are obsessed with their child's name. Although you might hear young parents saying that they did not think about the names of their children, this is nonsense. The name is everything. Destiny's Child's name will be crucial to marking her out as special.

For the Pope's Children, Destiny's name will be the first indicator of greatness. We can see the social aspirations of parents and this quest for uniqueness if we look at the changing patterns of Irish names over the past 25 years. The years have been tough on John and Mary. They were the Pope's Children's premier names. The most popular names by far. But something has happened. By last year, John had fallen to 22nd while Mary has plummeted to a lowly 45th most popular. In a bizarre symmetrical twist, Seán and Emma, both the 29th most popular names in 1979, have raced, hand in hand, up the charts to poll position.[11]

Amongst girls, there has been something of a name revolution. Not one of the top ten girls' names in 1979 remain in the top ten today. Where have all the Susans, Anns, Deirdres, Louises, Sharons, Catherines, Carolines, Lisas and Jennifers gone? They have been usurped by a slew of Emmas, Sarahs, Aoifes, Ciaras, Katies, Sophies, Rachels, Chloes, Amys and Leahs. Some names have had a field day since then. Hats off to Sophie in particular. She has rocketed up the charts from a miserable 166th in 1979 to chart-topping 6th last year, while poor old Deirdre, Ann and Susan have fallen out of the charts altogether. As befits the great blurring, traditional English rose names like Emma, Sophie and Amy are now in vogue, yet so too are old Irish names like Ciara and Aoife. While ironically, during a period when the Irish Jewish community has shrunk, Jewish names such as Leah, Sarah and Rachel all make it into the top ten.

The Pope's Children want their little ones to have cosmopolitan yet Hibernian names at the same time — as long as it has the diminutive *ah* or *a* at the end so we have little Ciara and her little sister Leah.

Although not so dramatic, the changes in boys' names have been substantial. Only David, Michael and James remain clinging on to the top ten positions, while Jack, Adam and Dylan have emerged out of nowhere. Jack and Dylan were not even in the top 100 names in 1979 and Adam was an unimpressive 97th.

We have also experienced a great variance and dispersal in names. In 1979, almost 40% of all boys were called John, David, Paul, Michael, Mark, Patrick, Brian or Alan. These were traditional, staid, common names reflecting a common culture where it would be pretentious to draw attention to the child by calling him something out of the ordinary. These were ordinary names for ordinary people. The one name, John, accounted for more boys christened in that year than the total of the forty-two least popular names put together. One in ten of the boys born in 1980 was called John or a papal derivative of it such as John Paul. This was a clear example of the 'don't step out of line' culture. Boys didn't have fancy names.

Today the situation is totally different. Reflecting the move towards individuality, Destiny's Child's search for uniqueness begins at his or her name. Let's call him a name no-one has ever heard of because he is special, gifted and different. He will be noticed from the off. He will be seen, recognised, marked down. He will not be like all the rest: he will be Destiny's Child. So we now have hundreds of special names.

Evidence from the US[12] explains why certain names are in vogue for a while and then fall away. 'Successful' sounding names have a fifteen-year cycle before they fall away and become common. The same pattern can be reasonably forecast in the Irish BabyBelt. Interestingly in the US — where they have data on names broken down by the wealth or education of the parents[13] — it has been established that it is not celebrities who dictate which names are on the way up, but the success of neighbours. If the bloke down the road who is doing well has kids called Claire and Aoife, this sets the trend in an area. So posh names only have a certain shelf-life. As the name becomes too popular, high-end parents soon drop it. The name gets shunted down the social classes and might disappear altogether, while other names will be on the way up. How else can we explain the popularity of Dylan and Adam? (Messrs Moran and Clayton can only take so much of the blame.) In 2020 will they still be in the top ten? I doubt it.

So not only are we getting a great blurring and dispersal but we are getting extremely rapid name-inflation and deflation. The fortune of names seems to be very volatile. One day it's in the top-ten, next it's out of the charts altogether. Why the name roller-coaster? What is driving it? Let's leave the newborn's bedroom and get to understand the philosophy of the Pope's Children in the BabyBelt. Let's get inside the heads of the Kells Angels. Let's read their dreams.

Chapter 5
The Expectocracy

THE NEW IRISH DREAM

All collars up, baseball caps and extra-firm hair gel, five young south Dublin lads — Drew, Pearse, John, Conor and Phil — came together to form A-men in March 1999. They wanted to conquer the world. If Westlife could do it, why not A-men? They looked great in suits, the image was right, they could dance, and the name — well, the name was perfect. A-men were posh — Donnybrook rather than Donnycarney — a fee-paying school version of Boyzone.

They all got on well. Conor and Pearse knew each other from school and from their days as mock politicians at the European Youth Parliament. Conor worked in the family business and did a sideline in karaoke. He could sing. He also knew Paul, the manager, who had great contacts in the Gaiety, the Panto circuit and, crucially, RTÉ.

Drew and Phil were second-year business students at Trinity and John was an old friend of Conor from schooldays. When one of the original line-up, Simon, pulled out, Conor asked Pearse, a UCD student at the time, to sign up on the explicit promise that there'd be no singing involved.

The rehearsals were in UCD. The guys learned a strict set of choreographed dance routines. These were high-energy affairs to backing tracks from Take That and Five. Original material was not discussed at that early stage, but envisaged after a recording deal. Their typical set was three numbers, lasting around 15 minutes. They were good and the irrepressible Paul said they were going places; agents had been making enquiries and it was only a matter of time before a record deal would be on offer.

Events moved quickly. They auditioned for RTÉ's 'Beat on the Street' in early summer 1999, were called back and three weeks later they landed the gig — two major events: one in the Square in Tallaght and the other in Eyre Square in Galway. Things were looking up. They followed up these gigs with a prestige interval performance at a fashion show in the RDS. The curtain raiser for the Peter Marks National Hairdresser of the Year Award came next and a fundraiser for their Alma Mater, the European Youth Parliament. A-men were on a roll. They were the talk of Kielys. Paul was forecasting the Point and maybe getting Louis Walsh involved. Then tragedy struck.

Conor found out that one of the guys was sleeping with his younger sister who was only seventeen at the time. The culprit was twenty — born in 1979/80 at the peak of the Pope's baby boom — but she was still in school. A monumental row ensued and the band fell apart acrimoniously. The music world would never know their real talent and we can now only speculate as to how far they might have gone. They drifted apart. A-men, the Donnybrook boy band who had the world at their Nikes, were no more, torpedoed by love, loyalty and family honour. Today, Pearse is practising at the Bar. He could have been a contender.

But for those brief months in that summer of love, A-men lived the New Irish Dream, which centres on the art of the possible. It is the dream of motivation. It believes that any Irish person can be or have whatever he or she wants. All you have to do is believe in yourself. It is the defining principle of the Pope's Children.

The Old Irish Dream — which was mother's milk to their parents and previous generations — was of Catholicism, nationalism, community, chastity, the Brits, the six counties, the Irish language, the famine, the underdog, getting a good job in the bank and the glamour of Grace Kelly. Things were offered up, sacrificed in this life for fulfilment in the next. This had been replaced by a New Irish Dream.

The New Irish Dream can be best summed up by 'I wanna trade up'. I want the biggest fridge, the best holiday, the newest car, the loudest sound system, the healthiest food, the best yoga posture, the most holistic world-view, the most talked about wedding and the best sex with as many partners, in as many positions as possible. I want it all and I want it now. I want to measure, compare and out-perform. I want to be recognised, appreciated and loved. I wanna be number 1 and no-one is going to stop me.

The Old Irish Dream was about us, ours and them. The New Irish Dream is about me, mine and yours. The New Dream speaks in the possessive case.

And New Ireland is acquisitive. This is not limited to income. We are also seeing status leap-frogging. When you get a nation where everyone regards themselves as middle class and there are seemingly opportunities for all, old barriers, which prevented people from 'rising above their station', disappear. So for a while you get a type of social anarchy. The system takes time to adjust to the new hierarchy. The old system can't get its head around the fact that builders earn more than surgeons, hairdressers make more than bank managers and car-alarm salesmen buy the most expensive houses in the country. Until this settles down, we see a constant jostling for social position. This carry-on is not new but it is particularly virulent.

Celebrity, fame and one-upmanship have become ubiquitous. We find ourselves in a world characterised by pester-power for grown-ups, where no suv is big enough, no model new enough, no orgasm climactic enough. It is a world where the brain of a seven-year-old has taken over the heads of the adult population, pestering, demanding and throwing away. Together, pester-power and the idea that the next kick will be better than the last has led to a bizarre Warhollian vision of the present, where everyone can be a star — even for only fifteen minutes. All boy bands such as A-men can be number 1 — if they can only keep their hands off your siblings. It is an 'Expectocracy' — an economic, social and political system where people's dreams and expectations dominate everything. The objective of the Expectocracy is immediate personal gratification.

In the Expectocracy, no-one is mediocre, average or not good enough. All you need is application. We are all brimming with unfulfilled expectations. There is no personal dream too deluded and no individual too ordinary to be brilliant. This is the self-help nation. No expectation is too high, too ambitious or too far-sighted. No child is too young for highlights, no bum too fat for hipsters and no singer too tone-deaf to be a Star. You just have to believe the hype and live the Dream.

THE 'YOU'RE A STAR' GENERATION

The exemplar of the New Irish Dream is the 'You're a Star' generation. On the last night of 'You're a Star' 2005, the national phone system crashed momentarily. Over 1.6 million texts were sent. More people watched the final than turned up to see the Pope. In the end, a brother and sister duo from Athlone won.

On their website they reveal a bit of themselves. Joseph McCaul feels that Nicholas Cage would be appropriate but Patrick Swayze could also do justice to the role of Joseph McCaul in his future eponymous Hollywood blockbuster. His sister Donna has pencilled in Jennifer Lopez to fill her shoes in the biographical movie that will be made about the McCauls when they reach the height of their fame. Lofty stuff, but what would you expect from the brother and sister who are the King and Queen of Ireland's 'You're a Star' generation?

'You're a Star' is the most successful TV programme in Ireland.[1] It shines a clear light on the Expectocracy. The two key selling points appeal to the individual expectocrat. For the contestants, the message is that anyone can make it, all you need is the self-belief, motivation and chutzpah. For the jury — the public who determine who is a Star — the message is that you are important, you count, you can change things, you have a mandate, no-one can challenge you, your view is as meaningful as that of the experts, you are powerful because you are the Starmaker.

The show itself is a strange hybrid — a cross between a conventional talent show and the frenzied parochial partisanship of GAA county club football. Like all talent shows, the different acts sing and dance, but here the jury votes less for talent than for tribe. People vote for their local hero and see regional conspiracies, rather than ability, behind the voting patterns. It's the 21st-century equivalent of a parish faction fight without cudgels, played out on TV and determined by text.

The partisan bias in the vote becomes clear if you read the emails on the show's website. Here is what Sinéad from Meath had to say: *'I'm sick of hearing everyone giving out about Ann Harrington (Meath). She looks fabulous, she has a great voice and she could put on a show to compete with any of the Eastern European countries. The Henry girls should have been voted off last week. Their interpretation of Vertigo was horrendous. It was like a bunch of Romanian gypsies doing a skit on U2. Why do you think Ray D'Arcy didn't ask Dave Fanning his opinion —*

because he would have said as much? I normally think Lorraine Maher is good, but she was woeful last Sunday. Voice too wobbly and nervous. We can't send someone like that to Eurovision. Áine O'Doherty is also not suitable for Eurovision. Ann is the last Meath contestant in it and everyone from Meath should get behind her and vote her through.'

Likewise, M. Casey from Kildare seems to see a Lillywhite mist first and talent second: *'Anyone who says Pete Fagan (Kildare) is not good enough for Eurovision needs their ears cleaned out. Vote Pete, he's brill.'*

Alan from Meath echoes Sinéad's sentiments: *'I think Ann (Meath) is by far the best performer in the show and would do us proud in the Eurovision.'*

Anonymous from Wexford has no doubt that only the Wexford girls Jade can perform for Ireland: *'The girls from Jade are doing us all very proud down here in Kilmuckridge/Monamolin. Here's hoping we'll get to hear more of their own songs in the future. The McCauls or Henry Girls would do Ireland proud at Eurovision. Keep up the good work, Jade.'*

Wexford votes for Wexford, Galway for Galway and Cork for Cork, conspiracies are seen and regional favourites are unearthed. Local passions are enflamed to such an extent that no cheating claim is too scurrilous and no allegation too outlandish. 'You're a Star' is the ultimate local hero rags to riches story. The stakes were high because until this year the winners stepped into Johnny Logan's shoes and went on to represent Ireland at the Eurovision. But like the victors of the Community Games in Santry playing in the Champions League Final, the results of such overblown expectations have been tragically underwhelming. In a competition that Ireland had a worrisome knack of winning when we picked winners professionally, we have barely registered a vote when proffering our 'You're a Star' heroes. Local politics works well for fixing footpaths; it's not so hot on spotting international talent.

Despite Eurovision failure, the programme grips huge swathes of the nation from November to March. It is manna from heaven for talk radio researchers and Monday morning tabloid headline writers. Every Sunday, voting leads to outbursts, tears and tantrums. There are countless Janet Jackson boob moments, tailor made for the press.

Because of the local angle, it is addictive. A local hero, maybe a receptionist by day who does Mariah Carey impressions on karaoke nights, has an opportunity to queen it up like Madonna on TV. It is celebrity made flesh and everyone has their chance, their moment in the spotlight, their star trip. Joe Duffy, the nation's king of chat, is delighted and admitted owing the following huge debt: 'I worked out that we got six controversies out of "You're a Star". It was like the All Ireland, it pitched parish against parish.'[2]

THE POP-NATION

Not only does it pitch old Irish parish against parish, but also it reveals that the New Ireland is a pop-nation. We have embraced a new disposable culture, where fame is fleeting, significance transitory and attention spans limited. Stories have to be generated and discarded; fast food has to be eaten on the run and the response to 'how are you?' is, nonsensically, 'busy'.

There is no better example of the pop-nation than pop-music. Old, slow, rigid, complaining Ireland did not do pop-music. The Beach Boys could never have come from Brittas; the Monkees with their bright, frivolous, up-beat, impossibly optimistic view of the world, could never have been from Sligo. Pop was for comfortable foreigners, not under-achieving Paddies.

Thinking back, it is impossible to imagine in the depressed 1980s an Irish pop act. Irish rock was serious and strenuous. Rock was about 'keeping it real' and, in the hierarchy, a tight rein was exerted by bearded traditional music enthusiasts — Brehon-like guardians of the flame — who cast long shadows over the music scene like grumpy schoolmasters. Irish music tended to be an earnest diatribe about empathy, poverty and drabness, coloured with limitless references to Martin Luther King, Nagasaki, disillusionment and general misery. It was *Angela's Ashes* in E flat. Irish music was about soul, angst, Ethiopia and the 'blacks of Europe' nonsense. When it was fun, like the Undertones, it was Bogside fun — the *My-Left-Foot*-of-punk sort of fun. It was fun with a social message. Whatever it was, it was not smiling pretty-boys in white tuxedos, perched on barstools doing Bee Gees covers. Music reflected the times. But times were changing.

Louis Walsh was the first to understand the musical significance of the Expectocracy. This eccentric man from Kiltimagh, working out of a small office with a mobile phone and a staff of one, led the charge. He asked, 'Why can't the Irish do pop?' After all we had been winning the Eurovision for years — the ultimate high camp, pop extravaganza. So why not out-boy-band the boy bands? Walsh twigged the new disposable nature of Ireland's pop-culture before any editorial headline writer, thinker, academic or commentator. He understood the value of a catchy pop chorus and recognised that the tweeney market — little girls somewhere between seven and fourteen — had not just exploded in Ireland but that their rich, overworked parents would always succumb to pester-power. He also recognised that Ireland could have three-minute heroes singing polished pop.

He realised a new generation was emerging who saw no barriers and wanted to push themselves forward. It was a generation that had the confidence, misguided or otherwise, to become stars. They were the people who believed that Nicholas Cage might just have the talent to do them justice. They were a generation of Irish dreamers. Walsh realised that the 'You're a Star' generation had already been born, they were hanging around every estate, singing into their hairbrushes in front of the mirror in every bathroom, they just needed to be discovered. Now they had a perfect platform.

But the 'You're a Star' show is distinct from other versions of the same format. It is not simply an Irish version of a cosmopolitan phenomenon. It is made distinctly Hibernian by the voting patterns, which are unique and pepper a cosmopolitan pop concept with local, deep-rooted tribal behaviour. It is musical GAA and the overall success is in the fusion of old Hibernian parochial, suspicious, partisan Ireland defined by townland, home and county with the new cosmopolitan Irish Dream, where no expectation is too lofty, and where there are no frontiers.

THE STARMAKERS — WHITE VAN DEMOCRATS

In the Expectocracy everyone wants to be mandated, so the flip side of the contestants is the jury. No only are all the contestants potential Stars, but we the public are the jury and the potential Starmakers. So the format fuses the expectations of both groups perfectly. This set-up satisfies the crucial Fox News slogan for success, 'We report, you decide'. It is the world of the new universal mandate — the 'have pre-paid mobile, can vote' universe and it is the ultimate expression of White Van Democracy. White Van Democracy can also be termed 'who the fuck do you think you are' democracy. Every time you text in your response to talk radio, vote in 'You're a Star' or give your tuppence-worth on blog sites under an anonymous pseudonym, you are participating in White Van Democracy. It is a mandate for those who never had one before and it thrives on the social anarchy that the great blurring affords.

The White Van Democrat is a ghoulish combination — the fury of road rage meets the voyeuristic empathy of Oprah. His view is pure, his vision unimpaired and his motives unimpeachable. He gets into his van, two foot above the rest of the traffic, runs his fingers through his hair and turns the ignition. He thumbs his wad, opens the TV page, checks his GSP and times his journey home. The Champions League is on TV3 at 7.30. He should make it. He smells of turpentine. He settles up with the Polish lads — in cash — calls herself, turns on the radio, adjusts his tackle and begins to fume.

Back in the studio the presenter, like a big game hunter, knows the White Van Democrat is out there, lurking menacingly somewhere in the depths of the Oscar Traynor Road. Like Robert Shaw in *Jaws*, he realises it is a long waiting game. He knows you're there and you know how to lure him. Experience tells the presenter to cast his line just after six. He does so artfully. Today's bait, driven by an *Evening Herald* headline is juicy: 'Do we need Nigerian guards?' he asks — half-indignant publican, half-social visionary. He calls in an ad-break like US marines call in air-strikes, sits back, takes off his headphones, sups his tea and waits.

The waters are calm at first. Initially the screen flickers, it then turns red as the angry texts stream in. The White Van Democrat scents blood. The airwaves go from tranquil to choppy. More bait. The presenter mischievously attributes a comment to an unpopular soft-left, liberal politician. He takes a traffic update, reads out some of the more inflammatory texts and waits. Textmen all around the city and out in the BabyBelt are frantically punching keys.

The producer screams that the system is coming down with texts. White Van Democrat is fuming but not ready yet to be reeled in. The presenter plays for time. The next item on his running order is not live yet and anyway, he is where he likes to be, toying with his quarry. He is the radiowave matador.

Time to do a poll, string it out and make a few quid, plus we can always call up the *Herald* and keep the story going tomorrow. Free publicity is the name of the game. Go for it. '*Just text 087100100 for yes or 087100101 for no if you are against African cops in your area*', calls out the matador in headphones. At a special low-call rate the money is flowing in. Maliciously the presenter invents a poll result — 80% in favour of black cops on Parnell Street. Our White Van Democrat is apoplectic. He cracks and phones in.

The matador kills his mic during a twenty-second traffic update. The red light in the studio flicks off. He checks the time. It is half six, time for the most expensive ad slots. He thinks of his job, his bonus and the ratings. 'Get that racist on the line immediately,' he screams at the producer.

White Van Democrat is through, he is alone but chosen. 'Tony from Clonsilla, good afternoon, you're on air, what would you like to say?' Tony rants and can hear himself in Dolby on the van's Blaupunkt. He manages to calm down and is more measured by the time the presenter interjects. An on-air joust ensues; the matador allows himself to be exposed, feigns injury and goes on to another caller. It's all part of the game but White Van Democrat doesn't even know the rules. As far as he's concerned he has landed a knock-out punch. He hangs up victoriously. His phone is now hopping with texts from other Democrats, all giving him cyber high-fives. He rounds the Santry bypass, slowly, measuredly, triumphantly, one hand on the wheel, the other pressing the phone keyboard. He is the tea-time champ who can text and drive.

He is content, calm now and thinking of golf on Thursday. He has voted, his voice has been listened to, his part played. White Van Democrat has exercised his mandate and all is well.

Our White Van Democrat is one of thousands of Textmen out there, festering in the traffic with a similar suite of opinions and vitriol — the Seven Notion Army. Like the sleeping, Chinese ceramic foot soldiers, these people were unearthed accidentally by reality TV and have captivated us ever since. They single-handedly drive the profit margins of TV programmes like 'Celebrity Love Island', 'The Restaurant' and 'You're a Star'. Every non-soap entertainment programme features them squarely on its initial pitch. For a TV executive these Textmen are crucial. If your idea taps into the psyche of the White Van Democrats, your programme will be commissioned. The reason is straightforward economics. The more texts, the more revenue for the programme; the more revenue, the smaller the budget for the TV or radio station; and the more interactivity, the more talkability and the quicker the programme becomes part of popular culture. Therefore, there is a bias on the part of TV producers and commissioning editors to pander to the White Van Democrat, reinforcing him, inflating him, making him feel entitled.

Once mandated, the White Van Democrat fades into the traffic, his 99 C Ford Transit indistinguishable from the others as they merge into the long, late evening chrome and metal snake that extends from the airport to Laytown.

THE POLITICS OF PARENTING AND THE ATTAINOMETER

The New Irish Dream demands that we accomplish things, conquer fears and achieve our goals — in this life, not in the next. As parents, the Pope's Children must give their kids a fighting chance to shine, to improve, to develop, to attain and, most crucially, to be Destiny's Child.

For parents in an Expectocracy, four factors take precedence over everything else. First, it is vitally important to remember that, at all times, your child's achievements are your accomplishments. Every little notch she manages over the average, every star she gets for spelling, each time she sings solo in the choir, all are direct results of your being a better than average parent. In the new suburbs, the most intense battle is between parents for the coveted best-parent award. In this race, the odds are stacked against two-income families, which are now the majority. If a mother works, she starts with a vicious and unforgiving handicap. The very act of pulling out of the drive, kids strapped into baby-seats on your way to the crèche at 7 am puts you at a disadvantage. Unlike golf, the handicap is not there to even things up. It is there to pass judgement, to trip you up, to expose your selfish 'me first, baby second' ways.

To get over this, your behaviour must be unimpeachable. In the politics of behaviour, you have to top the poll and be first past the post. You must double your efforts and have no aspersions cast on your commitment to good parenting. In the great suburban parenting battle you must show no signs of weakness, you need always to be committed. Remember, the others are always watching. No matter how sweet the stay-at-home mums might be at the school gate, or they might seem at the parents' association meeting, no matter how inconsequential the ballet lessons appear, no matter how tipsy you might think they were at the last party, they are always watching, waiting, listening and scrutinising. They are ready to betray you to the all-powerful parenting police — the KGB of SUV land — the guardians of Destiny's Child who are unseen but will display their wrath in an odd look, an innocuous dressingdown or an invitation not RSVPd.

The second rule for parents in the Expectocracy is that with everyone compressed into the middle, competition for everything becomes more intense. In the past, your social status was rigid, so you did not feel the same anxiety about under-achieving. If your Dad was not a lawyer, you would never be one so there was nothing to worry about. But today, with the New Irish Dream governing the society, if you or your Destiny's Child does not exceed, ascend or make the grade, there is something wrong with her as an individual. She cannot blame the system. She is at fault. The flip side of the Expectocracy is not disappointment, but humiliation, loss of face and banishment into the outer darkness of average-ness.

This heightened feeling of insecurity is made more acute by a media that informs, grades, opines and benchmarks everything. For example, any editor of a Sunday newspaper will tell you that nothing sells like the edition that publishes secondary school league tables. Parents scour the web to find out what school is better than the rest. They want to find out whether this grind-school is superior to another or, if they are real aspirants, they need to know whether this crèche has more Irish language speakers than the other one. Living rooms are a-buzz with parents logging on to www.ratemyteachers.ie on a nightly basis. So the information age leads to a neurotic babble of factoids, confusing people, making parents more self-conscious and heightening social anxiety.

The third crucial factor for parenting in the Expectocracy is that every child now will be Destiny's Child. This is the direct consequence of smaller family size and has led to what can be termed the 'preciousness index' of children. The preciousness index measures the uniqueness of your special one. It gauges just how special your child is. The preciousness index can tell you who is going to be the Jose Morinho of the class before he kicks a ball and which one is going to be Beyonce before she sings her first Old McDonald. It is a complex, but highly suggestive barometer of who is going to be the chosen one, the one that fate has picked, the Destiny's Child.

In the past when big families were the norm, this intense scrutiny did not exist. If you were one of ten, the chances of Mummy — or, even more remote, Daddy — doting over you were rather slim. In the New Ireland where children are scarce and families plentiful, parents' expectations have changed dramatically.

The fourth factor is fear of relegation from the good parenting Premiership. This forces some working women to go way over the top in the after-school activity stakes. Guilt is the driving factor. It is sometimes forgotten that 68% of young Irish mothers now work,[3] drop their kids to the crèche, childminder or granny, commute long hours and are guilty: trying to be a good mother, a good motivator and a good employee. They are the juggling generation. Because they are not around, it is crucial that their children are busy, so that they don't become couch potatoes because Mummy is making a useless bloody pitch to some idiotic marketing director with plastic shoes, who keeps staring at her boobs.

When I was a kid, mothers on our road did not go to work. There were some exceptions (my own mother for example), but in general, ours was a road of single-income families, Mummies always at home, on hand and Dads sitting down in front of their dinners at 6 pm. My memory suggests that we spent lots of time hanging out watching TV. We had no parentally organised or supervised after-school activities and we spent our weekends slouching around, under- rather than over-achieving. The keenness of mothers to get their kids involved in extra-school activities is part of the guilt of the juggling generation.

The Attainometer[4]

The American social commentator David Brooks in *On Paradise Drive* suggests that inside the head of every suburban American mother is a large devise which assesses her child's progress and achievements. He could have easily been writing about Ireland, borrowing from Brooks, we can term this Irish devise an Attainometer.

For your child to qualify as Destiny's Child, she has to score high on the Attainometer. This does what it says on the tin and measures, in the head of the Irish mother, the level of accomplishment of her child. You may think it imprecise, but it is exact and exacting. For example for 'early-schoolers', the Attainometer measures their grasp of the alphabet, writing, singing, sport, ballet and counting.

In the BabyBelt, the Great Suburban Expectocracy takes over and instead of children being free and fun-loving, their lives become regimented and tested. They have to achieve and they will be rewarded for accomplishments. Supervision, measurement, regimentation is the name of the game.

Low GI Jane — the Queen of the Expectocracy

Inside the head of every middle-class mummy, the large, shiny Attainometer ticks away relentlessly. Initially the Attainometer is linked to hours, days, weeks and months. It then progresses to years. Everything is benchmarked. She is much more interested in where her son is relative to the rest of the class. How does he compare? She is not interested in absolutes. Where should he be in Irish at six? Did you know that her friends' children can count up to forty, while she can't get past eleven? What do you mean your youngest can't crawl at five months? I know a great infant cranial osteopath who might help.

This carry-on is new, and the closest thing to it when I was a kid was a primitive form of the Attainometer: the little pencil marks on our kitchen wall which marked out height as our family grew from three through to five — broken down into half-yearly instalments. David aged four and a half; David aged five and so on. Every time I grew an inch my mum gave me a sweet and some cake 'to make you grow big and strong'. (These were the days before sweets were banned and replaced by lentils and yoga.) Like all kids, I cheated, inching up on my tippy-toes, trying to stretch my neck like the African tribeswomen who starred in missionary leaflets.

The modern Attainometer is a much more serious affair. And it doesn't matter how rich you are relative to the rest of society, what matters is where you are relative to your peers. So for example, if we leave the Kells Angels and move into the upper echelons of the Expectocracy, the motives, impulses and behaviour are exactly the same. It is all part of the great blurring. A rich Mummy will always be aware of the Attainometer which ticks away, measuring progress continuously. Take a rich yummymummy at the top of the Expectocracy who we shall call Low GI Jane. (She is a sucker for diet fads but she likes the science in the GI diet — it appeals to her A in honours Biology.) She is the role model for the aspirant Kells Angel. She has it all. She is the lifestyle Queen.

Her Attainometer is switched on just after conception which undoubtedly was fulfilling. The fit, healthy and well-matched sperm and eggs get to work immediately. No rough edges here. Perfect Blackrock swims manfully, against the tide, into the expectant, ripe 500-point Leaving Cert, Mount Anville egg.

While Blackrock is out practising his swing at Powerscourt with the guys, Low GI Jane, in between the bouts of nausea (which her mum incidentally told her just to put up with and not to annoy Blackrock about), is already planning pre-school activities for the baby. She worries about the immigrants more than the friends. You have to give your child every opportunity, particularly with those smart Chinese and Indian kids around. She knows that behind those pleasant smiles at the local Spar checkout, the Chinese are planning for their own little ones who will snap up all the scholarships to Trinity in 2022. Not only does your little baby have to outshine all the other kids at the school, but he has to out-think those inscrutable Asians who have joined the race recently. Remember what happened to poor Sonia O'Sullivan against those Chinese girls in the Sydney Olympics? Be prepared, be ready.

At five weeks, Low GI Jane has already stocked up on books like *What to expect at six months*, *How to be a Good Parent*, and *Positive not Pushy*. She likes the sound of the last one. That sounds more like her image of herself: breezy, effortless, non-perspiring achievement. Not too much struggle, not well-planned, just perfectly timed and executed. In many ways she was predestined, as Destiny's Child will be. It has, after all, flawless genes. Two rugger caps, a hockey colours for UCC, one L&H auditor, a barrister and three consultants in the past two generations — destiny is burned into that DNA. Oblivious, the little genius is swimming around in Low GI Jane's vitamin and supplement-enhanced amniotic fluid — progressing, growing, beating and succeeding daily.

The Attainometer is on, subconsciously measuring everything. Low GI Jane has studied the timetable. Frankly would you expect anything less? You don't do a B.Comm. with languages, rise up the corporate ladder and postpone your first child till you are ready for botox and not know how crucial the first four months are. At fifteen weeks she decides to tell the girls at Riverview. She pulls up in her BMW X5 SUV, perfectly highlighted blonde hair tied back, her New Balance Supplex sports bra making her look smaller on top than she is — which she quite likes at her age. Small is beautiful. She stretches her face in the mirror, the way women in their thirties do, smoothes her forehead and parachutes out the 10-foot drop from door to ground. The girls are ecstatic. Low GI Jane has it all, a perfectly successful career now on hold, a kitchen to die for, the caravan in Ballinacorrig and no IVF — how does she do it?

She is a fully paid up Mount Carmelite. At thirty weeks she's up in Mount Carmel every second week being monitored (after all at her age, thirty-five, she didn't want to risk anything). The gynaecologist, a great guy, although embarrassingly she did snog him years ago at Mount Merrion Tennis Club disco, tells her she is progressing well. Low GI Jane buys Wombssong, an intra-natal device which plays Mozart to the baby. Low GI Jane is content and well-groomed. As she rolls out her Malaysian yoga mat to perfect her pre-breakfast sun salutations, she gazes out the window at her teak decking and dreams of Destiny's first day at school.

At six months, she switches to pregnancy Astanga which focuses on strengthening the tummy and pelvic muscles. She can't go to seed and has heard too many nightmare stories of husbands leaving after the first one. Up at Riverview, she can't help seeing the vile consequences of Great Drooping. No tennis balls on chewing gum for her! So while maybe her once pert boobs won't pass the pencil test, there will be no flabby blancmange tummy, quivering in ill-advised swimsuits. And as for the corrugated obscenity of stretch-marks, no way.

Antenatal yoga is fantastic for toning, and Luke the Yogi is very cute. She likes the way he touches her and asks her to back into him to achieve the proper position for downward dog. She suspects he likes it too.

Her pelvic floor exercises are going well, although secretly she is not so convinced about the wisdom of the natural home birth — no matter what Gwyneth or Christy trumpet in *Vanity Fair*. She is chilled to the bone by the prospect of squatting in a bath in her kitchen under the stern eye of that dykey-looking midwife telling her to think of the opening of her birth canal as the blossoming of a beautiful water lily. Low GI Jane is equally sceptical of the idea that the child's birth is a fantastic natural journey which will forge a life-long bond between mother and daughter.

The problem with the antenatal yoga is that the other women are scathing at the prospect of a maternity ward and constantly refer to Holles Street as 'the industrial complex'. Low GI Jane finds herself — without really thinking — on a Wednesday afternoon in a drafty church hall with a bunch of Andrea Dworkin lookalikes chanting. She hears herself whispering *ep-i-dur-al* very quietly as she listens to the natural birthing expert who also doubles up as a homeopath, railing against the evils of the industrial, battery-hen process that is modern obstetrics. The other women in this chilly Church of Ireland hall with only one metred heater (typical Prods) are chanting some indecipherable Sanskrit muck about the birthing mother, the miracle of conception and the body's natural endorphins. Low GI Jane dreams of a glass of Pinot Grigio, Luke the Yogi at Riverview and a quick, painless Caesarean at Mount Carmel.

When she switched last year from corporate banking to fund raising and a few minor directorships, she thought she would have more time to oversee the new kitchen. But things didn't work that way. She needs to fly down to Africa one last time before the six-month flying ban to see those inspiring aid workers who are doing such marvellous things for the homeless HIV-positive child prostitutes. Those little faces and tragic sad eyes — perfect covers for the invitation cards on next Friday's fund-raising lunch in the Four Seasons. Everyone will be there — even Norma, who doesn't get out much these days. Maybe she won't fly out after all. She might leave the field work to those crusty New-Age types who get hooked on the charity anti-globalisation trip for a few years in their early twenties before joining Anglo-Irish Bank on graduate training programmes.

After all, who's going to kit out the new kitchen? They have punctured a large hole in the back of the house already and pushed back almost to the end of the garden. But it will be worth it — 85 square metres of pure kitchen. As she towers over the traffic in her BMW X5 SUV — 400 stone of metal carrying eight stone of well-preserved, uber-expectocrat, Low GI Jane dreams of the smell of cut grass, a glass of wine with the girls on her new solid teak deck, fresh coriander sprinkled on delicious avocado salads, spotless, pristine work tops and the little baby cooing away contentedly on the baby monitor. Low GI Jane can — and Low GI Jane will — have it all.

Chapter 6
Property Porn

THE GROUP TRIP

What gave birth to the Expectocracy? Why has Ireland changed so dramatically? Is this change unprecedented or have we been here before? Does every generation make the fatal assumption that their times are unique? And if we are in the sociological version of a full-wash, who or what is going to turn off the spin cycle?

The Expectocracy begins and ends with the property boom. The property boom — the soaring price of houses, the associated lending, building, commuting and working — has not just changed the economy, it has changed us — the Irish people — profoundly. In the same way as the English were changed by the Industrial Revolution, the Americans by the gold rush, the Argentinians by their boom at the beginning of the 20th century, the Italians by the Renaissance and the White South Africans by diamonds, the deep thing inside us that makes us Irish is going through a once-in-a-century convulsion. For the first time in Irish history, positive, not negative economics is the transforming instrument.

One way to look at the dynamics of an economic surge driven by an addiction — be it for gold, diamonds, tulips or houses — is through the group dynamic of a mind-altering trip. The property boom is a powerful addiction, it is a group trip and everyone is buzzing.

'This is the trip, the part I really like.' So said Jim Morrison, the most deified tripper of them all. In order to understand where the Expectocracy comes from and how powerful it is, we must appreciate that we are now hooked on that finest of all class A financial narcotics: property. Everyone has dropped at the same time and everyone is coming up together. We are all loved-up. In this heady effervescence, nobody is allowed to wreck the buzz. We are all in the same club. The music is pumping, whistles going, arms in the air, the entire nation is off its face on one giant trip and it feels brilliant. Initially, it was a bit tingly, we didn't know if it was working, we were touched by a bit of paranoia. Is it just me? Self-doubt reigns. Am I doing the right thing? What if this turns out bad? But then, gradually, the warm realisation that everyone is at the same carry-on dawns. Now it's full on. The roof lifts. Reality blurs and then disappears. Whoosh. It's now coming in waves. Jesus, I'm off my tits. So is everyone else, rubbing, smiling, happy. Feel the love.

We are all buzzing. It is impossible to have a conversation with anyone in Ireland without the subject of house prices turning up. Yes, it is a cliché, but it's true. Age, social class, colour or creed do not matter. The unifying topic is the price of houses, the fortunes made, the extravagances, the opulence or the dreary sameness of new estates. Everyone has their story.

A favourite of mine was an encounter on the back of a bus in Cork recently between a number of Irish tracksuits and a few Polish workers. The tracksuits were angrily taunting the Poles. Kitted out in full tracksuit mufti — all Burberry, Nike, baseball caps and male jewellery, sporting rings that you could land a helicopter on and topped with cropped hair gelled forward frantically — the preferred look of feuding families in Limerick. The Polish lads, who clearly could look after themselves, pretended not to hear. They stared straight ahead, resting their broad Slavic chins on the headrests of the seats in front of them, smoking their bus tickets and tucking their bomber jackets around themselves as if expecting something to be projected from behind. Trouble was in the air. My money was on the Slavs but the tracksuits, with two generations of chip-shop head-kicking behind them, were capable of anything. A few cans of Dutch Gold flew. A central European took one directly on the head. He looked at his three mates. They stood up in unison and turned as one, like any army troop. Trouble now. The biggest one, who looked like a Bond villain's enforcer, lumbered up the aisle and in a strangely soft voice explained to the tracksuits that he was only here to do the jobs the Irish wouldn't do, save money and buy himself and his family a little gaff back home. The tracksuits were taken aback both by his unthreatening tones, but also by his enormous clenched first which stated calmly, 'If you little fuckers don't chill out I will gladly defenestrate each of you in turn.'

One of the tracksuits broke the ice by asking surreally how much a two-bed flat would cost in Poland. He seemed genuinely interested. Vladimir responded, '€59K'. The tracksuits laughed and began rhyming off prices in Cork as if they were trainee estate agents. These lads looked more like burglars than investors and maybe they were both, but their knowledge of the property market was encyclopaedic. They explained to the Poles how they could group together and buy a place here, what was the best mortgage to get interest only or capital, and how, if the price went up here, the Poles could borrow against their Cork flat to buy in Poland. The conversation continued, comparing, contrasting and advising, full of anecdotes about friends and family experiences, profits calculated and rental yields assessed. This would not have been out of place at a stockbroker weekend at Ashford Castle after all the fine wines, fly-fishing and wife-swapping, but on the back of the bus in Cork city between a bunch of Norries and a few illegal immigrants, the mind boggles. It was the most extraordinary conversation I have heard in years. Welcome to the gold rush.

Although most the western world is in the grip of a similar property boom, nowhere as far as I can see is quite as addicted as we are. Since 1997, property prices have gone up by 197%.[1] Property and its various components are everywhere. In the same way as the Muslim world orientates itself towards Mecca, the entire fabric of Irish society faces the totem of the sun-god property and its various minor deities, kitchens, bathrooms, hardwood flooring, expansive utility rooms, maple decking or walk-in dressingrooms. Nothing defines you more than your house. Adults become delirious at the sight of other people's houses; there are more water cooler moments over apartments than the boss's indiscretions; and the views, well they are an entire lexicon to themselves. Property is the new sex, new black and new brown all together.

There are routinely more pages in the property sections of the newspapers than in the papers themselves. Turn on your TV tonight and doubtless you will see yet another property programme. Sometimes they focus on worried first-time buyers trying to get on the ladder. Maybe this week it's a sun-drenched series about house hunters abroad. Celebrity interior designers are like plastic surgeons suggesting an alteration here and extension there, to make your home look more beautiful, enchanting and desirable. Architects are the new Gods, and celebrity TV gardeners have turned Irish back lawns into varnished timber-deck platforms, full of water features and dramatic outdoor lighting.

The part of the Irish imagination which used to be taken up with dreaming of escape, writing a book or playing for Arsenal, now dreams of slate wet-rooms, gravel driveways and Belfast sinks. All kitchens are advertised with glasses of Chablis and smiling pretty girls with whopping orthodontic bills and suggestive fleshy lower lips, busily chopping coriander. All bathrooms have the same girls in a fluffy half-opened bathrobe gazing dreamily out of the *en suite* towards the Egyptian cotton sheeted bed. Photographers have had a field day, as have banks, building societies, advertisers, car dealers, crèche owners and Nigerians selling the *Evening Herald* at Newlands Cross. Everyone's a winner — and it could be you.

We are not a nation of home-owners but of speculators. Everyone is thinking of the next move. If you are where you live, then the only sure-fire way to exhalted status is another thousand square feet, a better address or a finer view. There are enough vested interests making out like bandits from the whole racket to make sure that the incessant cheerleading is cranked up to full volume.

If the cheerleaders are not telling us to move, buy, rent or sell, they are urging us to knock down, punch out, extend over, create, conceive, build out and improve. We feel like lesser humans if we are not caught up in the great land mania that sweeps all before us. We should be involved; only losers are not in the game. The land trip has changed the psychology of the nation and the way we see ourselves and others.

PORNO NATION
It's the blue skies that strike you first. Lighting up the scene behind every house, apartment, maisonette, new estate or development is a clear blue Andalusian sky, peppered with unthreatening faint nimbus clouds. You expect to smell tapas, hear castanets and see large cut-out bulls on remote hillsides advertising Seville's finest *jamon*. But you are

in Granard, not Granada. The ad is for a three-bed semi, not a sun-bleached hacienda, yet the dream is the same. Buy now, pay later, the sun is shining, the day will be lovely, the message is upbeat, the future is bright and the dream is alive. In this world nothing is grey, rainy or unsettled. There is no menace, just promise, optimism and possibility. We are in the land of permanent blue skies. We are in the world of Irish property porn.

We are awash with financial pornography, some soft and passive, some graphic and interactive. The real hardcore only appears on a Thursday. Embarrassed subscribers can have it delivered discreetly to the door — for a small fee. This is top-shelf material and should be kept out of our children's reach. It is the *Irish Times* property section.

Every house in the pages of this property porn mag is a bricks-and-mortar version of a playboy bunny with perfect 34D breasts — waiting just for you. All you have to do is call now. The property narrative is a virtual chat-line and property-speak has its own soft, suggestive vocabulary, designed for maximum financial arousal. Each 'for sale' sign beckons you evocatively with the thrill of capital gain and the lure of immediate social gratification.

Flick the pages and houses shine out at you, urging you on like touched-up glamour models, enhanced chests, tummies tightened, red lips full and lustful, mouth sensually half-opened, dyed blondes back-combed, waiting on white cotton sheets uniquely for you — the horny buyer. For this month's playmate, read property of the week. For Hugh Hefner and Larry Flint read Mark FitzGerald and Ken McDonald. Property porn is big business and it's legal.

Every house is an 'opportunity', every fetish catered for, no property peccadillo too weird to be satisfied. Would Madame care for gravel driveways, ebony stairs, a kitchen workstation and — a must for the modern suburban dinner party — an outside smoking area? If you have the cash, no questions asked. No problem, Sir, come with me. All can be bought for a price. You can be the Marquis de Sade of Irish property buyers with the most depraved suggestions and still come away satisfied. Each page of the glossy promises you a unique experience. Hush, hush. Perfection is for sale, all you have to do is borrow for the pleasure.

Like our bunny girls, all homes are well proportioned — all bay windows are generous, every living-room 'magnificent', every kitchen is spacious, integrated and stunning. All bedrooms *en suite*, all staircases sweeping and all halls imposing. The houses themselves, like the 'real live housewives' on a chat-line, come to life oozing charm and seduction to the prospective buyer. They are never garish, public or conspicuous but are discreet, 'tucked away', promising the privacy of a voyeur, despite being one of one hundred pebble-dash boxes built in Bishopstown in 1967.

Older houses are pitched, the way older women are in porn mags, at the idiosyncratic, discerning punter who wants a special type of experience. Light in old houses never just shines, it 'streams' or 'floods'. Houses display their 'original features' the same way as older madams possess experience, knowledge, insight and understanding. Older houses are gracious, nostalgic and evocative, never quick, brash or immediate. In reality, these 'original features' are rickety banisters, draughty window frames and gaps in the floor boards — guaranteeing unseen and usually unbudgeted-for heating bills that would keep Liberty Hall toasty all winter. But in the dream world of property porno, they make the punter feel that he is discriminating, informed and secretly part of a select group of aficionados that know their Louis xiv from their Louis Vuitton. Old houses make people feel special and ultimately posh. You have that most sought-after of attributes — you have taste.

In the same way as centrefolds have to be filthy, lewd and adventurous as well as discreet, private and gentle, Irish houses have to be all things to all comers. So while the ubiquitous lacquered deck speaks of balmy evenings, Riesling, barbeques and sockless deckshoes, the thick walls in the same period homes suggest robustness, hard winters and dryness inside when outside is mossy damp.

Bragging rights are essential if you are tempted to pay huge sums for bricks and mortar. Property-speak acknowledges this and the language changes to accommodate it. So the centrefolds do not just 'have' large rooms, they 'boast' features. 'This prestigious period dwelling boasts wonderfully bright, spacious entertaining spaces.' This conjures up images of reclining aristocrats, a sort of louche 21st-century Hellfire Club, entertaining decadently as opposed to career-climbing, stiff dinner parties where the wife's cleavage is on show for the sexless boss.

All renovations have been carried out meticulously by some expert or other, preferably imported, so the Portuguese stonemason or the Italian designer feature prominently in any sales pitch. If houses have views of the sea, they pompously 'command' such views. Every back garden is secluded, private and south-facing and all façades are handsome. Redbricks are solid, Georgian is elegant, bungalows are always stylish and terraces are impressive. In the great Expectocracy, nothing can be average, modest or normal.

No makeover is too outlandish. So, for example, a falling-down shell automatically metamorphoses into a 'once-off opportunity, presenting an outstanding challenge to someone with vision and style'. In this way, the shell begins to describe the type of person you are. Are you a boring, limited dullard who will settle for someone's design, layout or proportions, or are you an exciting person of style and vision with your own mind? Deep down, the question renovations pose is whether you are a maverick or a sheep. What you buy speaks volumes about the type of person you are.

Every problem is an opportunity, every downside a selling point. Inaccessibility becomes tranquillity. Congestion becomes vibrancy. A two-bit boreen with a Spar and a garage instantly becomes an 'old world village' as opposed to a New-Age illusion. Houses are always only a 'stroll away' from the village's heart despite the fact that no-one walks anywhere anymore and juggernauts trundle through, rattling windows at 100 km an hour!

In the world of property porn, all areas, like all models, are fashionable, exclusive and sought after. All house are prestigious, all neighbours ideal and discreet and all 'villages' heavenly. One recent advert suggested that Clontarf, on Dublin's northside, 'benefited from every conceivable amenity nearby'. Now Clontarf seems like a perfectly nice place, but every conceivable amenity — this covers quite a bit. If Carlsberg did suburbs, they'd probably do Clontarf!

With 70,000 new houses built last year, property porn moves from mild peep-shows into full-on fetish in order to shift these things. New developments are typically only a 'stone's throw' from the non-existent but 'eagerly awaited' rail link. In the same way as aged news presenters demand soft-focused lenses to obscure the wrinkles, the new estate sellers use distorted aerial views to obscure the vast distances between the building site and the rest of the country. Or the advertising performs optical feats. For example, an apartment block, let's say in Cherry Orchard, will have a touched up photo of Stephen's Green on its brochure as if to say, 'Dream hard enough and this flat will reposition itself from a west Dublin wasteland to the top of

Grafton Street'! For everyone, reality blurs.

Kinnegad suddenly becomes a commuter town, an hour from Dublin. They omit to specify that that is on a Sunday morning at nine. Distances from Carlow, Drogheda and Gorey are all similarly truncated and marketed as if these were quaint little streets just off the South Circular Road, rather than far-away provincial towns where people's grannies used to live and where we used to go on two-week holidays.

The new estates, characterised by the silver Toyota Avensis and the Sky dish, are typically billed as having 'stylish luxury with contemporary flair' as an estate in Delgany, Co. Wicklow was recently described. Who could resist spending their Sunday afternoon driving around blocked-up country roads searching for such a nirvana? It is the suburban equivalent of *The Beach* by Alex Garland and everyone suddenly becomes Leonardo DiCaprio behind the wheel, dreaming of the 18th, putting calmly for five under.

Druid's Glen features prominently in the ad for houses in Wicklow. Yes, Druid's Glen is in Wicklow, but so too are the amusements on the seafront in Bray — and you don't see bumper cars figuring prominently in semi-D ads. As well as golf clubs and smiling men in casual slacks, remarkably the ad for a certain Wicklow development stars a fallow deer. Quite what the deer is doing in the ad for a semi-D is beyond me. But of course, the deer evokes nature, open spaces, wilderness and expanses. Accentuate the positive at all costs because the flipside of the deer is the traffic, the four-hour daily commute, the exhausted neighbours and the absence of a footpath when you do eventually move in.

The most prurient small ad in the annals of Irish property pornography has to be the 'Take Five' section in the *Irish Times* supplement. This little gem compares the type of property that €200K or €300K or €500K will buy in Ireland and a similar property for the same price in other countries. Like the Reader's Wives or Swingers section of a porn mag, here you can compare what you have with what you could have, sit back, relax and fantasise, try to imagine what your own could fetch. In this Swingers' section, the car keys are always available, the prettiest wives always willing and the faraway hills always greener, and you get an idea about what like-minded folk are out there and what they are charging. There's also a touch of sex tourism about it. 'Look what you can get for your money in

Thailand'!

A typical example takes a pokey little Irish box and compares it to something at the same price in another country. For example, take a small two-up-two-down, turn of the last century artisan terraced house in Stoneybatter, with barbed wire on the tiny backyard, trucks on the street and traffic jams most of the day back to Cabra (which incidentally is termed Fabra by our gay community given that so many gays have moved in over the past three years). Compare this to a similarly priced but palatial Chateau just outside Paris, boasting stables, land and a direct rail link to Place de l'Opéra. Both are valued at €400K. We in Ireland are supposed to believe that the Irish market is good value.

In terms of value, however, it is a very useful tool to assess things in Ireland and even a quick peek should focus our minds on the excesses of our property obsession. We are now a nation that knows the price of everything and the value of nothing. Everything is a blur. And this brings us to how the whole system works, and why the economics of the property market has been the catalyst which has created the New Ireland.

Chapter 7

Vorsprung Durch Kredit

HANSEATIC HANDOUTS

Where did all the money come from? How did we go from being the poorest country in Western Europe with the lowest house prices, to the most expensive country in the union with the highest prices? How can the least populated country in Europe have the highest land prices? How did Ireland go from being a country with too many people and not enough money, to a country of not enough people and too much credit? How come we are now a large middle-class, aspiring nation that knows the price of everything and the value of nothing, glued to property porn with our 'You're a Star' attitudes?

Let's go back to the winter of 1992. House prices were 300% below where they are now, interest rates were at 100% and emigration was the problem — precisely the opposite of today's situation of rampant house prices, historically low interest rates and mass immigration. Ireland was in the throes of a currency crisis and it appeared that once again we were the dunces in the economics class. I was working as an economist in the Central Bank, the custodian of the currency, and it was increasingly apparent to us inside that the punt was on the verge of collapse. But there was a mantra that had to be repeated: no devaluation, no devaluation. When mantras take over from hard thinking, you know you are in trouble. This was the financial equivalent of a rain dance in a drought. No amount of repetition could obscure the fact that the Irish state was running out of money and we were seeing this every day as our foreign reserves dwindled from £2 billion to £56 million in three months. The foreign exchange markets were having a field day betting against us. Ireland did what all gamblers do in a tight corner: bluffed. A few of us were sent out like the puffed-up emissaries of a surrounded and doomed ancient kingdom to spin a line that we had loads of cash, loads of steel and we — little sovereign Ireland — would not be pushed around by the barrow-boys in braces.

I was the whippersnapper in one such delegation. We were all out of our depth, but I — the bag carrier — more so than the others. In a Marks & Spencer's suit and shoes with plastic soles, I was hardly Gordon Gecko, and the real Geckos smelt that a mile off. One particular Tuesday afternoon, we met a group of very worried German and Swiss bankers. It was one of the last days in the bunker — the final scene from *Downfall*. They had a very large exposure to Ireland. In fact they owned over £11 billion punts worth of Irish government stock and stood to lose a fortune if we devalued. It was our job to explain why a devaluation would never happen — which in hindsight sounded as hollow as a hooker's climax. As I spoke German, I introduced people and kicked off declaring our intent to defend Ireland's financial honour. When I'd reached my crescendo, capped by the monetary equivalent of 'no surrender' bluster that would have made an Apprentice Boy proud, there was polite applause, just one movement away from a slow hand-clap.

As the Germans got up to leave, one of them approached me. He looked older, richer, his watch was swankier and he was definitely fatter, than the rest. 'Mr McWilliams, your ability to lie for your country without even a smirk is truly remarkable! You don't know me. My name is Rudi Mueller, the Chairman of UBS — Europe's largest bank. Now that you have lied for your fatherland, would you care to lie for me?'

Ireland devalued the following Monday, and within months I was taking Rudi's deutschmark on the UBS trading floor — the biggest in London, speculating with the very braces brigade that had battered our currency. *Pecunia non olet* — money has no smell, as the Romans said.

But not only was devaluation day a good day for me, it was a good day for all of us, because it was the beginning of a process that would lead directly to EMU and to the low interest rates and never-ending credit which has kept the Irish economy so inflated over the past five years. Crucially as well, it marked the high point of the German economic empire which has been in decline ever since. The decline of Germany has changed Irish psychology and been central to Ireland's success. In fact, old, parsimonious Germans and their savings have shaped the new Irish Dream and the Expectocracy. Without them there would be no credit, and without credit we would not have had the property boom. There would not have been the great blurring of the classless society and we would not have seen the emergence of the Expectocracy. The Kells Angels would now be living in Streatham, Low GI Jane would be in marketing in Chicago and Destiny's Child would be an Australian citizen.

MEET UDO LINDENBURG

The hero of this Irish psychological revolution is an elderly German, who unwittingly broke our class system. Meet Udo Lindenburg. Udo is sixty-five and shares his name and bizarrely, his birthday, with Germany's most famous rocker. The other Udo Lindenburg is the Mick Jagger, Serge Gainsbourg and Bob Geldof of Germany all rolled into one. On the other hand, our Udo wears slippers, listens to Bach and keeps bees. He is fed up with people, particularly Easterners, sending him fan mail and the tax man sending him the other Udo's self-assessment forms. He lives in Bahnhof Strasse in Stuttgart — just three miles away from the Neckar Stadium where Ray Houghton's head and Packie Bonner's knees beat the English on that portentous evening in June 1988. Udo was born as his father, Carsten, was sweeping through Poland, preparing for Operation Barbarossa. Udo never saw him. His father was taken prisoner at Stalingrad and was part of a German prisoner chain-gang who built with their frost-bitten, bare hands the five Stalinist Wedding Cake buildings in Moscow. There is evidence from a released Austrian POW that Carsten outlasted Stalin but his release was prevented due to Soviet paranoia following the workers' uprising in Berlin in 1953. He died of pneumonia in appalling conditions in a camp at Borodino in 1956.

Udo's parents were Sudeten Germans who had lived for centuries in what is now the Czech Republic. His mother, Hannelore, was expelled along with her son, three daughters and elderly mother in 1945. On arrival in Bavaria, Hannelore became an original 'trummerfrau' or tapping woman — so called because these women rebuilt Germany's devastated cities using only the most basic tools. The name comes from the tapping sound of legions of widowed women breaking rocks and masonry with small hammers by tapping them incessantly. This was the sound of Germany rebuilding herself. They settled in the small town of Marktl am Inn where Udo went to school. One of his teachers was a very intelligent local lad whose love of football and history made a huge impression on Udo. They used to go for long walks on the banks of the river Inn discussing Bavaria, its history and its place in German culture. In the summer of 1954, Udo and his teacher were inseparable and they spent June glued to the transistor listening as West Germany beat Hungary to win the World Cup. They were delirious. His mother recalled that he cried all night the day his teacher, the young Father Joseph Ratzinger, left Marktl to take up his new position in Munich. The Lindenburgs, like the Ratzingers, were the generation of German rebuilders, the people who made West Germany into a powerhouse. They are made of stern stuff and lived lives governed by the three Ss — savings, simplicity and stoicism.

Udo's home is a tidy three-bedroomed apartment on the 6th floor which he shares with Gisela, his second wife. His only son, Holger, who studied up until his early thirties for free finally got a job with an NGO in Burma and moved out ten years ago. Since then Gisela's cat Swartzhy has lived in the lap of luxury with her own room amongst Gisela's 26 pairs of slippers. (Gisi, as she is affectionately known, collects slippers as souvenirs from holidays.) Udo and Gisela regularly write letters to the *Suddeutscher Zeitung* on what they believe is the inability of Germany's youth to put in a hard day's work. As for himself, Udo has been a valued and highly paid employee of BMW for years, working in accounts. He is a fully paid-up member of the trade union IG Metal despite being a staunch supporter of the Christian Social Union, the conservative Bavarian party set up by the Ian Paisley of German politics, Franz Joseph Strauss. Udo has always been Bavarian, Catholic and conservative. He regards Berlin as a foreign city and has no time for those wishy-washy Hanoverians who he says run Germany. Swedes, he calls them.

He is now sixty-five and ready to retire. Over the years he has saved a huge proportion of his income, and apart from the three weeks in Klein Deutschland in Majorca every July and a week on a nudist island on the Dalmatian coast where himself and other like-minded elderly Germans revel in getting their kits off and depositing towels on isolated rocks at 6 am, he does not spend much. He enjoys three evenings a week in his local *Kneiper*, drinking *Weiss* beer and eating *Wurst und Schinken und ein bissen Käse*. He trusses himself up in his bibbed lederhosen on special national days and holy days of obligation and um-papas around with other mustachioed sixty somethings. Gisela spends an inordinate amount of time in the hairdresser, gossiping, reading the *Bild* and tut-tutting about the decline of Boris Becker. Both are perfectly happy, God-fearing, law-abiding German savers in their sixties.

But if Udo does not spend his savings, who does? Someone has to. Otherwise, Deutsche Bank would not make any money. Up until 1992, there was no problem because reunification cost so much that the government borrowed huge amounts of Udo's cash to pay dole money for former communists in Cottbus, Mecklenburg and Dresden. But now that frenzied period is over. Many millions of Germans are simply sitting on their savings, not spending and getting very little interest. This is particularly worrying for the economy as the average German retires at 61 and spending tends to fall even further after retirement.

This is the core of Germany's and to an extent Europe's problem. They are simply not spending enough. For the banking system this is a disaster, because banks are money-lenders: they need to extend loans at higher interest margins than they pay out on their deposits. In addition, since the rate of interest is the price at which money is lent, if everyone is saving and not spending, the rate of interest falls as it has done for the past ten years. Because Germany still runs a massive export surplus with the rest of the world, money continues to flow into Germany, depressing the rate of interest even further. So if the Germans are not spending, the banks need to recycle this money out to other spenders.

This is where Paddy comes into the equation. Paddy is thirty and has no savings at all. In fact, he is the first in five generations of his family to have more than one bank account. He has eight accounts with three different banks. He needs the cash as he's on a spending spree and needs cheap credit. So where will he get it? This is where the Euro comes in handy. The Euro, because it is the same currency between Ireland and Germany, allows Paddy to spend Udo's savings. In fact the effect of the Euro was to give Paddy, who is on a bender,

buying rounds and first to the bar, the PIN code to Udo's bank card.
The reason is very simple. Before the Euro, Irish people could only
spend as much money as we saved. If we spent any more than we
saved, interest rates would go up here, encouraging us to stop
spending and start saving again. The advent of the Euro has opened
up to us the savings of over one hundred million Europeans. Because
many of these Europeans are like Udo, old, rich and parsimonious, the
rate of interest is very low. This suits Paddy who is young, indebted
and *flaithiúil*. So we can borrow as much of this cash as we want, and
because there are only 2 million of us working and spending as
opposed to 40 million Germans working and saving, our spending, no
matter how outrageous, will never of itself push up interest rates.
(Although we are certainly trying to test this theory!) Therefore, the
Euro has facilitated a massive transfer of cash from old, rich German
savers such as Udo to young, free-spending, over-borrowed Paddies at
a rate of interest that suits Paddy. This is allowing Paddy to buy his
new 06 BMW seven series which Udo made in the first place. As long
as old Udo does not go on a spending spree, which is unlikely at his
age, interest rates will remain low and allow young Paddy to borrow
and spend, extend the kitchen and buy the finest state of the art
German-made, American-style Neff ovens. So the system is simply a
circular flow of cash, ending up in many cases back in Germany. But
it has liberated Paddy.

Udo does not realise that his savings pattern and those of millions
of Germans like him are the oxygen of the Irish miracle, no more no
less. But there is no miracle, there is only a large overdraft. Without
Udo there would be no credit and without credit there would be no
New Irish Dream. Without Udo's savings there would be no cheap
loans to finance the massive spending splurge in the country. There
would be no cheap loans to finance the housing market, nor the
equity releases to finance the next skiing holiday. Without the cheap
money there would not have been the massive take-off in shops, cafés,
take-aways, pubs, restaurants, car dealerships, mobile operators or
advertising campaigns in order to buy the latest gadgets. The great
boost for the Irish is that there are millions of elderly, solvent
Germans like Udo Lindenburg and they provide us with an almost
unlimited supply of cheap loans. Never before in peacetime Europe
has there been a transfer of money like this from one sovereign
country to another.

But Udo's money would not have had such an amplified impact on Ireland had it not been for land and property. Land plays a crucial accelerator role in multiplying the impact of cheap loans because property is the booster rocket which launched the great Expectocracy. The impact of land and property, and the interaction of the banking system with it on the credit market and the availability of loans and cash, have all propelled us from a stolid, dull 'Respectocracy' to a vibrant, if self-conscious, Expectocracy.

HOW THE WHOLE THING WORKS — THE LAND STANDARD

A few years ago, the following letter arrived at my retired parents' house.

> Dear Mr McWilliams,
> It has come to our attention that you bought your house in 1957 for €1,000. Today, we have had it valued at €700,000. We believe that this offers you a once in a lifetime opportunity to liberate equity.
> Yours sincerely,
> Mr Bank Manager

My Dad called me: 'Son, I've heard of liberating Kuwait and liberating Iraq, but what in God's name does liberating equity mean?' It means that one of our supposedly prudent banks is urging my father, a 75-year-old pensioner, to borrow and spend against the value of his house! Now I realise that bank managers are under pressure to increase margins, but this is taking the biscuit, don't you think? However, this is happening every day. Irish banks are lending hand over fist.

There are three separate forces at work here. The first is the law of insecure middle management. Let's not forget that behind all the slogans like 'working together' or 'your partner', banks are simply moneylenders and the more money they lend, the more money they make. So yellow-pack bankers, whose status both within the bank and outside has been dramatically eroded by ATM machines, are at pains to exceed lending targets set by senior bosses. The middle manager does not see my father as a person in this transaction, but sees his suburban house as collateral. My Dad is simply the conduit to the asset. If the banker can get his hands on a bankable piece of collateral such as the house, he can make an easy sale and thereby hit or exceed his target. After all, if he does not hit the target, there are plenty more suits coming behind him who will.

The second force at work is the law of shareholder value. Bank bosses' salaries are linked to the share price of their outfits. So it is in their interest to get the share price up above the average. The problem, however, is that the people who ultimately own the banks — large pension funds — expect too large a return every year. How can a business like a bank which is involved in a typically low-growth, mature industry like money-lending make returns on equity of 20% plus as expected by the pension funds and banking stock indices? The only way they can do this is by working their workers to the bone, capping costs and capping pay and lending recklessly. Therefore, and ironically, our own pension funds are driving our banks to lend to us with abandon. So the prospects of your pension fund when you retire are indirectly linked to getting you into debt when you are working.

The third and most important factor at work in the lending frenzy is the impact of land on the balance sheet of the bank. If the price of land is rising in tandem with the amount of money gushing into property, the banks will be able to lend more against it. The balance sheet starts to play tricks with them. Counter-intuitively, the more money they lend, the safer it looks in terms of the ratios they use to assess secure lending. So it becomes a self-reinforcing dynamic where the more money they lend the more they feel they should lend. So credit becomes the crack-cocaine of the financial industry. The initial hit leads to euphoria but it wears off quickly, leaving the junkie needing more. And like the addict, all the economy's senses have been blurred by credit so it doesn't know when to stop. We have all become hopelessly addicted to the soothing balm of credit, and the banking system is desperately dependent for its living on the price of land, houses and property. The banks can be regarded as the dealers — the middlemen — who cut up the deals, take a fee and keep the addict hooked. But because of the impact of the lending on them, their balance sheets, their bonuses and share price, they are as addicted as their clients.

So the banks break the prudential rules set down by the authorities. Take for example a story I heard the other day of a typical first-time buyer. Liza works in the cosmetic business. She is freelancing and is therefore not on a steady income. Work has not been too bad lately but is very erratic. Like many of her peers in their late twenties, she has decided to take the plunge. Fed up with renting, she has just put down €4,000 to secure her first apartment. She lied to get the cash. She knows that she has lied about her income to the broker and the broker knows it too. She has invented 'nixers' which she claims her annual P60 misses and she assures the broker that these will plug any monthly financial gaps.

The broker is also well aware that rent from the second bedroom is absolutely crucial to meet the monthly repayments. Without that, Liza will probably default. Liza has already moved back home to save and intends to stay there for the first year. She will initially rent out the new place. Her broker secured 93% of the cost of the property. This figure is close to six times her earned salary and yet a bank in Ireland is willing to give her the cash. She has no idea whether the property is good value or not, all she knows now is that she is on the ladder. Liza is going to take a big cut in her disposable income in order to have her own property. In fact, her mortgage (at the lowest interest rates in her living memory) will be twice the rent she pays at the moment but she is willing to take the plunge because she feels that every year she waits she is being left behind. Who could blame her? In the past seven years, housing has been the single biggest creator of wealth in the country. Even the government gives you a tax break to buy a place and the banks are only too glad to lend, reinforcing the link between land and credit at every stage.

So standing back we see that Ireland operates what can be described as a land standard like a version of the gold standard. In the old days, banks printed money based on some ratio of the amount of gold they had in their reserves. This was called the gold standard. The amount of money in circulation was inextricably linked to gold. This system had the strong point of preventing delinquent tyrants from printing money whenever they wanted to finance some venture or other. However, the downside was that in ancient societies when they ran out of gold they had no money, or when gold flowed in too quickly, extra money was printed to accommodate the new gold, and typically inflation, house prices and the cost of living rose dramatically. Ancient Rome and Imperial Spain are extremely good examples of what happened when the gold system becomes debased. They should be regarded as cautionary lessons for us and our similarly rigid and fallible 'land standard'.

The problem with the Irish land standard is that the soaring price of land and houses is intricately linked to the profitability of our banking system and the roaring supply and availability of cheap loans. Both are part of the problem. Unfortunately, because rising property prices keep the banks looking profitable, the banks have a vested interest in ensuring that the great Irish land rip-off remains in business. This is why credit is rising so quickly. The flip side of credit is always debt.

Let's have a gander at how the system works in practice. Take a house worth €300,000. It is used as collateral to borrow €270,000 to buy another apartment for investment. The extra €270,000 goes into the system. The golden rule of monetary economics is that the more money in the system, the greater the upward price pressures on all other things. Thus, the extra cash sloshing around in the system puts upward price pressure on houses because there is too much money chasing too few houses. This makes the original collateral now increase in 'value' to €330,000. And so on. The bank extends another loan on the same collateral, failing to distinguish the chicken from the egg.

On top of this mechanism is the fundamental problem that everyone is in on the trip. The bankers, brokers, developers and advertising salesmen, estate agents and the state itself have a significant vested interest in keeping the whole system operating at full throttle. To do otherwise would be to entertain economic collapse, so everyone continues to believe the hype. Equally, the houses price rise gives everyone a warm feeling in their tummies. If the house up the road goes for €400,000 and you bought yours for €200,000, you feel wealthier and subconsciously push the boat out a bit more when it comes to your credit card, next holiday, car loan or overdraft.

Because of this self-propelling mechanism, the system has no brake and it is impossible for it to slow down of its own accord. Not only does the machine not have a reverse gear, it has no neutral and feels like a car constantly revved in third gear. The only thing that can stop credit from gushing into every nook and cranny of the economy is if Udo and Gisela begin to spend like they did when they were in their thirties; but they are in their slippers by 8 pm watching repeats of 'Verboten Liebe' — the long running German soap. So the combination of Udo's recycled savings and the land-related amplification means that the Irish economy is now a credit junkie — and only more gear can keep it functioning.

THE CHRONICLE OF A DEBT FORETOLD

In Gabriel Garcia Marquez's *Chronicle of a Death Foretold*, the story of a gruesome murder unfolds. A young woman gets married, but on her wedding night is found not to be a virgin. The incensed groom vows to kill her lover and conscripts the bride's two brothers to carry out this act, in order to maintain their families' honour. Everyone in the town is aware of the impending fate of the lover — Santiago Nasar — but no-one warns him. The genius of the book is that the reader becomes complicit in this act of wanton silence. We implore the villagers to tell Santiago to run, but they fail us. In the end, we become witnesses and, ultimately, accessories to a horrible end. Everyone could see what was going to happen, the murderers had even declared their intent but nobody was sure they would execute it, preferring to hope that something or someone would come along to save the day.

In Ireland, rapid borrowing over the past five years tells a similar story, albeit less gruesome: Chronicle of a Debt Foretold. Everyone knows that payback time will come, but we are all hoping that some miraculous intervention will bail us out. We want to warn ourselves and our neighbours, but fear that the act of warning itself may waken the sleeping dogs. So we remain silent, petrified in the face of a rising debt monster.

Let us look at the figures. In 2004, for the first time ever, our overall debt levels surpassed our income levels. Yet this in itself is not the issue. The issue is the pace of growth of indebtedness. In 2003 the ratio of debt to income was 94%. One year later, that figure had jumped to 120%. If we continue at this pace, by 2010 our debt burden will be twice our income. This is financial delinquency on a monumental scale.

By the end of this year our debt burden will easily pass 130% of income. Does a debt burden of 130% sound familiar? Well, it should, because this is the figure our national debt hit in the mid-1980s — prompting fears that the IMF would have to intervene to save the economy. Why did a public debt burden of 130% then trigger political upheaval, capital flight and, eventually, remedial action, while a private debt burden of the same magnitude today makes one headline and then fades, with no prospect of corrective measures? The reason is clear: commentators mistakenly believe that there is some material difference between public and private debt. There is not. Debt is debt no matter who incurs it. To see how this works, look at the example of the Asian Tigers where their collapse in 1997 was entirely driven by an inability of the private sector to pay its debt. When the banks called in their loans they did not discriminate between public and private. This will not happen here because of Udo and Gisela, but if rates were to rise, the fact that the debt is private would make no difference to the repayment schedule. The timing of any payback is outside our hands and in the gift of Germans like Udo Lindenburg who, thankfully, are hardly registering an economic pulse.

THE NEW VENETIANS

In addition to the domestic financial impact of EMU, Udo's money, the property boom and the increasing levels of debt at home, there have been significant geopolitical developments abroad which have benefited Ireland and the Pope's Children unexpectedly. These have reinforced the positive impact of Udo's credit. Before we analyse the likely future path of the housing market, let's look at these positive global trends.

This summer, thousands of Irish tourists will visit the old walled city of Dubrovnik on the Croatian coast to savour one of Europe's gems. What many will not realise is that the history of Dubrovnik offers us the blueprint for Ireland over the next twenty years.

It is clear that something went right for Dubrovnik in the Middle Ages. From its marble streets to the immense baroque cathedral, the heavily fortified harbour and the oldest pharmacy in the world, ancient Dubrovnik exudes affluence. Moreover, with the world's oldest orphanage (founded in the 14th century) and one of Europe's oldest synagogues, it's clear these people were both enlightened and tolerant. So where did the cash come from? Why did it dry up? And where is the modern-day equivalent of old Dubrovnik?

The Dubrovnik Republic was one of a number of very powerful city-states that emerged in the Middle Ages of which Venice was the most powerful and influential. When the rest of the bigger powers were wasting money and talent fighting wars, a few smart, small, nimble states saw that there was a serious and profitable niche in the world's trading system. As long as a city-state juggled its allegiances and avoided any military showdowns with the big boys, it could trade and export its way to prosperity.

The elders of Dubrovnik realised that the city was poised delicately, occupying a crucial strategic point in the Adriatic, half way between the expanding Ottoman Empire to the south-east and the rapidly developing Renaissance markets of Italy, France and Flanders in the north-west. Instead of involving themselves in wars, military alliances and territorial adventures, they set about building up the finest merchant navy in the Adriatic and honing their diplomatic skills to avoid conflict.

Dubrovnik's immense wealth was generated by trading with Renaissance Europe in lead and silver from Turkish-occupied Serbia and Bosnia (the silver mines still exist in Kosovo today) and silks and spices from the Levant. Indeed, the Republic's most famous son, Marco Polo (born on the nearby island of Korcula), epitomised the swashbuckling, capitalist adventurers of the time.

Working on the principle that flattery gets you everywhere, Dubrovnik managed to keep the Turks sweet by offering annual donations of gold and silver to the local Muslim Pasha in Bosnia. This allowed the city to remain Catholic, which ensured brownie points with the rich Papal States to the west. Indeed, Dubrovnik was the only Catholic city in Europe to get a Papal dispensation to trade openly with the infidel Turks.[1]

In the first example of a national branding campaign, Dubrovnik, by the early 17th century, had opened trade consulates in eighty cities from Alexandria to Marseilles. This golden era of peace and prosperity allowed the city to grow and the aristocracy to indulge its passion for fine art and architecture.

At the same time, the Republic remained tolerant and open to minorities, attracting talent that was fleeing prejudice elsewhere and thus reinforcing Dubrovnik's competitive advantage in human capital. Its golden age faded when Dutch, and later British, fleets began to dominate global trading and the Atlantic, Pacific and Indian oceans usurped the Mediterranean as the key global trading route. Gradually but definitively, the era of the powerful, enlightened city-state passed and was replaced by the hegemony of large, 'might is right' regimes that saw geographical size as an essential prerequisite for economic wealth. Dubrovnik became a type of trophy prize fought over by Napoleon, then Austrians, later Italians and Germans and, most recently, Serbs.

In the past ten years a kind of city-state has re-emerged. Following a 300-year absence, the city-state or rather the small, agile state is again a dynamic and powerful source of economic wealth creation. Ireland is one such country and the only one in Europe (others being Singapore and Hong Kong). We are using the Dubrovnik approach. We are trading as much as we can, making ourselves available to investment, and trying, where possible, to produce goods of high value that are more the product of inspiration than perspiration.

Granted, the US — a large country by any standards — is still top dog. But its very domination allows the smaller countries to thrive, free of security and other geopolitical fears. These days, size of army, abundance of raw materials or depth of population doesn't matter so much. In short, the world is facilitating the re-emergence of something akin to the Renaissance city-states.

Ireland is particularly like ancient Dubrovnik because of our reasonably elegant diplomatic tight-rope act. Our relationship with Europe is like Dubrovnik's with the Turks. We have got into bed with the EU, tying ourselves politically to Brussels' orbit while not merely retaining but actively encouraging a rather promiscuous economic relationship with the US. While much debate centred on whether we were Boston or Berlin, based on the premise of an absolute choice between one or the other, this was in fact false. It misses the point. In the new global economy, which values dexterity and flexibility over hard and fast choices, Ireland is neither Boston nor Berlin but a hybrid, a type of Bostlin.

Like ancient Dubrovnik which had to keep the Pope on-side to trade with the Turks, we have played a smart game by smelling, feeling and sounding American (to corporate America) but making sure that everyone else, particularly the Brussels mandarin clique, believes we are fully European. As a result, cosmetically at least, our politics are European. But when the chips are down — as on Iraq — we hold our nose and do what is necessary. We don't strike poses — as if the world cared a toss for our moral posturing. We facilitate the Yanks at Shannon. Anything else is bad for business. It's called being all grown up.

Ireland is the first Ameropean society in the world. We are a 21st-century city state — we are a hybrid nation, sometimes regarded as the most western outcrop of the most ancient European civilisation while at the same time feeling like a congested New Jersey. We are equally at home in Buffalo or Brussels which allows us to play both off against each other. But this means we have had to be extremely deft in diplomacy. This diplomacy begins not in the boardrooms of Iveagh House but in the minds of the Pope's Children.

THE GEOLOGY OF ECONOMICS

The future value of the city-state model can be appreciated if we look around the globe at what is happening to the world economy and understand that some of the old certainties may not be around indefinitely.

An interesting way to regard the global economy of the future — the theatre where we the Irish will have to perform — is to view the relationship between the world's economic power blocs through the medium of geology, where the earth's rigid outer shell, the lithosphere, is broken up into an extraordinary mosaic of oceanic and continental plates. Just underneath is another layer: a more fluid, plasticky surface, called the aesthenosphere. This is the uppermost layer of the earth's boiling core, which bubbles away below.

When the pressure in the bowels of the earth gets too intense, the core bubbles and, occasionally, where the lithosphere is thin or cracked, it explodes into violent volcanoes. More typically, the plates are in constant slow motion, sliding glacially and peacefully over the liquidy aesthenosphere.

Where the plates interact and nudge against each other, important geological shifts take place, such as the formation of mountain belts, earthquakes and volcanoes. Probably the best-known is the San Andreas Fault in California. The fault line is about 1,300 km long and in places tens of kilometres wide.

Along it, the Pacific Plate has been grinding horizontally past the North American Plate for ten million years at an average rate of approximately 5 cm per year (which is about the same speed as your fingernails grow). There are around ten other main fault lines across the globe, so earthquakes, both on land and under the sea, are relatively easy to locate, but predicting precisely when they will happen is almost impossible, as we saw with the tsunami.

Ireland could be regarded as living on the economic and political equivalent of the San Andreas Fault, where the huge continental plates of the US and Europe grind up against each other. When the world's financial lithosphere is calm, we prosper in what economic geologists might term a false sense of security. When the giant plates move in opposite directions, we find ourselves in an uncomfortable position. We are consistently compromising, altering, adjusting and re-balancing.

Such constant juggling has had an impact on us, our political system, our expectations and our national philosophy. This Ameropean geopolitical stance is very evident in the chat before elections. Irish politicians, commentators and the electorate in general display a split personality in claiming that we can deliver the tax system of Texas and the social welfare system of Sweden. Our discussions centre on the utopia of lower taxes and better health, education and social security services. You can have one or the other but not both. The roots of this dichotomy are old and hark back to the fact that over the past thirty years, Ireland has positioned itself politically at the heart of Europe (initially to move out of London's orbit) but economically we have moved away from the European model and jumped into America's boudoir.

The European political move has meant that our politicians adopt the language and posturing of the European left-of-centre consensus, with its ultimate promise of a strong state providing a functioning safety net. Yet this rhetoric is in direct contrast to the realities of being part of the us economic space.

We have adopted American policy on taxation, investment, trade and business attitudes. We have stopped short of the American 'get-a-job-bum' attitude to the poor, preferring — but not delivering — the less unpalatable European 'the-state-will-provide-from-cradle-to-grave' approach to poverty.

So we are a bit like the jockey riding two horses. When the horses are moving along in tandem together, the jockey's position is tenable and almost comfortable. When our European rhetoric does not undermine our American values, we — like the jockey — can ride both steeds effortlessly. But when the two horses move in opposite directions, we have to choose.

EUROPE'S DIFFICULTY, IRELAND'S OPPORTUNITY

What makes Ireland very unusual is that it is the only EU nation that benefits more when Europe is weak and America strong, than the other way around. The fusion of monetary economics, trade flows, immigration, demography and investment flows explains this. When Europe is in recession, Irish interest rates are extremely low to reflect this. But because we are much younger than the rest of Europe and young countries spend more, we get a free lunch. We get German interest rates that fuel the Irish boom. On top of this, when Germany is weak, the dollar is strong against the Euro. This makes Ireland look cheap and hyper-productive to American investors, creating more jobs here, reinforcing the injection of German cash because as our incomes rise, we can borrow more without necessarily feeling the strain. In addition, we still do twice as much trade outside Continental Europe than with it. So we benefit disproportionately when the rest of the world is growing faster. In contrast, we do not get a huge payback from a robust Europe. Also, because migrants from Central Europe are so essential, we benefit when unemployment is high in Germany and France because it makes their decision to come to Ireland easier. Many underestimate just how significant immigration has been. Ireland is benefiting from the last fire sale of white Christian immigrants that the world is likely to see. All the Poles, Balts and central Europeans are choosing Ireland and we are benefiting from their brains and brawn.

Thus we are unique in the European Union in that it suits us better to have a weak rather than strong Europe. So we are a bit like a parasite feeding off a bloated and sclerotic Europe which is too lumbering and slow to swat us away. But this bizarre set of divided loyalties holds true not just for economics but for politics too. When Europe is economically fragile, the ambitions of some of Europe's more deeply federalist politicians are thwarted. Europe can only expand when there is a tail wind of positive economics at the national level. If people are worried about their jobs, the last thing they are going to do is support what is perceived as a pampered elite and their superfluous ideas and potty projects. This is what we have seen in this year's constitutional votes in France and the Netherlands where the metropolitan elites are completely out of step with the ordinary voters all across Europe. This development is unambiguously positive for Ireland. As semi-detached Ameropeans, the prospect of a strong federal Europe challenging America properly in either foreign affairs or global economics might force us to choose, which is something we are loath to do. The art of playing both sides is: never commit to either. This is always easier when the relationship between your two suitors is just ever so slightly unequal.

Furthermore, in the same way as we benefit from a strong American economy relative to Europe, American global hegemony has done wonders for us. So let's look at the American Leviathan, the world's first hyper-power from the angle of Irish self-interest alone.

Since the end of the Cold War, the US's grand strategy has been to maintain its overwhelming military, political and economic preeminence. For that, we should be thankful — not because the strategy has been remotely designed with Ireland's interests in mind, but because, as a by-product of US dominance, we have had the opportunity to flourish economically, intellectually, politically and socially. Until now, the Americans have acquiesced in that grand strategy because the costs appeared to be tolerably low.

Over the years, great powers have had two basic strategic options: they can pursue dominance, or they can try to maintain a rough balance of power between states of relatively equal power, each having its own sphere of influence. America has chosen the former course of action.

By providing security for Britain, France, Germany and Japan, by defending their interests in far-flung places like the Gulf, and by intricately involving them in a system of mutually enhancing alliances, Washington prevented any of the old powers from ploughing their own furrow. This global policy, which is known as 'reassurance', has cost the Americans billions of dollars. It has also facilitated unprecedented levels of economic, political and social cooperation among the states of Western Europe with the EU and East Asia with ASEAN. Without the US security blanket, it is hard to see how the EU would ever have evolved into the peaceful structure it is now, of which Ireland is a member and from which it benefits greatly.

The collapse of the Soviet Union did not diminish the feeling in Washington that a stable world order depended on the US remaining pre-eminent. The policy is now referred to as 'adult supervision'. As well as ensuring that the US looks after the military interests of Europe and East Asia, it also entails the US safeguarding (in their own minds) our interests, so that we do not feel the need to develop military forces capable of projecting our power.

The war in Iraq is a good example of this. It is clear that the war is as much about resources as it is about regime change — but resources for whom? America derives most of its oil from Alaska, Venezuela, Mexico and Texas; only 25 per cent of its oil comes from the Gulf. By contrast, Europe, Japan and increasingly China get the lion's share of supplies from the Gulf region.

The American logic is that they will protect our interests in order to prevent us from protecting ourselves. This is especially the case in Asia where, in the coming years, the possibility of an arms race between China and Japan cannot be ruled out.

Underneath this American military umbrella, the economies of Europe and Asia have flourished at unprecedented rates. The system that the US has fostered has led to enormous improvements in the standard of living for most of us. Politically, Ireland has been able to express itself in Europe, feeling like an equal at the top table for the first time ever. Do you think this would have been possible in an EU dominated by the military aspirations of France, Britain, Germany, Italy or Spain? I somehow doubt it. American hegemony has put manners on them.

Our increase in living standards has been the result of cherry-picking from both the European and American way. By attracting foreign investment on the one hand, and taking advantage of the European pool of savings on the other, we have profited in ways unimaginable only a few years ago. The technology transfer from the US to Ireland has also been unprecedented in the past few years. All this has been possible because of, not in spite of, American hegemony.

We arguably benefit much more from the Pax Americana than the Yanks do themselves. For small countries it is the ultimate free lunch: we get peace without humiliation, for the first time in history. In contrast, the medium-sized old powers have been made to dine on humble pie — and this, in my book, is no bad thing. At the same time, the US leans sufficiently on the likes of Pakistan and India to keep them from pushing the button.

America's use of the dollar and its economic muscle in buying off allies and foes has been referred to disparagingly as a 'global protection racket'. Perhaps it is. But is it not preferable to the alternative of a bullying China or Russia, an expansionist Germany or Japan, or an arrogant, imperialist Britain or France?

Pax Americana has been very positive for small states such as Ireland. It has emasculated traditional medium-sized aggressors such as France, Germany, Japan and Britain, to the benefit of smaller, weaker nations such as ourselves.

However, Venice, Dubrovnik, Hong Kong and Singapore all had their financial crises, despite highly supportive outside influences. The most important development in Ireland over the next five years, for the Expectocracy, the 'You're a Star' generation, the Pope's Children, the Kells Angels and Low GI Jane, will be where the property market goes from here. In the next chapter we look at the likely chain of events. Sometimes in Ireland, given the unexpected nature of the boom, we tend to think that it has never happened anywhere else. Well it has. And, in the same way as it is important to examine the global changes which have facilitated Ireland's boom, it is equally important to be aware of the international lessons gleaned from similar property frenzies around the world.

Chapter 8

RoboPaddy

THE SEVEN STAGES

Charles Kindleberger's seminal work (1945) called *Mania, Bubbles and Crashes* sets out the seven stages of a property boom cycle.[1] Kindleberger, a renowned economist, looked at trends in a variety of assets over hundreds of years and concluded that most booms follow more or less the same seven-stage pattern.

Stage one is the introduction of looser credit. This occurred in all recent property booms particularly in the UK, Japan and the Scandinavian countries in the 1980s. Cheaper credit and lower interest rates encourage people to borrow more and reduce the monthly cost of a mortgage. This leads to a wave of money flowing into bankable assets such as property. How did it happen in Ireland? Our interest rate environment changed dramatically in the 1990s. In 1993, after our devaluation, Irish interest rates began to fall as EMU became more likely. Money flowing into the country and the cost of credit fell progressively from 15% to 5% and later down to 2%.[2] This meant that borrowing was never cheaper and, accordingly, people were spending like drunken sailors. Prices of houses started rising rapidly and this fed a frenzy where people thought if I don't buy now the prices will go up more, thus fuelling the boom.

By the late 1990s, the second stage of Kindleberger's cycle had kicked off. He refers to this as Euphoria. The euphoric stage is where everyone is beginning to make a little bit of easy money and they envisage themselves as a type of suburban Irish Donald Trump. People who wouldn't know an investment from a kick in the head start to wax lyrical about property prices, investments and accumulation strategies at dinner parties. Property porn abounds. No shack is too grotty for a make-over. Words such as imagination, flair and dreams are bandied about when referring to garage extensions. Not having vision becomes a serious taste crime. Property supplements begin to get thicker, glossier and more prosaic. Recently the property section in *The Irish Times* was bigger than the actual paper itself. Lifestyle sections start devoting entire sections to the joys of triple-headed showers and wet-rooms. A euphoric property-owning country begins to believe its own rapturous propaganda.

The warm glow of Stage-two euphoria is followed by Stage three — the gearing stage. We have discussed this in the last chapter. The gearing phase is when the banking system begins to fuel the boom excessively, mainly because it must. Banks are in competition with each other and they play a finely nuanced game, lending enough to keep the boom going, while ensuring that they don't drown in credit which might cause the whole deck of cards to fall down. It is an almost impossible high-wire act, balancing prudence and profligacy. With borrowing growing at 25% per annum and incomes growing at 4%, it is not hard to see that the banks are playing a dangerous game.[3]

Gearing leads to Stage four of Kindleberger's boom — the mania phase. Mania sets in. Houses are bought off plans for astronomical amounts. The money is never a problem as the highly geared banks are falling over each other to facilitate this. People camp out overnight to get their hands on new properties and there is an air of intense panic surrounding new offers. This stage is best summed up in JP Morgan's observation that, 'Nothing so undermines your financial judgement as the sight of your neighbour getting rich.'

In Ireland this mania has spilt overboard, with Irish investors charging around the globe looking for properties. Our lust for property, inflamed by the allure of the *Irish Times* pornographic centrefold of Take Five, finally climaxes over half-built developments in Bulgaria.

Inevitably, the wanton financial abandon of Stage four leads directly to Kindleberger's Stage five — the bubble stage where all value, sense of proportion, etiquette and monetary decorum are thrown out the window. The banks have to finance the bubble because not to do so would cause their entire structure to collapse. The punters are likewise caught in the full monetary headlights, unable to do anything else except continue to place bets. The nation is caught in a collective denial. We know that the Emperor has no clothes but all of us are so dependent on his favours that none of us will call out. This kind of collective behaviour is called the bystander effect in psychology. It refers to the observation that when a group of pedestrians pass a man who needs help, most do not stop, whereas if there is only one pedestrian, he will typically offer help readily. The same goes for property. As long as everyone is doing it, even the sceptics get carried away in the euphoria. The bubble phase can last for a considerable time and is usually pricked when interest rates go up, leading to the penultimate stage. However, as there is a global bubble in property, a crash elsewhere would lead to a rapid reappraisal of value all over the world. For example, a fall in us house prices could easily trigger a fall in Ireland without interest rates here ever going up. Confidence is the key and it can be sapped in a variety of unexpected ways.

During the bubble stage, builders who have purchased recently at high prices realise that there might be a narrowing window of opportunity to sell on at a profit. Thus the building industry moves into top gear and house and apartment construction go through the roof. Huge supply threatens to overhang the market but as long as the party and its cheerleaders are in full voice few worry.

Stage six is the Stage of Distress. This is when certain people discover that they are stretched. The properties they bought as investments remain un-let. Rents begin to fall. They realise that property yields below the rate of interest can only be sustained while there is a hope of capital gain. They put their properties on the market to try to pay spiralling debts. The properties do not sell quickly. Media reports turn negative, replete with stories of impending difficulties, and there are the first whispers of bankruptcy. This is what economists call negative contagion. If the positive contagion brought us to these heights, the negative contagion will drop us back to earth.

Distress quickly gives way in Kindelberger's cycle to the final phase of *Torschlusspanik* — German for 'shut door panic'. The roots of this expression come from the many financial crises experienced in Germany and Austria in the 19th century. It is easy to picture a 'shut door panic' where everyone puts his/her property on the market and tries to prevent a stampede of selling by trying to shut the door to other frightened sellers. People want money, not assets. 'Give me cash', is the cry. Selling then becomes overwhelming, and the banks — in a mirror image of the upswing when they financed anything — withdraw credit all over the place. A credit bonanza is quickly followed by a credit crunch and prices tumble, bankruptcies abound and bargains are everywhere. And the whole cycle starts again.

An interesting game is to try to pinpoint where the Irish property market is in the seven-stage cycle — somewhere between four or five possibly? Optimists may pretend we are in the early stages, while pessimists will claim that we are firmly in the sixth stage and only the very human sentiment of denial is preventing us from seeing clearly.

STAGE FIVE SYNDROME

What do you think? Where are we? I have been wrong on this for some years, so don't listen to me. You decide. But what I will do is give you some pointers which show that I think we are in the bubble phase. You make up your own mind.

RoboPaddy

There he is sweating, laden down with paperwork, with unsightly wet patches under the arms, squinting up at the monitor to see just how long the Ryanair flight from Teeside to Dublin will be delayed.

What does he care! He has just picked up half a dozen council houses in South Shields, just outside Newcastle, for half nothing. RoboPaddy, like Robocop, is an invincible good guy. Like Robocop, he is an indestructible force, driven by his own mission which is to buy as much foreign property as humanly possible. RoboPaddy lives on his wits, by the seat of his pants. He is curious, adventurous and loves life.

He has never been to Newcastle before today and has only spent the one afternoon driving around in the company of a matey Geordie salesman. It's not too bad really. The conversation revolves around Newcastle United, Shay Given and Gazza. The city is in the middle of its own buy-to-let boom. Rick the salesman sells about 40% of his stock to Irish investors. They deal quicker and in bigger amounts than the equivalent English buyer, ask fewer questions and cough up deposits on the spot.

Rick purposefully drives him though the better areas, the leafy redbrick suburbs with clean Waitrose shopping centres, red pillar boxes and alarmingly precise road signs — all staples of upright, balanced, suburban England. The place is a shrine to red Vauxhall Astras, Courage Pubs, dyed-blond hair, sports leisure wear and Argos male jewellery endorsed by Rio Ferdinand.

The salesman is careful to take RoboPaddy down by the river, past the new gleaming dockland redevelopment project — most of which has been snapped up by other RoboPaddies off plans. They pass the university with its Indie band posters, well-fed kids in baggy pants and high-yielding student blocks. RoboPaddy enquires about rates, rent rolls and tenancy agreements, does a few back-of-the-envelope calculations and asks Rick to keep an eye out for any Victorian redbricks if they come up.

They progress under the flyover with motorway signs to places RoboPaddy is vaguely familiar with: Edinburgh, Leeds, Manchester, and Middlesbrough. His knowledge of English cities is entirely based on the Premiership. He could name their football stadiums quicker than their upmarket residential areas. In fact, he could be buying in the Neilstown of Newcastle and he wouldn't know the difference. Past the flyover, Rick swings left into Carlisle Road Villas. It is one of these just-above-water council estates. RoboPaddy is buying council houses. The British social security pays the rent and the Newcastle firm ensures that one of its heavies sorts out any rental disputes. The houses are all pokey little places where the struggling live. The tenants are never seen by RoboPaddy. All he cares about is the yield, which in these sort of places is close to 10% — about 7% more than he is getting in Dublin. There is the typical newsagent's grilled window with 'It could be you' Lotto ads seducing the chain-smoking, overweight, single mums whose hoop-de-hoop earrings could pick up Sky television.

This is Ant and Dec land — the interface of middle England and under England which the Labour government is intent on privatising and of which RoboPaddy is a main beneficiary, or at least he hopes he is. He checks out the show house, which has been vacated and tarted up for him. Neighbours peer over walls and from the white mini-vans parked in the driveways.

He's seen enough, shakes on the deal and by the time he is sitting down to his pale ale at the formica tables of Teeside Airport, fruit machine flashing away as another work-shy, feral Darren or Lee gambles away his Giro, RoboPaddy has added to his portfolio. 11% yield. Where would you better it?

You also observe him at Bulgarian property exhibitions in the RDS, laden down with brochures about to sign up for Pomeroy Investments (which went bust last year), having just paid a deposit for four penthouses in Kusadasi at the Turkish stand. He's bought off plans in Dubai feeling that he had enough in Budapest, Alicante and Cape Town. He spends a lot of time in airports, typically at the bar of Ned Kelly's Irish pub.

In the past there was always a disproportionate presence of Hassidic Jews in international airports. Hardly visible in major cities, they seem to live in airports. The reason is that they are trading, travelling and acting as links between the various Hassidic centres of Antwerp, Golders Green and Crown Heights, Brooklyn. In recent years, Hassidic man is being replaced by an equally exotic character — RoboPaddy. RoboPaddy is equally odd looking and has a similarly distinctive garb. He tends to have a permanently red hue, yellowish eyes and a tight, acrylic Celtic away strip, acting as a harness for a fine, corpulent, stout belly. His trousers are worn low — in the fashion of an overweight rapper. He looks like a sun-burned Biggie Smalls as he mooches around the ex-military airports of Europe.

He is an irrepressible animal and very wealthy or at least very indebted. It is fairly common for him to have been a civil servant up until the mid-1990s and then bought a place in Dublin on SIPTU's free-interest-rate-scheme. One thing led to the next and before he really thought about it, he had fifteen places in Manchester, two in Aldershot and a pair of student housing schemes in Waterford. The bank that wouldn't have let him in the door ten years ago now calls him a 'high net worth' client and has assigned him a 'banking partner'. It will finance almost anything, as long as he puts up the collateral at home. With prices going up and up in Ireland, credit is plentiful.

No place is too far flung — Shanghai, Rio or Montreal — to prevent him buying off plans, no country too risky not to bet the house, no property flogger too oily to be doubted. Success has brought a swagger, but he's still good fun, down to earth and always the last to bed on the foreign trips, singing and drinking until the bewildered gigolo barman at the Four Seasons in Budapest heads for his bed.

RoboPaddy's entire scheme is based on borrowing against

properties at home to finance properties abroad. The banks will not take the risk on a foreign property so everything is leveraged to the hilt from properties in Ireland. Thus an original house in Dunleer, Co. Louth which was bought in 1989, plus his house in Kilmainham, became the financial catalyst for a chain of purchases which may well end in Shanghai. This is what could be termed the Dunleer Paradox. The financial robustness of the decision to buy in Shanghai is not assessed by any research done by the lender on the ground, rather it is a charge taken on the Irish property and the borrower gets his cash.

Unfortunately, because RoboPaddy is only human, the very act of getting his hands on the cash tends to vindicate his decision to buy in the first place. He is left with a false sense of security because the banks have not given him a thumbs up for Shanghai as he thinks; rather the bank has taken his house in Dunleer as collateral and will move to take this if things go sour in China. Thus RoboPaddy has performed the most amazing feat of risk transfer. He has reduced the risk for the bank immeasurably and increased his own dramatically. In China, interest rates are well above 10% for those wanting to borrow to fund housing. By borrowing at 2.5% here, RoboPaddy has exposed himself to four times more risk (2.5 divided by 10) than the Chinese market would be prepared to give him for the same property in China. Does he know something they don't know? Well yes and no. No in the sense that he has not even seen the apartment, has no idea of the rental market and less about his prospective tenants. But yes in the sense that he knows how the Irish game works. He knows that if he can hang on to this flat for a year or so and things don't go bang at home, some other Irish RoboPaddy will buy it from him. So it's a large pyramid scheme and the governing rule is not to be Paddy Last.

By virtue of RoboPaddy, an original 1980s house in Dunleer, Dundrum or Dunmanway has become the anchor of a global property portfolio and RoboPaddy bears all the risk. So who is making money? Well, the banks and the giant RoboPaddies who in many cases are developing the sites. Bank of Ireland and AIB make more profits per customer than any bank in Europe — €346 and €352 respectively,[4] while the giant RoboPaddies are building places in Bulgaria and Hungary specifically to sell to Irish investors who have been priced out of the Irish market. In this way, the success or failure of an apartment block scheme launched at the RDS off plans has nothing to do with Kusadasi but will be driven by market conditions in Limerick or Letterkenny.

Giant RoboPaddy knows how to play the game. He adopts an 'all drinks free for girls before eleven' approach to marketing his developments in Spain. In the same way as the nightclub owner operates on the principle that the more pretty drunk girls you get in to your club, the more you can fleece the free-spending testosterone-driven lads, Giant RoboPaddy works on the principle that you need to keep little RoboPaddy happy, get him out there, the sun will go to his head and he will buy two apartments off plans. Giant RoboPaddy then banks the deposits with the bank, the bank releases the financing and Giant RoboPaddy has his entire block financed without putting much of his own equity in. If he is good, the entire risk of the project will be passed on to little RoboPaddy before the block is even finished.

This means he has to cough up a few quid in advance by chartering a plane and flying a group of little RoboPaddy investors out to Marbella. There, he will have done an off-season deal with a hotel, putting them all up in decent suites for half nothing. The little RoboPaddies don't know this and psychologically they are in a very different place. They are made. They feel like players. The frenzy then begins. A few drinks and a showhouse is all it needs. Because the little RoboPaddies want to show-off to people they have hardly met before, they get involved in a bidding war amongst themselves. They tend to lie about what they have done before as everyone is petrified of looking like a rookie. The head salesman mingles with them, ordering drinks and dinner and telling them that there is a 20% discount for this special party. There are probably a few of the developer's *agent provocateurs* in the group. This was a ploy used by the English for years in Irish history. All you need is a rat in the group and it was because of this experience of infiltration that the IRA developed their cell structure in the 1970s. Unfortunately there are very few cell structures in Marbella at 1 am in the company of a pre-paid Serbian lap dancer.

The little RoboPaddies are Expectocrats in the great Expectocracy and they can be picked off one by one. But remember they are happy. They have not only bought a dream, they have a place. They can talk about 'my place in Spain'. They can be as deprecating or as brash about it as they like but they are 'place people' and place people are a cut above common or garden holiday people. They are also in that rarified class that previously was elusive: they are investors. The bank back home simply takes a charge over the family home in Bishopstown, Raheen or Claremorris and the property pyramid gets higher.

Investor yield chasing is one of the most conspicuous amber flashing lights of any market. It means that for the same return the investor has to take on more risk and go to far-flung places where the risks are unquantifiable. A few years ago in a previous existence, at the height of the late 1990s boom in stock and bond markets, the bank I worked for involved itself in increasingly esoteric transactions, seeking to maximise yield. This led to investments in all sorts of assets in all sorts of countries. One of my favourite places to visit was Bulgaria and when the bank was buying a hotel complex on the Black Sea coast I found myself as the lead negotiator. But when I see hundreds of RoboPaddies swarming around Bulgarian property exhibitions taking advice from salesmen at face value, I am always reminded of a balmy evening on the Black Sea in 1997.

The moll, all legs, stilettos and big hair, got out of the Ferrari and demanded a Harvey Wallbanger. The gangster was more subdued, but the mobile hitched to the belt of his Armanis did give him away. 'Mr McWilliams, I would like a word,' he said in halting English with a heavy Bulgarian accent. Across the beach, beyond the 1960s-style beach tents, the Black Sea stretched for miles. 'One million dollars.' He didn't repeat himself and knocked back his beer.

The blonde at this stage was getting giddy and I was nervous, having just been part of a team that had bought a beach resort for a western bank. Now the local hoodlum, who also happened to be an official in the region (Varna, one of Bulgaria's finest tourist stretches), was looking for his cut. When you come up against corruption like this, the first reaction is one of incredulity, followed by anger and resignation.

In our case, it was quickly established that this character was only a small-time bluffer who could be seen off quite easily, but I have no doubt that somewhere in the legitimate purchase price of the resort was more than a few Bulgarian levs for the local hard chaws. I don't think it has changed much and I am not singling out Bulgaria over anywhere else. There's more than enough of that carry-on here for us to be pointing sanctimonious fingers at anyone.

The point is that when investors chase yield, they are driven not so much by the opportunities in the new country as by the lack of opportunities at home. This also holds true for the developers, the larger RoboPaddies. The reason many of them are building in foreign places is that they simply cannot afford the price of sites in Ireland. So how does a smaller developer continue to be involved in the Irish market without being in Ireland? He builds in Spain, Cyprus or Portugal and sells it in Ireland. His margins are probably higher this way and he taps into the property frenzy without paying the Irish site premium.

Many of our 'investing' RoboPaddies have sizeable portfolios, deep pockets and are selling as well as buying (which is always a good sign) but many are 'investing' abroad because they are priced out of the market. Everyone is a bit twitchy at these dizzy heights but everyone thinks that they will get out before the suckers.

And this is the name of the game in Stage five of the boom/bust cycle: do not be Paddy Last. Most RoboPaddies are buying property abroad on the back of equity withdrawals on their Dunleer semi-D's or something similar. The Irish banks, which are finding it hard to make the silly valuations and profits demanded by their shareholders, have to generate huge volumes of business to make money. They are thus facilitating practically every proposed equity withdrawal. The Irish property market is therefore being leveraged at least twice. If anyone believes that the banks are staying within the multiple of income guidelines when it comes to lending, they need to have their heads examined. So the 'Dunleer' equity withdrawal is in effect a credit derivative that is driving up property prices in Budapest.

Forget that the locals couldn't afford to buy at the prices the Paddies are paying. The locals do not matter in this hermetically sealed Irish pyramid scheme. It's Paddies who are buying from other RoboPaddies and the exit strategy is to sell to another RoboPaddy when they want out. As long as the pyramid-scheme keeps going, fuelled by equity withdrawals, abundant credit and low interest rates, RoboPaddy can make money by playing 'beggar my neighbour' with other RoboPaddies. The golden rule of the RoboPaddy pyramid scheme is: don't be Paddy Last.

Golf lessons

Another Stage five sign is the mania for golf. Meet Billy Bunker. Always clean-shaven, eyes clear, hair parted on the left, he is the picture of the corporate man. He is only half a stone overweight and he's nearly thirty-five. He grips his Big Bertha clubs purposefully as he throws them into the back of his company navy 05 Merc 200 Elegance. He is the putting prince of the Grange Golf Club in Rathfarnham. During the summer he tries to be on the tee by 6 pm. It's difficult to slip off before 5 pm — bad example to senior vice-presidents — but he manages to sneak his Elegance out of IBM's staff car park. He usually has INXS blaring on his Bose by 5.15 pm. He calls one of the guys on the hands free. He likes the way you can pick up the surround sound anywhere in the car.

Today he is in full mufti — Pringle socks, golf shoes, diamond V-neck and lemon Nike visor. He is modest, clubbable and highly respectable, with a weakness for pastel-coloured slacks. But underneath he is steely and not above cheating which he prefers to call gamesmanship. He loves the psychology of the fairway. He has employed the same tactics at work and it has facilitated his rise to Global Head of Logistics — a coveted prize. He is a 'quick-stepper' who likes to start walking just as his opponent is swinging and he always lets his opponent find an errant shot; he has noticed that it makes them angry and they lose their focus. He always walks to the next tee before his opponent has finished his putt and has affected an irritating habit of jangling coins at a crucial moment and, worse still, loudly ripping the Velcro off his glove incessantly. All this focus, single-mindedness and ambition have allowed him to become a member in double-quick time.

There is something extraordinarily morbid about golf club politics and the rather unsavoury process of becoming a member. We all know people who spend their waking moments busily networking, like Billy, in the hope of being elevated to the inner sanctum of an old, established club.

Given that this ritual usually involves waiting for a member to croak, it seems a bit distasteful. However, social etiquette aside, doing the chicken dinner circuit and waiting in line is probably more palatable than coughing up for membership of one of the new clubs that have sprung up around the country.

In the mid 1990s, membership of one of the swankier clubs on Dublin's outskirts cost around £2,500; this year it will set you back €40,000. Indeed, banks are financing loans for memberships and at least one enterprising individual has made a healthy crust trading golf club memberships, buying them cheap and flogging them on later.

Edward Chancellor in his history of financial speculation *Devil take the Hindmost* used the mania for golf as an indicator of the excesses of a property boom because in the 1980s, a similar craze gripped Japan. As the economy boomed, so too did golf. The game was a central feature of Japanese corporate life and a permanent fixture in the *shain ryoko* or company outing. Membership and position in the club denoted a certain privilege and bestowed a clear hierarchical structure on what is a very position-conscious society. As property prices boomed, banks fell over themselves to lend to golf course developers, seeing golf clubs as a property play.

In 1982, one of Japan's leading newspapers, the *Nippon Keizai Shimbun*, launched the infamous Nikkei Golf Membership Index which calculated the average price of membership in 500 clubs. From its base of 100, the index rose steadily to 160 in 1985 and then took off in the 'bubble' years of the late 1980s to peak at 1,000 in June 1990. The market in club membership was sustained by salesmen who earned commissions flogging membership certificates, with banks financing up to 90% of the so-called 'collateral'.

The golf club index became one of the most accurate indicators of the Japanese property market's boom/bust cycle. By 1992, the index had more than halved as the collapsing property market caused trade in memberships to dry up.

Ireland is in the midst of a similar golf craze. Billy Bunker types are replicating themselves all over the country. Between the day we devalued and 2004, the number of courses increased from 280 to 413 and the total number of registered golfers rose to 276,389 from 157,804 while the rather anachronistic description 'lady' golfers increased from 30,982 to 54,727. There are now more golf courses in Ireland than children's playgrounds.

Of course, everyone knows that there are really two types of clubs, the old and the nouveau. The old clubs are long established and are *owned by the members in common* — ownership rights accrue to membership. Those in Dublin include Milltown, the Grange, the Castle, Elm Park, Portmarnock and Royal Dublin. All are located in choice suburban areas. These clubs are nigh on impossible to get in to. They are over-subscribed and so the speed of the queue at the front is dependent on the amount of members going out in wooden boxes at the back. This over-subscription has an effect on the price of entry. For example, the Grange's full member entry fee is currently a mere

€16,000. This is substantially below what the market could bear but there are other significant costs — principally hanging around the clubhouse for years on some limited form of membership (junior or pavilion) and sucking up to every bar-room bore who might have some influence on the arcane selection procedure for membership. Truly this is a debasing purgatory for all but the very ambitious, like Billy Bunker. Thus many people are happy to go off to the newer courses.

And it is in the nouveau where we see explicit Stage five syndrome. Over the 1990s there was a large increase in proprietal courses — those where no ownership rights accrue to membership. Thus, the elite like Michael Smurfit (whose bust of General Patton in full military uniform which Smurfit himself wore at his own sixtieth is a sight to behold) who owns the K Club, end up owning the courses, not the members. These new courses include South County Dublin, Powerscourt and Carton House. Members of these clubs can have their membership terminated by the owners after five years. Thus they pay €50,000 to join for the privilege of paying a few grand per year and then can be booted out after five years. What a deal. But at least you are free from the extraordinary mania for rules and committees where the pedantry is awesome and terrible to behold: woe betide the man who fails to wear a tie at the appointed hour.

However, the new clubs are not immune. A much reported story[5] about Dermot Desmond apparently blocking Noel Smith's attempt to become captain of the K Club is priceless. Here are two titans scrapping over an honorary position in a golf club. That's golf for you, though; little things that appear meaningless to outsiders are of huge importance to insiders. This extends to the etiquette of the game. There are a million and one spoken and unspoken rules governing behaviour on the course and in the clubhouse. And in an extraordinary display of snobbery there are 'artisan' members in clubs like the Grange and Dún Laoghaire. These are generally local working-class men. They have their own clubhouse and have limited playing rights — essentially they can play at first light. Once a year there is an artisans' day, when they are paired with members for a round and all retire to the artisans' clubhouse afterwards for a few scoops. In the Grange they don't have a barman but each artisan does a while behind the bar on rotation.

Abstracting from the ludicrous snobbery which blights this

otherwise wonderful game, the prices of this most fantastic social indicator have gone up ten-fold since 1995. Banks are topping up mortgages to finance this type of carry-on in the same way as Japanese banks financed club membership on margin in the late 1980s. In terms of prices, Ireland is now in Japanese territory. Remember that the Japanese golf club index began at 100 in 1984, peaked at 1,000 in 1990 and had fallen to 160 by 1992.

Less in-your-face than membership but equally instructive has been the decision to sell old member-owned courses to take advantage of the property boom. Dún Laoghaire recently cashed in. It was reported that 'the club's members agreed overwhelmingly to sell its grounds to developers Cosgrave Brothers in return for a new 27-hole golf course and a new clubhouse with ancillary facilities at Ballyman Road, between Enniskerry and Bray, as well as €20.3 million in cash.'[6]

Bray golf course did likewise, reputedly in a 'deal worth about £10 million to Bray, including a £2 million cash settlement. There was to be no scrimping in terms of the course or the clubhouse, down to the cutlery and accoutrements. The facility would be a magnificent 1,765 sq. m (19,000 sq. ft) structure that offers a view not only of several holes but the surrounding countryside.'[7]

If you want to get a good view of what Stage five of a property boom/bust cycle looks like, take off your visor, lean back on your Big Bertha and take a long look down the fairway.

Trophy assets and big willies

Another flashing amber light signalling Stage five syndrome is the scramble for trophy assets. Japanese speculators began snapping up trophy golf courses in the US.[8] In 1991 Cosmo World, an investment vehicle, bought the Pebble Beach resort of hotels and golf courses in California for $831 million which was a record-breaking sum at the time and prompted many commentators to warn about the Japanese takeover of the US. Golf courses in the US had special significance for Japanese buyers as they were seen as the bastion of American capitalism, and the Japanese taking them over would draw a close to the Japanese defeat in World War II. Even Japanese politicians started to speculate that the main reason for Japanese economic success was ethnic purity rather than the mixed-up melting pot that was the US.

In a similar vein, today Irish developers are buying exclusive and historic clubs like the Wentworth club — home to the World Match Play series in deepest blue-blood Surrey. There is an element of trophy shopping here. There may even be a sense that it was the Paddies who used to build and caddy at places like this not so long ago but now they are walking proudly through the front door and buying the place. The tables are now turned. 'Asset envy' among the super-rich speculators leads them to buy trophy sites and assets in London, outbidding even the Arabs — the ultimate trophy shoppers. In the same way as the Japanese of the 1980s bought the Rockefeller Centre, Hollywood's Colombia Pictures and the Exxon Building in Manhattan, Irish big swingers are waving their willies around buying the Savoy, half of Knightsbridge and other landmark sites in the City and Canary Wharf. (There was a time Irishmen blew up landmark buildings in London, now the Irish are buying them up.) A recent example of trophy shopping was the crazy bidding war for the Jurys site in Ballsbridge. Trophy shopping whether at home or abroad is a typical Stage five syndrome. These buyers are brash, public and in-your-face. Yields are normally very low on these types of purchases but they are more of a willy-waving exercise than a pure commercial play.

And speaking of willies, a classic Stage five syndrome is what is called the 'erection index'. This suggests that the top of a bull market in property is around the corner when the height of a new building exceeds all previous records. For example, the Chrysler Building was finished days before the 1929 crash, as was the Empire State Building. Likewise the world's tallest building, the Petronas Towers in Kuala Lumpur, was finished months before the Asian Crisis of 1997, while Canary Wharf was completed just as the British market imploded in the early 1990s. Back in Ireland, there are plans now to build the tallest building the city has ever seen down in Ringsend. We have the U2 tower in the dock basin and there are also towers planned in Donnybrook and Kilmainham. A 32-storey tower has just been granted planning permission at Heuston — this is twice as high as Dublin's highest building. Meanwhile six 12-storey towers are being planned for Sandyford. The logic behind the erection index has a bit of economics added to the large dollops of rich man's vanity. When the price of land gets so exorbitant, builders have to go up. The higher they have to go up is a reflection of the ratio of the site value to the break-even point. So, for example, break-even point may have moved from six storeys to ten in the last year or so. By 2005, a certain architectural swelling can be seen in Dublin's building plans. The erection index is stirring.

The demographic civil war

Quite apart from financial warning lights flashing amber, there is a significant social problem emerging which suggests that we are in bubble territory and that the political pendulum may swing against the property obsession.

There is something of the Bimbo about the Kells Angels because, for all their education, these Pope's Children are not getting a great deal. Financially, they are the most stretched Irish people ever. They have been shafted by the property boom. An interesting way to look at the paradoxes of the Pope's Children is to view them through the prism of a demographic civil war. This idea was first made clear to me by the English socialist Tony Benn. I interviewed him a few years ago and, leaning back in his volume-lined study, pipe in one hand, tape recorder in the other, Benn, then 78, fixed his gaze on me and pronounced: 'Young man, the old and the young have one thing in common: they are both bullied by the middle aged.'

He summarised perfectly one of the central dilemmas of Irish society where one age group holds all the wealth and most of the power.

An overlooked and potentially explosive dividing ground in Ireland is between the Jagger generation and the Pope's Children. Like their idol, the Jagger generation are now in their late fifties and early sixties. They are the ones who keep the Rolling Stones back catalogues in business, who read Van Morrison biographies and who go for regular check-ups at the Blackrock Clinic. Let me just make it clear that we are not talking about some pre-planned conspiracy by the Jagger generation. In fact it is almost an accident that happens to have culminated in them having it all. As some of these people include those who were student radicals and editors of music magazines, they tend not to realise that they are now 'the power'.

It is, of course, natural that the fifties generation will be the ones in power, but because of demographics here, they are much less representative of the general population than they would be, for instance, in Britain where they constitute 27% of the population, or over 30% as in France and Germany. Here, those in their fifties only represent 11% of the population and yet they dominate business, the law, the media and politics. This tiny cohort of our population controls almost all the levers of power.

The Jagger generation, born between 1945 and 1955, are making out like bandits, while the Pope's Children — the Stakhanovites of Ireland — are all grunt, no power. This is most evident in the housing market.

The past ten years has seen an enormous transfer of wealth from the young Pope's Children to the Jagger generation via the instrument of the housing market and land prices in general. The Jaggers bought their houses in the 1970s and 1980s and they have profited enormously from the subsequent rise in property prices. The losers have been the Pope's Children who can't afford to buy anywhere except the BabyBelt and those who live in the cities must rent at exorbitant prices.

Thus, while the Jaggers have seen their stake in society greatly increase, the Pope's Children are the worker bees, slaving away deep in the belly of the Celtic Tiger with little bar huge debts to show for it. The transfer of wealth from the housing boom is unprecedented. Historically, these financial spoils have been reserved for invading armies and the like, but not in Ireland where it has just been a matter of luck.

We live in a society where the young work to excess to make the middle-aged. Every 10% rise in the price of houses is equivalent to a 10% tax hike for the young who are trying to get on the housing market. Another way to look at it is every 10% increase in the price of houses adds an extra 14 km commute on to the day of the next batch of Kells Angels. In contrast, the same 10% price-hike adds 10% to the wealth of the Jagger generation and ten more holes on the golf course on the Algarve.

Theoretically, in a democracy there are meant to be electoral checks and balances that militate against excessive political power being exercised by the rich, but these are not working because the BabyBelt does not vote. Party politics, the Dáil and the government have passed them by. In the last election, the BabyBelt did not turn up to vote. Does this mean that the Kells Angels are not political? Probably not. After all they put Naomi Klein's *No Logo* on the top of the bestsellers list for months, but they are profoundly cynical about national politics. They couldn't be bothered. A bachelor farmer from Achill is twice as likely to vote as a Kells Angel, so too is a Jagger generation lawyer in Sandycove, Foxrock, Terenure or Clontarf. In fact, the two areas of Ireland where the Pope's Children are present — the new suburbs and the inner cities — vote least.[9]

This opting-out trend contrasts with the rest of Europe where voting patterns follow education. In Ireland, when you were born, rather than letters after your name, is much more likely to determine whether you vote or not.

So the Stakhanovites of the country, the Pope's Children who work hardest, commute longest, pay most taxes, have the biggest mortgages, have children, pay exorbitant crèche fees and keep the profits of multi-nationals operating in Ireland sky-high, participate least in politics.

As a result of the increasing wealth divide due exclusively to property prices, a demographic civil war could break out in Irish politics. This may well lead to some governmental efforts to curb the property boom which, of themselves, might puncture the bubble.

Failing a political tremor, the boom will last as long as credit remains abundant. And the only thing that can guarantee this is if Udo Lindenburg lives indefinitely. So maybe the government should invest all Ireland's technological talent into a futuristic scheme to cryogenically freeze the entire German geriatric generation. Keeping them alive — just about — is the only way to guarantee that the credit keeps flowing. Wherever we are in the cycle, one thing is clear: without the property boom, the credit and the resulting spending we would not have the New Ireland or the New Irish Dream. The 'You're a Star' generation would not exist.

One of the most interesting and arguably overlooked aspect of the past few years has been the impact of the credit boom on our psychology. How has the boom changed us? How has it changed our basic social DNA? Are we simply the same people, only now some of us have a Lexus, second homes and credit cards, or has the credit itself changed the society? Has the credit boom changed the Irish mentality, how we view ourselves and how others view us?

Chapter 9

The Protestant Catholics

CREDIT, THE 21ST-CENTURY LIBERATOR

Back in the days of Daniel O'Connell, the original Liberator, religion excluded people. In the eyes of the British government, if you were Catholic you were suspect, unworthy and dangerous. You could not vote and you certainly could not have access to credit or anything close to economic power. Although the anti-Catholic laws here were particularly harsh, they were not unique.[1] Anti-Catholicism was one of the gelling agents of the British project. It permeated British culture from top to bottom, from the bar on Catholics occupying the throne to 'Guy Fawkes Night' in the villages. For centuries, stoking up anti-Catholicism was the populist trick of choice in Britain. Being a Catholic excluded you.

Up until recently, there was a much more subtle form of exclusion in post-independence Ireland. It wasn't religious bigotry, racial segregation or gender oppression (although all those issues were there). It was credit discrimination. Only respectable people got credit. Only respectable people had bank accounts. Only respectable people had access to loans. While we had a political democracy, we lived in what can be termed an *economic respectocracy*, where nepotism, respectability, favouritism and networks determined your ability to draw credit. The poor had wages, the middle classes had overdrafts. The economic effects of this are self-evident. They are unambiguously negative for all. In the same way as excluding women from economic participation in some Arab countries has hampered the development of these countries, excluding the non-respectable from credit did untold damage to our economy. But quite apart from the economic impacts, the psychological effect of moving from a country where credit was rationed to a country where credit is freely available cannot be underestimated.

Psychoanalysts regularly try to identify pivotal events in someone's life that may hold the key to understanding subsequent behaviour. Why did the murderer change, with no warning, from being a quiet church warden into a cold-blooded killer? Or why did the rapist leave certain clues behind? Why did the multi-millionaire seem unhappy and unloved? Why his irrational hatred of women?

Similarly, it is possible to examine the economic tea-leaves of a nation to explain why certain political or social traits emerge. Amazingly for a country whose economy has been seen as a model for others, we have chosen in general not to see economics in an explanatory light. Economics has been afforded a small role in the way the Commentariat has tried to understand the change in the Irish psyche over the past few years. Yet economics, the property boom and the associated deluge of credit explain the New Irish Dream very persuasively.

While much commentary has focused on the impact on our psyche of the demise of the Church, the betrayal of the political system, the end of the IRA campaign in the North and left-wing ideas or right-wing ideas, the most liberating development in the past fifteen years has been the emergence of credit. This credit has washed over us like a liberating, democratic, soothing balm. It has eased the deep neurotic pain of being economically second rate and healed us of the great Irish affliction whereby we can only be financially successful when we are in New York, London or Boston. Credit has harnessed our energies for the first time ever, at home.

Credit has been a great liberator. Delicious, reasonably equitable credit has shifted some of the most tight-assed, rigid social structures and it has allowed a degree of social mobility, aspiration and freedom unfathomable only a few years ago. Credit has allowed business to flourish which otherwise would have been squeezed by deficient cash flow. Jobs, incomes, good fun, late wild nights, one-night-stands, great weekends and all sorts of other goodies have stemmed directly from our new cash — and this should be celebrated.

Most importantly, the credit avalanche buried an economic ecosystem where respectability underpinned our class system. The old class system was the ultimate Respectocracy. He who had credit was king and to get credit you had to have credibility; in the old repressive climate, respectability was the key to credibility. So the respectable were on top. In the Respectocracy, doctors, senior executives in semi-state companies and other professionals held the commanding heights. The banks were populated by old boys who did deals with their old mates based on the premise of Respectocracy and networks. Those who were not respectable could either emigrate or live off scraps. Credit was the arbiter. In response to class-based lending policies at the main banks, credit unions sprang up all over the country. Go to any working-class area in Ireland and nestled in the cluster of shops beside the post office, the grotto to the Blessed Virgin Mary and the bookies, you will find the credit union, waving two big artisan fingers at the established banks.

Today the big cheeses of the old order have been replaced by builders, car-alarm salesmen and the self-employed. No longer do you need to be a golfing partner of the bank manager, a guard or a career bore with some insurance company to get a loan. Now all you need to have is a bit of property and a good sales patter. Contacts and networks still mean a lot, but not as much as they did. The wave of cheap credit has liberated the country and nullified the old credit class system.

Just think about how it used to be. A few days ago I was in the back of a taxi in the lashing rain. 'David, do you know what bread and butter pudding is?' Joe asked in the rear-view mirror and before I could answer he continued. 'Well it always reminds me of bad weather, mornings like this when you can hardly see in front of you, wind howling and rain chuckin' down on you.' It was pouring as we sneaked up the bus-lane, past hundreds of stationary commuters — blokes texting talk radio stations, women shouting at bored kids whose faces are distorted by Mickey Mouse sun shades on rear side windows. Joe drives a taxi. He played for Shamrock Rovers in their pomp which makes him a bit of a local hero with football aficionados from the Borough. Now with his golf-course perma-tan and his slicked back hair, he looks younger than fifty. Bernie, the missus, was the Irish 'Come Dancing' Champion in the 1970s and spends summer weekends, when Joe's on the golf course, in Blackpool, ballroom dancing. Life is good. Joe works when he wants, doesn't work nights, couldn't be bothered taking drunks' fares and pays as much tax as his accountant tells him he has to. Three foreign holidays a year, two grown-up daughters and one investment property — things have worked out well.

His father worked on the ships and Joe can remember weeks when his father was caught in bad weather at sea and no wages arrived. His mother responded by making bread and butter pudding and the whole family lived on it for days on end until the old man docked. Bread and butter pudding was the antidote to credit. If he was gone for a while, his mother would send Joe down to an aunt in Dún Laoghaire on a 'message'. The message was a sealed envelope with a few quid in it to tide the family over until the Dad docked and sorted everyone out. People like Joe's parents did not have bank accounts, credit facilities or overdrafts.

Typical of many thousands of Irish families in the 1960s and 1970s — whether the Dad was working in England or here or on the labour — the existence was from day to day, week to week or at best, month to month. People's time horizons rarely extended beyond the next week or month and never stretched out beyond a year.

Apart from health, pregnancy and physical longevity, the crucial determining factor in people's perception about their own future is money, cash and credit. We are not talking about the difference between being rich or poor here. We are talking about the ability to get your hands on cash today, to plan for tomorrow.

Credit is a great liberator — it facilitates the future. When you have no credit, everything is immediate and the future does not exist. Today governs tomorrow.

As soon as credit becomes available either to an individual, a society or a class, something strange happens to time. Time travelling becomes possible. With credit, the status quo that has characterised humans for millennia is turned on its head — today no longer rules tomorrow, tomorrow governs today and the three Ps dominate: planning, postponement and progression.

With planning comes plotting, mapping, targeting, achieving, comparing and benchmarking. In short, the future — and most importantly your future — becomes projectable. One of the main manifestations of this is further education. Further education is the luxury of those who can postpone earning a crust today to earn a better one tomorrow. The last census registered a 38% increase in Irish teenagers going to college; many are the first ever in their families.

In the 1960s and 1970s, only the already rich could entertain the future and plan, invest and wait for the dividends. Without credit, the Irish working class could not postpone the lure of cash today. Only the middle class postponed. In many ways the crucial difference between the classes was the credit divide.

The time and mindset-altering effects of credit on entire classes is often overlooked. So the onset of credit in this country in the mid-1990s did not just allow people to buy Gucci, Kenzo and Kompressors: credit allowed hundreds of thousands of people — the Pope's Children — to move from instant gratification to the great middle-class state of postponement. The transition and gap years — favourites of the Pope's Children — are the ultimate expressions of postponement.

The biggest driving force behind the great Irish class compression of the early 21st century is that we can all dream about the future because of glorious credit. Yes, free education, better health care and a variety of other much heralded factors helped emancipate the Irish working classes from under-achievement, but the main factor was credit. Credit lubricates the society as oil does a rusty hinge and it facilitates planning; but, more importantly, it allows us to live in the future rather than live in the present as Joe's mother had to. To live in the future is to be middle class.

So within a generation, we went from a country that dreamt of past struggles and was rooted in the cash-strapped present, to a society that lived in the future, that dreamed, expected and chose the future over the present. The working class has become the credit class.

In the time it will take you to read this book, €100 million in credit will have been created, washing into every nook and cranny of the economy, flowing into each family and impacting on each and everyone's expectations about the future.

Credit drives the price of houses, which gives people the perception of financial security, which allows them to postpone. Credit pays today's bills in the absence of today's income. It pays college fees, grind school fees and the hire purchase on the latest suv. It allows us to live in the future, to make plans to see into the next decade or two. It gives 130,000 of us the confidence to change jobs every year, it encourages 100,000 of us to change houses every year and 150,000 the ability to live out our retirements today by buying holiday homes abroad.[2]

Credit has created a New Ireland — an Ireland that lives in the future rather than the past — an Ireland enthralled by the New Irish Dream. Credit, contrary to much commentary on the vapidity and vacuousness of our society, makes people happy. Blurrily so.

Yet within this blur, there have been winners and losers. In addition to credit, changes in the way people are paid and why they are paid has also undermined the foundations of the old Respectocracy. In the new Expectocracy, there is a new form of economics which impacts on our position and our incomes, which I shall call Keanonomics.[3]

KEANONOMICS

Recently my father came out of hospital after a long illness and, in contrast to the hype about the dreadful health service, our family's experience in the public hospital was brilliant. The nurses were angels, charming, efficient and patient. They held his hand when he was frail and touched his brow when was running a temperature. They were humane to a fault.

The day he got out, I was given a pair of tickets to see Pavarotti in the Point. I knew that he had been a life-long fan and nothing could announce his return to the world (to himself as much as anyone else) better than getting spruced up and heading into the concert with my mother.

Just as they pulled up to the Point, the announcer on Lyric FM stated solemnly that Pavarotti had just cancelled the concert because he had a throat infection. Concert off. Undeterred, my parents said they would go to the National Concert Hall to see what was on. If they couldn't see Pavarotti, they would listen to someone else probably equally as good but less famous. After battling with Dublin's traffic restrictions, counter-flows and one-way systems, they finally arrived at the Concert Hall. It seemed strangely quiet for a Saturday night. They approached the desk and the woman politely informed them that all performances had been cancelled as Pavarotti was singing in the Point.

Ultimately, the upshot of Pavarotti's streptococcal infection was that no-one in Dublin heard any classical music that night. Pavarotti may be the best tenor in the world and hearing him would be worthwhile. However, that night my parents would have been very happy to hear maybe the second-best tenor or one-hundredth-best tenor, but they couldn't. Those guys would not get a chance to sing. Their stars were eclipsed by the Sun-God of tenors, Pavarotti. Pavarotti was the winner and they were the losers and no-one gets the chance to see losers.

Modern communications from Lyric FM, to DVDs, CDs and in my Dad's case records, had brought Pavarotti into everyone's lives and overshadowed all the other very brilliant but not quite brilliant enough, tenors in the world. Years ago before the advent of these technologies, a journey-man tenor (as the name describes) could make a good living on the circuit and be happy doing what he did best, singing, entertaining and milking the modest applause. But not now. Why listen to Joe Bloggs for €15 when you can buy a Pavarotti gift-box for €29.99. So all the cash goes to Pavarotti; none to Joe Bloggs.

In *The Winner Takes All Society* Robert Frank and Phillip Cook expertly outline the forces that drive huge differences in rewards in a variety of jobs. They highlight sport as being a leading indicator for what is happening in other professions. And as US trends seem to re-appear in Ireland with a lag of a few years, what better person to elucidate this than our finest footballer, Roy Keane.

His weekly salary is twice the annual industrial wage and since he signed his new contract United have won nothing. In another world he would have taken a pay cut, but not in the world of football. Is Keane worth £80,000 a week for playing in a faltering team and when his individual performance can only be seen in the context of the players around him? No of course not, no player is. But the market for football talent dictates that that is what he gets. Look at players who have played with Roy over the years. Take Nicky Butt, clearly less talented, less effective, but is he £30,000 a week less effective? I'm not sure. The crucial issue is that Keane is a winner in the winner-takes-all markets that affect our society.[4] And the difference between winners and second best is enormous.

But in recent years the Roy Keane market for talent — where the best is paid multiples of the second best — has stretched its tentacles into other jobs. The old expression 'No-one remembers second place' is true not only in sport, the performance arts, media and music; it is slowly permeating every aspect of our lives, jobs and careers.

Ireland now has superstar barristers who coin it in at the bar. We have superstar solicitors who bring in the biggest clients. We have superstar architects who get paid twice as much as the next lad to build something very similar. We have superstar surgeons going to private hospitals. We even had the case of the superstar CEO of Bank of Ireland who came to an unedifying end and got paid a superstar €2 million pay-off — that is one hundred times more than the nurse who saved my father's life gets paid in a year. No wonder people want to get into high finance.

The proliferation of the Roy Keane theory of economics is due to the mutual forces of competition and communication, which are raising the stakes at every level. Let's take the example of the barrister. Ireland is a litigious society and the stakes down at the Four Courts can be very high. The recent case between two well-known titans of the Irish business community evidences this well. At issue was at least €120 million, maybe more. The side with the best case, as presented by the best lawyer, wins. So is the lawyer worth €2 million, €3 million or €1 million? Maybe he is worth €7 million, no-one knows exactly. The participants know that if they win, they stand to gain enormously, so they pay whatever it takes. The barrister in question, therefore, has no real benchmark to put a value on his services other than some fraction of the likely loot. Like Keane, you can't put a value on him, but Man United know the value of winning trophies in terms of merchandising, TV rights etc., so Keane's wages are some fraction of that and a top-up so that Abramovich won't snap him up.

Now, how does the Keanonomics theory of economics differ from the traditional theory of labour economics which described how wages are set? Traditional economics indicates that the price for, let us say, a barrister, is set by the supply and demand for barristers. If we have more barristers, the cost of barristers will fall because they are all more or less the same and the expensive one will be replaced by the cheaper one bringing down the hourly cost. This is the logic that underpins competition and deregulation. However, it does not work like that. We have more and more barristers down at the Four Courts but they are going into the game precisely because of Keanonomics. They want to be the top dogs in the winner-takes-all market for barristers. They have no interest in going into the business if entry depresses their likely future wage. There is no evidence that the wages of barristers have fallen over the years. But there has been a growing gap between the best and the rest. Meanwhile jobs that are not characterised by these conditions — such as teaching and nursing, where the wages are set across the board — begin to fall back relative to the Roy Keanes of the Bar, the medical profession or the design trade. The combination of credit loosening our rigid class system and the exertion of Keanonomics has led to rapid status inflation and deflation. Many of the old Respectocrats have lost out in the Expectocracy and this is having a profound effect on our society.

THE SLIPPING STATUS

'Vulgarians at the gate' is the cry of the slipping status snobs. How can those people afford that? Ireland was better in the old days when people knew their place. While the country may be getting rich via the Wonderbra effect, certain members of the old, solid middle class are falling behind, and they don't like it. The following table examines those who have done well and those who have been left behind.

Status Winners	Status Limbo	Status Losers
People successfully generating their own income	*People with the potential to generate their own income*	*Public sector professionals/ establishment employees*
• Entrepreneurs/ Builders • Artists • Writers • Musicians • Media people • Creative/ Innovative but need to be successful, either critically or financially	• Doctors • Solicitors • Journalists • IT workers • Politicians • Depends on the individuals, the area in which they're working and the money they're making	• Teachers/University lecturers • Civil Servants • Bank Managers • Gardaí • Priests • The old reliables. Haven't had to change and adapt in the past so now are pretty much unable to. Fixed incomes, familiar roles, little room for major development within the job

If we break it down into three groups, we can see clearly that in broad terms the old reliables have seen their position slip. The key to the recent changes in people's status has been the ability to generate your own cash. This has profound implications for people's status and self-worth.

The biggest change the Expectocracy has wrought is via Keanonomics, whereby it is not what you do that is important but how you do it. So the term professional which used to refer to a type of job you did, now refers to the way you do that job. Anyone who does any job professionally will see their status rise in the Expectocracy and a professional who does his job unprofessionally will see his status and income fall.

Although it is unfair to single out teachers in particular, the decline in the position of the teacher in society has been quite stark. The teachers' miscalculation of the public's mood in the recent strike suggests that we are looking at a profession in status freefall.

Years ago, the school master was a big cheese. Not any more. In fact one of the signals of that loss of teachers' status has been the gradual disappearance of the school master who has been replaced by the school mistress. The feminisation of certain jobs is a tell-tale sign of a loss of status. There are a variety of reasons for this. The main one is that women typically see through the corporate flannel quicker than men and choose jobs that suit their lives rather than lives that suit their jobs.

During their strike and attempts to get a 35% pay increase, the teachers were shocked at the public reaction which was not supportive. The teachers forgot that the Expectocracy demands a certain standard, and people's collective memories of the odd rubbish teacher made them militant in the face of a profession that seemed to think it could get anything it wanted. The distinction between professions and professionalism was never more stark. Teachers regularly cite friends who were in university with them making multiples of the teacher's salary as indicative of the fall in their status.

Teachers also suffer from being in an inflexible job where the average dictates rewards, so the good and bad teachers get paid the same. We all have memories of useless as well as inspiring teachers, yet only the teachers who leave the state system and go into the grind schools get paid something like the value society puts on them. This in itself is significant because the grind schools have a narrow and explicit objective which is to get little Johnny into Trinners or UCD. The professional bar is set so as to make the aim quantifiable. If the teacher achieves this, like the salesman hitting a sales target, he gets a bonus. The problem for teachers is that the Expectocracy wants targets, benchmarks and immediate indicators of success, whereas most good teachers regard teaching as a greater process of preparing pupils for life (or at least that's what they tell us), so immediately the aims and objectives are out of synch.

The Expectocracy has changed the class system, rates of pay and status in our society. However, quite apart from the impact on the individual — whether Joe the taxi driver, the teacher or the nurse — there has been a collective change in our psychology which is quite a departure from the philosophy that governed Ireland before the boom. In many ways, we look and feel more like Americans than Europeans, where money and possessions are highly valued. This is new in Ireland and, in fact, conflicts with our traditional philosophy and the way we saw ourselves. The Expectocracy has changed the Irish story. It has turned us into New-Age Catholics who think like old-fashioned Protestants.

THE PROTESTANT CATHOLICS

'It is easier for a camel to get through the eye of a needle than for a rich man to get into heaven.' This is probably the only parable I remember from school, not because of the sentiment but because of the imagery. It was one of the few where the image jumped or rather waddled out of the page at me. The picture of the fat rich man is timeless. However, like many other images, that has now been turned on its head because these days, the rich are thin while the poor are fat. But for practically the entire history of humanity, bar the last ten years, rotundness was associated with wealth. The picture of the fatty struggling to get through the eye of a needle, while the lithe, penniless pauper limbo-danced through, effortlessly, was always going to stick with me.

Practically all the Pope's Children will have remembered this one. The sentiment was quite simple — being rich could well be a hindrance in the hereafter. Material possessions said nothing about your spiritual status. In fact the more you had in this world, the harder it would be to do well in the next. Catholicism held that there was an explicit inverted relationship between being rich and your moral status on earth.

For years, poor Irish Catholics could be comforted by the parable of the rich man. Likewise, 'The meek shall inherit the earth' (Matthew 5.5) is helpful when you are rock bottom poor.

Following mass expropriation of land by the English, status in Ireland came to be conferred by religion, language and ethnicity. If you were Catholic, Irish-speaking and Hibernian you had no status; you were an *untermensch*. If you were a Protestant, English-speaking planter your status was guaranteed. The idea that the new rich settlers were robbers has always been the subtext of Irish nationalism. Until recently, the combination of the rich man parable and the secure knowledge that the vast majority of the traditional rich had, in effect, stolen the land, making their wealth illegitimate, allowed most Irish people to look down on the rich from the standpoint of spiritual superiority and historical legitimacy.

Thus the poor Irish had narratives and myths, both secular and religious, in which they found not only mere solace for their station but even an assertion of superiority. They would inherit the world — if not in this life, then certainly in the next.

These stories were the narratives of Catholics, Hibernians and left-wingers alike. They were universal and cosmopolitan in their reach and they acted as great levellers for those who found themselves poor, not least because they militated against linking poverty with self worth, status and your sense of yourself.

But there were other narratives, Protestant ones, and particularly those associated with the Calvinist variety of Protestantism. They made a direct connection between wealth, material success and personal virtue. This Calvinist precept, combined with the emphasis in Protestantism generally on individual conscience and individual initiative, formed the mental template for the emergence of modern capitalism. It is no accident that capitalism first developed in countries like England and Holland with strong Calvinist traditions, or that it has flourished most luxuriantly in God's own Puritan republic, America. Or that its greatest theoretician, Adam Smith, was a product of Calvinist Scotland.

Industrialised capitalism gradually produced a meritocratic society. Since World War II, in particular, the belief in the social mobility of individuals, in their ability to rise due to their own efforts and exertions, has become the norm.

And for many millions of us, the meritocracy has allowed us to prosper irrespective of colour, class or creed. In Ireland, in the past ten years we have seen huge social mobility, most of it upwards. Of course this has not been true for everyone and there are pockets of persistent under-achievement as well as instances of rampant nepotism, but for the majority of us, the meritocracy has been beneficial.

Over time it has become the most normal way of looking at the world, and governments are now less inclined to provide cradle-to-grave care. They are now legislating against discrimination so that equality of opportunity is in some way upheld. In many ways, this has allowed governments off the hook, but nonetheless this is how most Anglo-American societies, of which we are one, work.

The problem for the poor is that if you live in a meritocracy and you are not rich, you can't blame the system, the aristocracy or anyone else. So if you are poor, there is something wrong with you, personally. Another difficulty is that, by explicitly linking your place in the social order to merit, wealth and possessions take on a moral quality, as they have never done before. If you do not have either you are therefore without merit. Also, possessions in a meritocracy allow you to benchmark your status at a certain time, so the constant tyranny of relativity emerges, bringing with it envy and angst. No longer is it good enough to be comfortable: you have to be *more* comfortable than your neighbour. As the Expectocracy is a superannuated version of a meritocracy, this problem is amplified in 21st-century Ireland.

With the emergence of the free market as the economic underpinning of the Expectocracy and the only economic system that has actually worked in this country, the values of Irish individuals have become more Protestant than Catholic, where the community has been usurped by the individual.

Ireland is now a nation of Protestant Catholics, where you are what you own. The good citizen is now the one with the fastest car, the biggest house, the newest fashions or the biggest bank account. Your address, Hermes or Maybach confer status — and people will do anything to get status. Daniel O'Connell, the original Liberator, would turn in his grave.

This is also leading to a bizarre new type of economics which is turning the old rules on their head, and creating a whole new theory of economics which could even be a core subject on the Junior Cert by 2020.

Chapter 10
The Economics of Envy

MIDNIGHT AT THE OLYMPIA THEORY OF ECONOMICS
Sorry son, I don't know you.
Ladies, two at a time each please, girls.
I said, I don't know you.
Alright, but if I see yez messin' yez are ou'.

In the drab pre go-go days of the early 1990s, Dublin punters who wanted an after-hours drink had to make do with a limited number of late-night establishments, one of which was the immortal 'Midnight at the Olympia'.

At midnight, a queue formed half way down Dame Street with punters prepared to pay £12 to see brutal outfits — the likes of Smokey on their fifth 'reunion' — as a pretext to getting a few extra gargles. If you could slip past the monkey suits, you were in. (Remember, this was the era of 17% interest rates, emigration and double-digit unemployment and we were still prepared to part with good cash for the seductive attractions of warm beer in a plastic cup!)

You arrive at the gig, get your watery lager and sit down with your mate to have a chat. When the band comes on you roll your eyes up to heaven but, as the grog kicks in, you find yourself singing along to 'Who the fuck is Alice'. You are, rather pathetically, in the zone. But this is what you paid for. You are happy. You have your pint, your mate is chatting, you can see the stage and the night is moving nicely to a close.

Then, without warning, the big bloke in front of you stands up. Initially, you crane your neck to try to see past him but he's a big, wide, GAA type so eventually you have to stand up to see the stage. You paid to sit down with your mate and have a few scoops but now you are standing awkwardly. You get used to it and ultimately begin to sway. Then the bloke in front of you puts his girlfriend on his shoulders. Blocked now by a fifteen-foot waving triffid with an arse the size of a small housing estate, you are stumped.

Someone taps you on the shoulder. It's getting out of control now. With some effort you focus. 'Never seen this wan in my life.' In a squeaky Malahidealect accent she gesticulates, smiles (well grins really) and points to your shoulders. You leer back and before you know it, you have some young wan on your shoulders, your pint is spilt, your mate is nowhere to be seen and you begin to have dirty thoughts (would you?) — all quite difficult under the circumstances. The whole of the Olympia is suffering the same plight. The place looks like a ghoulish greenhouse — an entire theatre, forty rows deep, of flailing, sweating, hormonal triffids and not a pint in sight.

Remember that you came for a swift sharpener with an old mate. Finally, the bloke in front of you stands on the rickety flap-up theatre seat. Up on the seat with you and tipsy Marie from Malahide and all you wanted was an after-hours pint. If only everyone had remained sitting we could have all saved ourselves the dreaded morning-after 'walk of shame', and saved the Olympia its huge personal insurance bill. But no, the opposite happened. In order to see the stage, I had to react to the bloke who originally stood up. Every time he stood up, put his girlfriend on his shoulders or balanced on the back of the chair, he unwittingly threw the gauntlet down to me and I had to react.

This is precisely how the Irish economy works. To rate in the New Irish Dream, to achieve parity of esteem, you have to have it all and have it now. No-one can overshadow you and if they do, it can't be permanent. If it is permanent, you are a loser and therefore not worthy in the Expectocracy. So the collective psychology of the nation is one of anxiety: everything one person does, buys, wears, learns or accomplishes sparks a reaction in others, not only because these things look, feel and smell nice, but because they confer status.

This psychology impacts on the economy in a simple way. The economy — of which consuming accounts for 68%[1] of the total — operates like a large consumerist version of Midnight at the Olympia.

Every purchasing decision you make affects the buying behaviour of your neighbour, in the same way as every time the bloke in front of you stood up, you had to as well. This Pavlovian response might be prompted by a fleeting glance at a designer bag, a lip-gloss, a suggestion in a magazine or a yearning to be somewhere else, but the process of wanting to acquire things is both definite and real.

Increasingly, Irish people are beginning to move into small tribes defined by the type of people they believe they are and the type of products they believe represent that tribe. So the simple urge to spend which used to be defined by the instant shopping moment of, 'Oh, I like that' has been replaced by the more complex, 'Oh I am like that'. This process, half-psychological, half old-fashioned snobbery, is contagious. Hierarchical shopping is like a chicken-pox virus in a crèche: when one kid gets spots, they all do.[2]

MUTUALLY ASSURED CONSUMPTION

Recently, my father was in a state of shock after a visit to the local garden centre. Our faithful Qualcast had broken and he needed, after twenty-five years, to price a new lawnmower. He was quoted above €2,300 each for a Honda lawnmower![3] Now I was of the view that Honda made motorbikes but no, lawnmowers are a great seller. So remember the Dad was trying to buy a simple mower and this is what he was offered: a garden beast of a Honda with a 17-horse power, Kohler OHV engine with electric start, a 48-inch, 10-gauge powder-coated cutting deck, Hydro-gear IZT wheel motor/pumps, 6.5 mph forward, 3.5 mph reverse speeds, 125-lb. electric PTO clutch, 1.5–4.5 in. cutting heights, 5.4-gallon petrol tank, 18 x 9.5 in. rear tyres; 11 x 4 in. front tyres, includes hour meter and cup holder and a two-year limited warranty.

According to the salesman, this hydrostatic-drive engine is the cream-of-the-crop, with more convenience features than other mowers. It bags, mulches and has side-discharge capability. There is also a blade-brake clutch which lets you stop the blade without cutting the motor so you can empty the bag without having to restart the engine. The young man went on to tell my mesmerised father that you can cut the grass in the Sierra Nevada mountains with such a machine which has fifteen different heights, an indestructible rotary blade and a swivelling back axle.

You might find this stuff hard to believe until you realise that purchasing such a monster also gives you such delights as free membership to the Irish Chapter of the British Lawnmower Racing Association whose motto is, 'Turn a weekend chore into a competitive sport'. The British Lawnmower Racing Association, or BLRA to the *cognoscenti*, organises three specific championships each year: the Great Maze, the World Championship (open to Irish entrants) and the Grand Prix. You might snort at lawnmower racing but here's a little known fact — in 1975, Stirling Moss made his first return to motor racing since his near fatal crash at Goodwood in 1962 at the British Lawnmower Racing Grand Prix. According to Irish enthusiasts, Moss, driving with all of his old skill and with great enthusiasm for this new sport, won the British Grand Prix for lawnmowers in 1975 and again in 1976.

So not only can a suburban Dubliner follow in the footsteps of a Formula One giant but he can engage in a bit of lawnmower snobbery on a Saturday afternoon. The last time I checked, the front and back gardens in Dún Laoghaire were pretty flat, straight things; not a drumlin, let alone mountain in sight, so the only reason Irish men are buying a type of mega-lawnmower is for fear of lawnmower envy. In the past, men were envious of only one attribute that another man might possess. Not any more. Lawnmower envy is alive and kicking in the suburbs. Someone is looking out of the window in their 'exclusive development of distinction' and jealously eyeing the neighbour's lawnmower and going one better. Every time you buy a swanky lawnmower, you throw down the gauntlet to me to go one better. In the past, a Mercedes in the suburban drive conferred status. Not any more. Any old knacker can have a Kompressor with ice-blue feature headlights. Forget Mercs — their status has fallen. In 1994 there were fewer than 500 Mercedes sold, today there are over ten times that so they are common as muck. For real status one-upmanship, posh lawnmowers are obviously where it is at.

Similarly, every time you buy a swanky mobile phone, the next guy does too. When you buy Jigsaw, the girl next door buys Joseph; you buy DKNY so she goes for Dolce & Gabbana; you counter with Gucci and she slaps back with Prada and so on.

This behaviour is classically evident in the car market. A mate of mine has a 4x4 and he justifies this not just because he obviously needs it to negotiate the treacherous, off-road terrain of Donnybrook (it's a jungle out there you know), but also because to him it's a matter of life and death. Maybe he derives a certain 'know-all' pleasure being seated at the right-hand of a seven-speed gearbox, 9 ft up, towering over the minnows below and being able to see the 3-mile tailback into town. Who knows?

His own logic for such an off-piste, out-sized tank is simple. He claims if he's involved in a crash, he will be safe. Ok, in so far as it goes, but what happens when the possible victim, who might value his own life like the rest of us, borrows cash to buy an even bigger 4x4 for protection?

Within ten years, the Naas Road will look like downtown Baghdad, as if the entire 102nd Airborne has descended with convoys of Humvees bumper to bumper backed up to the Red Cow roundabout. (Rumour has it that one of our most successful property developers has one such machine. It will be interesting to see what he graduates to, particularly as one of our best-known criminals has just imported the mother of all Humvees.)

The traditional laws of economics are based on the almost extinct idea of rationality. Thus when a society is faced with a problem like congested roads, the rational response should be to buy smaller cars and mopeds to get around more efficiently. No way, José! In Ireland we respond by buying huge 4x4s that take up more space!

Traditional economics is also based on the fundamental value-for-money premise. The basic rule is that when the price of something goes up, the demand goes down. But in consumer-driven Ireland, when the price goes up, the demand goes up!

This can also be regarded as the consumer version of the old arms race. When the Soviets put a man into space, the Americans had to do likewise simply to be seen to be in the same race. Then the Americans put a man on the moon and the Russians responded by putting two. The Americans send a probe to Mars, arm themselves with thousands of warheads and explode a bomb in the Nevada desert. The Russians respond. Finally, Ronald Reagan adopts the Star-wars programme and the Russians run out of money. So the American willie was bigger after all.

Before the New Irish Dream dominated, this type of competitive consumption was limited to 'the moneyed classes' as evidenced by Georgian follies around the country. However, today we are all members of the 'moneyed class' or at least the credit class. Relatively easy access to credit allows everyone to shop to impress. In the extreme, this means that people will work harder with the express sole intention of consuming more.

THE AUTOFASHIONISTAS

Although we are seeing similar patterns all over the Western world, the Pope's Children have made conspicuous consumption and keeping up with the Smurfits something of a national obsession. In this atmosphere, probably the cruellest thing a government can do to a nation that is caught in the brace of status anxiety is to change the way we number car licence plates, to allow us to signal automatically to everyone, 'Look, I've got a new car.' But this is what we did when we introduced 1987 with the initial 87 D plate. It is a cruel, heartless and mean thing to do to us. Many's the relationship has gone by the wayside as a direct consequence of the 05 plate. Doubtless, there are children going without shoes this very day as a result. Yet the frenzy continues unabated.

Every year, grown men and women swoop down upon car dealerships in a lunatic state, demanding to have the first reg of the next year. To be out of the blocks and on the road in January is the Autofashionista's equivalent of a synchronised orgasm. You can spot an Autofashionista a mile off. They are the ones that, in the first few weeks of January, look intently into their huge mirrors to see whether you are checking out their rear-end licence plate. I suppose it is a car buyer's version of, 'Does my ass look good in this?'

Since 1987 an extraordinary plate-rush has ensued. Over half the new cars bought in any year are bought in the first three months of the year. This puts huge pressure on salesmen, dealers and makers to have everything ready for the January rush. Conrad Schmidt, BMW's man here, is characteristically German when he suggests that this January frenzy 'is more marked here than anywhere else in Europe'. It's a lot more marked, Herr Schmidt. In fact Germany, Europe's largest car market, hardly displays any seasonal buying variations at all.

However, we should be thankful for small mercies because what would our plates be like if we had personalised plates as they have in the UK?

Recently, a small bought man who works for a fat rich man asked to meet me for what could have been a difficult encounter. This was to be our parting meeting. He came armed with his SUV. It is rather comical to see a small man try to get into a huge SUV. I suggested stirrups. It reminded me of a child taking her first pony lesson. I felt like giving him a hard hat just in case he fell backwards. But he made it into the cabin. His little legs dangled over the clutch and brake like a child on a high-chair, but thankfully for both of us (because it was excruciating), the flick of a switch lowered his auto-throne, allowing him to reach the pedals. When we eventually pulled into the hotel car park, I felt like giving him a ramp to allow him slide down from where he could, like a choreographed 1950s swimmer, hand the Lithuanian valet the pointedly branded keys in one flawless move.

Would Napoleon have driven a SUV? Hard to know, and obviously not all SUV drivers are short, but you do get the impression that anyone driving around in such a contraption is possessed of some sort of size complex. My main worry is for the thousands of children who suffer needless vertigo each morning as a result of being suspended at Ferris-wheel height, trussed up in their padded car seats, looking down over the suburbs. It will be hard for them not to have an inferiority complex in later life once they realise they are normal sized. I doubt very much if any will be able to drive an ordinary car when they are eventually thrown the keys on their seventeenth birthday.

In 2004, SUV sales rose by 37.8%, in a premium car market that grew by 22.5%. The BMW X5, a sports utility vehicle, ironically driven by people who do not do a lot of sport, judging from those who waddle out of them regularly, has a price tag of over €121,000. It has an eight-month waiting list. This is a familiar story. The price is not important as demand far exceeds supply. The SUV is now the car of choice for the Autofashionistas and in another great perversion of the laws of economics, as the price of petrol rises so too does the demand for these 17-mile-per-gallon[4] fuel-guzzling panzers. In this regard, we are even more *flathúil* than the Americans. Over the first six months of 2005, American demand for SUVs collapsed in response to the increased price of petrol, causing the bonds of both Ford and GM — the main makers of giant SUVs — to be downgraded to junk status.

Not here, in the world of the Pope's Children. We can't get enough of them. Tom O'Conner of VW explains that he has waiting lists for the €103,000, 5-litre V10 Touareg (which sounds disturbingly like Toe-rag). The Volvo XC 90 is not far behind, with airbags that remain inflated during roll-over accidents for those rich, wannabe stuntmen out there on the Raheen Road.

Have you ever seen a 4x4 in a ditch or off-piste as they like to say in Ranelagh? No, me neither. But it's worrying to know that the latest generation BMW X5, called the X Drive, has everything you would need for the dangerous, unpredictable Howth Road terrain. The basic premise of the four-wheel drive is to enhance traction, so you don't go squelching off into the great Andean mudslides on the Merrion Road. Thankfully, the new BMW X Drive proactively searches out the best traction before it is lost — invaluable in the rush hour grind, don't you think? If you are not tempted, what about the other top seller, the Lexus RX300? This offers as an added safety feature new knee airbags as well as torso, abdomen and pelvis protecting extra-large side airbags so you can host your four-year-old's birthday party, complete with wall-to-wall bouncy castle, on impact. But, this year, for fashion conscious yummymummies and Coolock hip-hop rappers, the real value is in the badge — and the model is the BMW.

NESTING IN THE BABYBELT

Autofashionistas may be in your face, but a more subtle example of the Expectocracy at full consumer tilt can be seen in the wedding frenzy which afflicts the BabyBelt each summer. The Pope's Children are nesting. Marriage rates are up by 25% since 1995.[5] There will be over 20,000 weddings in 2005 — more than any other year since 1974. This is big business — the Irish wedding industry is worth €400 million per year and this figure is rising rapidly. The nation is in the grip of Marriage Fever. And every wedding ups the ante for the next one.

In *Bobos in Paradise* David Brooks details how the *New York Times* wedding announcements are a great place to observe the changes in up-scale American society. Similarly in Ireland, a good place to begin to study the wedding mania and its social connotations is the upmarket mergers and acquisitions column, otherwise known as *The Irish Times* engagement column in the 'Social and Personal' pages.[6] Here we can see who is merging with whom and who is acquiring what at the top of the pile. Every Saturday the good burghers of the BabyBelt open their lives to us on the editorial page of *The Irish Times*. People who announce their unions in *The Irish Times* are different. They are sending out signals, indicating who they are, where they are from and where they are going. You can hear the admittance ledgers of the big private schools for 2018 filling up as you glance through the names and addresses.

Thus, less-than-exclusive *arrivistes* become genteel. First-generation money can feel comfortable, educated and secure, sitting snugly beside august letters to the editor, penned by Horse Protestants with cardinal letters after their names.

More than any other vignette, the *Irish Times* wedding column is a deep and subtle gauge of the next privileged class. It is not bohemian, cool or street. It indicates submission, resignation and narrow ambition. You will find the next senior partners of law firms there. It is the insiders' club and the ultimate stamp of respectability any couple can bestow on their fornication. It is a siren call for a successful, fertile, solid future. So Trinity marries UCD, lawyer beds down with doctor, AIB marries Anglo-Irish, Beauchamps marries Arthur Cox, Southside marries country, Blackrock marries Mount Anville.

Faltering old money marries rampant new money and both parties are delighted with the deal. The mergers and acquisition page is genetic self-selection of the most perfect form. Good schools, unimpeachable genes, strong bones, thick hair, white teeth, vitality and solidity get thrown together in a flawless system of social fingerprinting. Educational achievement is matched with breeding, rugby meets hockey, Shanahans cops off with Thorntons and gap-year fuses with trainee. Wesley marries High School, Monkstown marries Clontarf, Templeogue marries Bray, Sandymount marries Booterstown — just think of the property portfolio alone.

Take a random announcement. Dr Emma O'Brien and Dr Adam Byrne are to tie the knot. 'John and Therese O'Brien (Dillon), Whitehorse House, Skerries are delighted to announce the engagement of their daughter Emma to Adam, son of Michael and Annette Keeney, Birdswell Manor, Montenotte, Cork.' Two doctors — perfection! What addresses — a House beds a Manor. These people have never seen their neighbour's washing, thrown a neighbour's football back over the garden wall or had rough kids from the local estate trick or treat at their door on Hallowe'en. No rough edges there.

This is a merger made in Volvo heaven. John and Therese are obviously people of some significance as their house suggests. Only the accomplished live in houses so vast that no address is needed — nothing vulgar, no numbers, not even a common street. Whitehorse House intimates solid, old, Georgian, certainly harking back to a time before Bovale and Park developments suburbanised the city. Whitehorse House conjures up a long, winding gravel drive with beech trees, a couple of golden pointers asleep on the lawn under the magnificent willow, a tradesman's entrance and possibly a brace of fowl hung over the green wellies outside the scullery with its double Belfast sink. Whitehorse House is all damp Burberry jackets and tweed. Whitehorse House's kitchen is underground where the cracked flagstones echo. The thick kitchen walls are off-white and the suitably tatty tea-towels are hanging over the Aga.

John and Therese are people of substance, not only wealth but brains as well. Their daughter Emma, the doctor, was top of the class, 500 points in her Leaving Cert, fluent in French as well as mathematically minded — pretty perfect material. She is now mating with another doctor. Their kids will be bright, healthy and rich. They will breed with similar kids and off the cycle goes again into the next generation.

Degree holders marry degree holders, Sutton marries Terenure, Milltown marries Rathgar, Greystones marries Malahide, Sandycove marries Ranelagh. Neilstown does not exist in the 'Social and Personals'. Ballyfermot never hitches Dalkey, and in the past five years not one person from Tallaght — Ireland's most populous suburb — announced her wedding in *The Irish Times*!

Just below the gushing announcement, discreetly positioned every week in the bottom left-hand corner of the page, we hear the opening salvos of the wedding war. Directly below the news of Lorna Dunne and Conor Fitzpatrick is an ad for jewellery valuation by a man called C. Clarke whose credentials are the following very impressive sounding B.J.I.G., R.J Dip. and G.I.A. Obviously Mr C. Clarke exists to rank brides according to the value of their ring. The more handed down, the better. Inherited always beats bought.

Underneath the valuer lies the ad for *www.RugArt.ie* of Sandycove for handmade designer rugs. These are perfect as a wedding present for the new house — as they signal taste rather than mere wealth. Rugart's slogan is ludicrously inappropriate — 'I have spread my dreams under your feet. Tread carefully because you tread on my dreams.' This of course is from W.B. Yeats when the bard was referring to his love; the good people at Rugart have managed to mutate this into a description of a carpet.

But this selection reflects the discerning, literary education of those who shop at Rugart and by extension those who announce their marriages in *The Irish Times*. According to their website they can 'provide that dream rug' — which is what exactly?

Rugart also appeals to your creative side by suggesting that you create your own rug. Here they are tapping into the 'I can do anything' mentality of the 'You're a Star' mind. Not satisfied with being the youngest surgeon in Skerries, our bride-to-be can out-rug the Iranian tribesmen who have being doing this for millennia. What versatility! Underneath is another ad. This time it reads: 'Exclusively yours for weddings, Marlfield House, Gorey'. Marlfield is an up-market place and doubtless you wouldn't be getting out of there for less than €20,000.

From the minute the announcement goes into *The Irish Times* the Weddingometer starts to tick. The Weddingometer is a large internal clock in the head of the bride. It gauges, measures, benchmarks, compares, assesses, ranks, rates and analyses every minute detail of the wedding's progress, its organisation and crucially its execution on the day. The Weddingometer is both qualitative and quantitative. Taste and style are just as, or even more important than, scale and reach. The Weddingometer has the precision of a clock, yet the ambiguity of a social climbing judge. One false move can be fatal. One inappropriate flower, one unimaginative hymn can tip you into negative status territory. For a young couple in the great Expectocracy, nothing should upstage your big day. It is a unique opportunity to showcase your strong breeding, your straight teeth and your ascending status. Wedding *faux pas* are not easily forgotten.

The Weddingometer has started to tick: by the time the bride is up the aisle, thousands of euros will have been spent on everything from flowers to placemats, dresses, cards, drink, food, bridesmaids, photos, cars — all designed to make this day the best wedding in Ireland, the wedding of your dreams, the wedding that will out-wedding all your mates, the wedding that will push the Weddingometer into a state of mechanised nuptial delirium.

The Point Depot in lilac

Enter any moderately proportioned hotel on a dark, dreary Sunday towards the end of winter and early spring and you will be ambushed by the smell of Mac foundation, hairspray and baby pinks, soft whites, ribbons and general schmaltzy glitz. This is the nirvana where 'dreams come true'. Welcome to the Wedding Show — Ireland's great nuptial road show. Today we are in the Point Depot — Dublin's largest indoor venue. It is thronged with the Pope's Children, mostly 20- and 30-something women, from Juicy-Couture track-suited blondes to highlighted brunettes in suits. Some have forlorn looking fiancés in tow, others are marshalled by gushing bridesmaids and many have their mothers with them. Row after row of lilac and pink stands are crowded with girls loudly discussing the merits of various products.

The sound system blares out a looped 'My Girl' by the Temptations and leaflets are thrust by the type of women whose faces crack when they force a smile. The focus is almost exclusively on the dream. Live your dream, your dream day and so on. Running a close second is the 'be different!' mantra. Personalise this and individualise that — from wine labels to match boxes.

The Expectocracy's equivalent of the fairy godmother is the Wedding Planner who can wave her wand here and a tacky carriage with be-feathered nags will emerge, a sprinkle of fairy dust there and the bride's teeth will change from Marlboro Light yellow to J-Lo white enamel. The wedding planner is the queen of dreams and overdrafts. For a fee, she can create the perfect VIP day.

With such pressure it is not surprising that half of Ireland's weddings end with a bawling bride in the jacks and a drunken groom at the bar ordering double vodkas and Red Bull.

One wedding planner has a suitably Gothic ad. (There is a big Gothic thing going on with wedding planners. Helpless maidens and dashing princes that keep recurring in a cross between Shrek and Saddam Hussein's boudoir.) This agency sets the scene with a blatant white lie, claiming that 'no two couples are alike'. They offer the Full Service Package. It promises the following: 'A most comprehensive package. It is inclusive of all of your planning needs from budget development, creative event design, site and vendor selection, meticulous planning, etiquette advice, development of event schedules and timelines, and on-site event management.' It sounds more like Microsoft's AGM than an Irish Big Day Out.

I was intrigued as to what exactly etiquette advice is and who might admit to needing it. As for the Enchanted Occasions website, it is full of Arthurian imagery of Gothic virgins with long flowing locks being carried away on horseback by dashing vaguely camp princes in tights. However unbelievable the queenish princes are, the idea of an Irish virgin on her wedding day is even more bonkers. Given that the average girl loses her virginity in her late teens and doesn't get married now until she's thirty, it's a hard circle to square.

'If another person asks me for doves, I'll bloody kill them!' So says one of Ireland's top fairy godmothers who has seen a huge increase in demand over the past three years. When she meets the spellbound ones, they discuss weddings they have been to, what worked and what didn't. In the benchmark file somewhere deep inside the Weddingometer, every prospective bride is gauging, dissing and sniggering at a friend's best efforts. In no time at all the 'to-be-avoided-like-the-plague' errors are listed. This particular fairy godmother only deals with wedding budgets above €30,000 and the most juicy commission was the big €1,000,000. Lots of doves there, one imagines. What exactly does a wedding that costs one million euro feel like?

The average Irish wedding costs €20,000 and, as the Pope's Children are getting married in great numbers, typically parental cash is brought in to finance the impact of celebrity weddings on mere mortals' expectations. *Hello!* weddings set the tone — from J-Lo's pink diamond ring and Brad Pitt's self-designed (but obviously not very effective) ring to Vera Wang's celebrity frocks and Britney Spears' gift of tracksuits to all her guests.

Photographers make out like bandits at weddings, plus they get fed and watered as well and usually end up scoring some drunk girl who has peeled off from the main group. One celebrity photographer describes himself as 'relaxed and unobtrusive'. I would have thought that this would be a basic requirement rather than an advertised extra. Why not go for the 'fidgety and interfering' photographer next time, just to calm the nerves?

Bridezilla gets touched up

As a girl has to look her best all over for the big day and the honeymoon in the Maldives, lots of maintenance is required in the run-up to the wedding. Wendy has a reputation for being the gentlest waxer in town and she is inundated. She never advertises but waxing is the ultimate word-of-mouth business and her currency, like her wax, is hot. It's mid-May and Irish girls are getting ready to bare all on hols, weddings, parties or just getting themselves ready for the summer. Everyone wants to be seen and made feel lighter, cleaner, sexier. Wendy's waxing business is up 65% this year. The bulk of her clients are women between twenty-five and thirty-five but this figure goes right up to fifty-five. She reckons it is only in the past five years that the business has really taken off, largely as a result of 'Sex and the City'. (Come to think of it, before 'Sex and the City' I thought a Brazilian was a footballer.) This year, the Brazilian or Landing Strip is still very popular, although Wendy Wax has seen a significant rise in the Playboy or Hollywood. Most girls claim it heightens sensitivity, some are doing it for their men, but most are doing it because of the same peer pressure that forces them to buy bigger cars, hire larger marquees and caused them to turn into Bridezilla in the first place. When Bridezilla comes in, Wendy Wax is sitting down; she jumps up, bright smile, and pulls her Juicy-Couture tracksuit bottoms *down*, not up.

This is Midnight at the Olympia below the navel. Most of the girls are still fairly self-conscious and Wendy chats away to them about all the usual stuff, holidays, TV and fashion. That is her gift. She makes everyone feel at ease which, when Bridezilla has her legs wide apart, is quite an achievement. Wendy doesn't usually dye, but Urban Wax in town does and it comes recommended by many of her friends. Bridezilla even went on to rollercoaster, i.e. to get advice from other girls. She'd quite like a Tiffany Box this time. Wendy will do it — just for the special occasion. The hot wax is much less painful. She gets up on the table, in position. The wax is bubbling away like a fondue beside her at 60 degrees. Wendy stirs away gently, talking about the latest Jimmy Choos; Bridezilla rhapsodises deliriously about the Manolos she'll have for the wedding. She barely feels a thing. Wendy smiles down at her, maternally.

Her smile is wide, teeth straight and bleached, lips bud-like. She's had work done, thinks Bridezilla. Wendy Wax looks younger than her thirty-six. Bridezilla asks her straight out.

– *Yes, just a bit of collagen. Looks great, doesn't it?*
– *How much?*
– *€500.*

Within two days, six days from D-Day, Bridezilla has her new lips and she looks great. Surgery is all the rage now, particularly Botox. How many permanently surprised looking women do you see around?

And it is not just limited to Dublin. Did you know that Kerry is the boob-job centre of Ireland? I thought their Kerrygold jerseys looked particularly well filled this year at Croker. Well now, at an average cost of €5,850, I know why. The originally well-endowed chests in Sligo are going the other way: it is the boob reduction capital of Ireland. Mullingar is the colonic irrigation centre of the country, with more hosing out in the Midlands than anywhere else, at €120 per session. Meanwhile, the sun in the sunny south-east is obviously having an impact on the skin of the locals, because Wexford is where we are seeing the most facelifts in the country, setting the punters back €6,000. For my money the best is yet to come. Have you noticed how Wicklow men tend to be more aggressive than most? After all, are they not the lads who kidnapped the Gaelic football ref and trussed him up in the boot of a car? Well, now I offer you the answer. Penis envy, plain and simple. Wicklow registers the highest number of penile enhancement operations in the country. There you have it. In the Expectocracy, size matters.

Part II

Two Tribes: The Decklanders and the HiCos

Chapter 11

Intermezzo

Up to now we have been discussing what could be termed the catalyst and the revolution. The changes sparked by the economic turnabout have indeed been revolutionary in their scope. The Wonderbra effect has pushed us all together, lifted us up, enhancing us all. The resulting emergence of the Expectocracy is one of the most profound developments since Independence and indeed, for the man on the street, may be of much greater significance. In addition, the primacy of economics as the dominant philosophy in our culture is probably now exceptional for a small European country. These events have changed the way we look at ourselves and the way others view us. The Pope's Children are the pivotal generation in this transformation. Everything has blurred.

The next part of this book contends that there are two broad tribes emerging. The first tribe, the Decklanders, has benefited materially, emotionally and psychologically. They have flourished under the Expectocracy. They live in a consumer paradise called Deckland. Deckland is more of a state of mind than a place and it is defined by many qualities, not just income. So, for example, an exemplar of Deckland in Dublin is Foxrock, which shares more psychologically with towns like Mullingar and the new estates around Celbridge than it does with Ranelagh, Kenmare or Westport. Deckland has embraced the American way. It wears a new, shiny, laminated exterior. It is full of new things and the newer the better. The Midnight at the Olympia approach to economics reigns here. It is crammed with new cars, new houses, new hair, new nails and new aspirations. It is the home of the Expectocracy, fuelled by cash and an optimism which resembles America more than Europe. Its story is one of opportunity, economic uplift and the Wonderbra effect. Given our Irish weakness for a narrative of economic under-achievement, financial failure and commercial pessimism, the upbeat clarity of Deckland is novel. Financial liberation has come and the Decklanders feel most liberated.

On the other hand, there are many who regard Deckland and its American material obsessions with suspicion. There are plenty of Irish people who feel that there is more to us than *Heat* magazine, Brown Thomas charge cards, property prices, o6 registrations, Man United away strips and Puerto Banus.

These types feel that there must be more to Ireland than a vast ATM churning out crisp fifties. They are looking for something else, something deeper, something authentic that can't be just bought. They are searching for the distinctive in all this blandness. They are looking for the something that makes us special. They are searching for community in all this individualism. There must be more to the Irish than SUVs. Otherwise, we are just suburban America with shitty weather.

They are asking what it means to be Irish. What makes us different? In this search for the authentic, they have delved deep into our Hibernian past to find that which makes us unique. They are looking for a distinctly Irish way of life rather than just an American standard of living. But when they examine themselves a bit further they realise that they actually want both. And why not? The positive energy of the Expectocracy has infected them like everyone else. Unlike previous generations of Irish Hibernophiles who, after our colonial history, found that to elevate their Irishness they had to reject other influences, this new tribe wants to combine the best of both.

They want to be both special and rich, they want the Gaelscoil and the fancy double-doored fridge, they want Kila and the Killers, they want the connectedness of spirituality and the freedom of liberty, they want to belong and yet lose themselves. They are Hibernians but they want cosmopolitan goodies. They realise that globalisation and the cosmopolitan world provides us with our material wealth, but unlike the Decklanders they don't believe that this is sufficient. They are the fusion of the best of our Hibernian culture that makes us special and the best of the cosmopolitan culture that has created the Expectocracy. They are the counter-revolutionaries to the Expectocrat revolution. They are the HiCos — the Hibernian Cosmopolitans.

Before we check out the HiCo tribe, let's have a look at the Deckland tribe in all its plumes.

Chapter 12

Deckland — A State of Mind

THE KELLS ANGELS, 'ONLY AN HOUR FROM DUBLIN'
The original 'only an hour from Dublin' was immortalised in the broadest Navan accent — not an 'r' to be heard — in a radio ad by Crannac furniture co-op in Navan. The year it was first broadcast was 1979 — the year of the Pope's Children. The Crannac factory, as befits the kosher economics doctrine of the time, was a workers' co-op which had traded behind the barriers of protectionism. It was run by Gael Linn who also established a special marketing company, Irlandia, to market Crannac furniture and other Irish manufactured products in the UK.

The Crannac factory finally closed down in 2003 and next year the site will be home to 150 apartments and 36 houses in an 'exclusive' development overlooking the Blackwater. Up the road, on the old site of Navan carpets, will be Blackwater Retail Park, home to Woodies DIY — the portcullis of the BabyBelt: 800,000 sq. ft of retail heaven. At the other side of town, on the old site of Navan Steel, 40-odd acres are being developed for another massive shopping centre, as is the old Navan dog track across the road. Just up from the dog track, where there used to be old traditional furniture makers, there is a furniture retail park, with shops such as Home Zone and Versatile. Versatile won the Bathroom Industry Award last year — the Champions League of the bathroom industry. Versatile offers specialist bathroom designer services using the finest Italian and German models. A little further into the town on Fenian Terrace, Pierce Brosnan's old two-up, two-down house is for sale. Rumour has it that it will be the first Irish house ever auctioned on e-Bay.

Navan is blurring. Apartments are replacing businesses, homes replacing workplaces; nothing is made here any more. Navan is a quintessential 21st-century mini-economy existing on services, credit and property mania. The property boom has also ensured that the DIY and self-improvement disease has reached Navan, so furniture makers are replaced by bathroom designers, local products replaced by hi-spec Italian versions and Navan Carpets replaced by Woodies DIY — from which you can create your own dream decks.

Just outside the town is little Dublin. In 'Little Dublin', as Johnstown is known locally, there are two bars, O'Dwyer's for the Dubs and O'Brien's for the locals. Little Dublin has over 2,000 houses in it and a Jackie Skelly fitness centre where overweight commuters can burn off the flab. But €280,000 buys you a three-bed, timber-framed semi and you wouldn't get that anywhere in Dublin.

Further out, past one of the busiest Mercedes garages in the county — Newgate Motors — we move out to the home of the Kells Angels. As well as the Book of Kells and Colmcille's 9th-century house, Kells is home to Jack Fitzsimons whose famous book, *Bungalow Bliss* — the manual of architectural plans and contracts for affordable bungalows — was hugely popular here in Ireland since its first printing in 1971. It was the subject of virulent debate about the building of new homes in the Irish countryside. Fitzsimons' book is a fascinating social document; like any planning document it is full of fantasy and aspiration. The figures sketched in its architectural plans are perfectly formed and poised contemporary beings, and the hills sketched in some of its plans are perfectly curved Arcadian idylls. When compared to the panglossian images sold in the polished brochures for such estates like the Glebe in Archdeaconry just outside Kells, Fitzsimons' bungalows may indeed have been blissful. Incidentally, Fitzsimons lives in a beautiful 17th-century lodge beside the heritage centre.

The population of the town has doubled in eight years and villages around Kells have also seen their populations swell. On sports day at the local national school, Carlonstown, there are more Dublin accents and registrations than local ones. This is home to the Kells Angels, the commuters who are on the road by six every morning. In the villages around, such as Mullagh — which has seen more houses built in the last two years than in the previous two millennia — the minority are original natives (let's call them the Mullahadjeen) who regard the Kells Angels with a certain amount of both bewilderment and suspicion.

You have now entered Deckland. Deckland is more of a state of mind than a place. It is home to Dulchies, commuters, wooden decks in back gardens replete with patio heaters and barbeques. It is the epicentre of the Expectocracy, jammed with the aspirant 'You're a Star' generation. In every provincial town and village around all our major cities there are local versions of the Kells Angels and the Mullahadjeen, living cheek by jowl, their identities blurred, all striving to make it in the Great Expectocracy.

DIY DECLAN[1]

In Ridley Scott's sci-fi classic *Blade Runner*, the future is a drab town full of video arcades, fast-food joints and populated by oriental types. The sun never shines, the clouds are just above your head and it never stops raining. Scott clearly had Bray in mind. Brayjing — as it is known by the locals — is Chinatown-Sur-Mer and offers a perfect slice of modern Irish life. It is one of the fastest growing towns in the country. It is another example of how a provincial town, in this case the former, stand-alone, capital of North Wicklow, has become a commuter dorm, firmly in the BabyBelt. Its immigrant population is vibrant and fake tan parlours and gyms are making fortunes. However, Bray's position as suburban centre supreme was solidified, not just by the opening of the country's first swingers' nightclub outside Dublin a few years back, but by its monumental Woodies.

Little sheds more light on the Expectocracy than our DIY stores, and Woodies is the home-grown exemplar. Around the country, Woodies stores are positioned perfectly at all the key access routes to the BabyBelt. With military precision, Woodies have placed themselves strategically at every clogged bottleneck around the city, in Tallaght, Lucan, Swords and the Naas Road. One hundred years ago you would have had a British garrison on such strategic sites — today you have a DIY superstore. Woodies is the Serengeti of the suburbs. Wherever there are Kells Angels there are Woodies. Woodies is on the Headford Road in Galway, on the way out to the commuter towns of Tuam and Headford. In Cork it's on the Kinsale Road. There are huge

DIY shops in Athlone, Kilkenny, Carlow, Cavan, Clonmel, Newbridge, Tralee and Waterford, as well as in Glasnevin, Sallynoggin, Coolock and Sandyford.

It is a rich savannah where the Pope's Children roam wild on their day off from the office. It is a perfect observational starting point for watching their rituals, foibles, mating habits, hopes and dreams. Settle into the large cavernous aisles of Woodies, the nooks and crannies of the patio heating department, and note the precise etiquette governing the Pope's Children at play.

In *On Paradise Drive* David Brooks notes that one of the best places to find the new face of the suburbs is in Homebase, where a character called Patio Man can be seen. In Ireland, patios are not in vogue, but decks are and there is no better place to see the Irish equivalent of Patio Man than in a DIY superstore. There was a time that you could gauge the social hierarchy of Ireland by who was sitting where at Mass on a Sunday morning. Not any longer; as religious observance has fallen away, home improvement has become the national obsession and Woodies is the place of worship for DIY Declan — the main man of Deckland — who moves around assured, confident and self-controlled. He knows the creed, the ceremonies and ritual of his tribe, the Decklanders. You have seen this type before: he is the one who tries to read the motor supplements of Sunday newspapers in shops on Sunday mornings without buying the paper. He is in his element in Woodies. Significantly, he is not just a member of the DIY church, he is a practitioner. Not for him simply buying the finished article: he builds, creates and transubstantiates the simple wood into the holy host of the completed deck. DIY Declan is the high priest of Deckland. He is not alone. Like evangelicals in Central America, decking devotees are springing up all over the place. Suburban back gardens, thanks to Diarmuid Gavin, are now altars of lacquered timber, wooden railing, barbeque grills and patio heaters. As the Woodies brochure suggests you can:

Bring your home into your garden, making it even more enjoyable by introducing timber decking. Create your own suntrap, a tranquil corner for a quiet read, or the perfect location for the summer barbeque. Warm and soft to touch, the natural beauty of wood will perfectly complement the peace and changing seasons of your garden.

But wait a second, suntrap, summer barbeques, tranquillity? Are we talking about the same place here? Is this not the country where Noah's Ark still trades 356 days a year? Is this not the island that experiences the most rainfall in Europe? A place which is permanently damp, where a 'scorcher' is the one cloudless day in July? Are we not the race whose collective memories of summer holidays are of hours in the Austin 1100, condensation dripping down the windows while the parents try to find Achill Island in the fog? And yet, despite this, hundreds of thousands of the Pope's Children dream of the Great Outdoors in their small back gardens.

No new estate comes without decking. Garden furniture is a must for the New Irish Dream Lifestyle. In the Expectocracy even the weather can be dreamt away. Maybe it comes from watching 'Neighbours' too much, but in stark contrast to all the meteorological evidence, we are convinced global warming will happen tomorrow, the temperature will rise and Ireland will bake. Why else would a confident Tesco announce 'summer times' outside furniture sales on the last week in May? We seem to believe that, overnight, we will look like second generation Eye-talian chippers in Fairview, dark, sallow and vaguely foreign. By mid-July, a dusty Mistral will blow over Baltinglass, bringing with it choking Saharan sand. The RTÉ weathergirls will be in a state of permanent shock — scorchio. In our dream, semi-detached, pebble-dashed estates will morph into white-washed, Spanish terraces with rolling views down from the Pyrénées to the Mediterranean.

If you can't have the second apartment in Alicante, then at least pretend, by spending vast amounts of money, time and effort kitting out your back garden every May with the accoutrements for summer in Andalusia. Sales of timber decking have quadrupled in the past few years. Likewise, sales of charcoal for outside grills and patio heaters fly out the doors of Woodies, only to end up rusting in the corner of the garden or being used by the children as a monster prop. Ireland shouldn't do barbeques, not just because of the weather but because we can't grill properly. How many times have you risked salmonella on a chilly July evening from undercooked barbequed burgers? But flying in the face of all the evidence, and for some insane reason, the Pope's Children have decided that barbeques are as central to our culture as Braais are to Afrikaners. Irish barbeques are the Wimbledon of suburban entertaining — rain always stops play.

But decks, decking and Deckland are part of the Dream. Deckland: a state of mind. It is an aspiration and what's more (in a country obsessed with property prices), a good deck can add 10% on to the price of a house, which explains why, along with a Sky dish, new semi-Ds in the BabyBelt are never complete without their deck. No matter how small or pathetic, a deck or, as it's called, 'an outside entertaining space', is essential.

In Deckland the Dream takes over. All evenings are balmy, all chicken drumsticks tasty and succulent, all grills are the perfect temperature, all steaks medium rare and all your guests are impressed and, importantly, slightly envious. The deck says something about the type of person you are. It complements your expansive kitchen. You display a similar straight uninterrupted line from your dual refrigeration system in the kitchen, to your Omega Elite gas barbeque grill with its porcelain-coated cast-iron cooking surface. DIY Declan is that type of person: straight, uncomplicated, unassuming — a very safe pair of hands. He has BMW three series written all over him, from his pressed chinos to his no-nonsense ring tone and his little mid-thirties paunch. He is secretary of the work summer soft-ball league at Microsoft.

In Woodies he is at home. He has a mission. The gazebo will be built raised above the existing cedarwood deck. He'll make it in tropical hardwood. The contrasts will show-off his fine workmanship which, like his internal audit at work, is meticulous. Only after he has bought the wood, talked knowledgeably about the designs, the curves and the railing, only after he has mentioned 'fast-setting concrete' at least half a dozen times, establishing his bona fides with the other deckmen who hang out in Woodies on Sundays, will he choose something as frivolous as a grill. The key to a successful and enriching day at Woodies is never to come looking for something assembled. It is also crucial to be seen as a DIY man of substance — you have to be pitching roofs, making furniture, laying blocks or putting down railway sleepers. Merely buying grills, patio heaters or grass-seed doesn't count. Real DIY men are confident and always call the sales assistants loudly by their name-tags in that overtly chummy DIY way.

DIY Declan surveys the wood. This is the part he loves. This ritual separates the wheat from the chaff, the men from the boys. Only Woodies aficionados here. You are now in a zone which is for men only; men who work with their hands and subscribe to *Powertools*

Monthly. These are the sort of blokes who know their clear yellow cedar from their knotty yellow cedar, who can tell clear grain at fifty paces; they know the meaning of T-straps and post-cap connections. These lads are comfortable in Dublin GAA jerseys, drink in places like the Cat and Cage in Drumcondra after a match, and trade up to Malahide or Greystones. These places have big, open spaces with the promise of large gardens which are perfect for expansive decks and snooker table lawns. Declan expertly feels the tropical hardwoods. He rubs them down again, knowingly rubbing against the grain. He stands the 2 x 6 boards up and eyes the tongue and groove as a sniper looking down the barrel of a gun. He runs his licked finger down the tongue. The other Deckmen sense he knows his onions. There is maximum Woodies respect in the air. Declan breathes it in, filling his smoke-free lungs. He is ecstatic as he feels the admiration, and envisages his Malaysian Meranti hardwood gazebo, just at the bottom of the deck with a curved staircase up to its different level. He will have a multi-level decking masterpiece in time for the third-quarter, regional sales target party which he is hosting for the first time. He points out nonchalantly to the assistant that his Metabo Steb 105+, 1 horsepower, quick-change blade, variable pitch-saw action and accurate bevel set will allow him to carve pagodas into the end rails of the gazebo. The very mention of the Steb 150 — the Rolls Royce of jigsaws — invokes appreciation. He senses woodworker envy. He readjusts himself.

He strolls confidently towards the patio section. There are always cute housewives in this outback part of Woodies, fussing over the colours. They will know a readjusted true DIY man when they see one. He wants state of the art; he wants the barbeque griller's barbeque grill. He likes the sound of the Viking — strong, Nordic, reliable and unflappable. He can see the sales target party now. The sun is going down. He is flipping steaks, drinking Rolling Rock, in total but understated control over his 660 sq. ins of cooking area. The Viking Magic Regal II with its Flavour Grid, which vaporises drippings, has just cranked. No waste. He will casually engage the finance director in conversation about the impact of the dollar on our bottom line. He always refers to the company as his or ours. The boss is standing beside one of the set of film director's chairs that Declan picked up in Woodies, performing perfect air golf swings. The director's chair is a nice, artistic touch. Declan knows that even in the sports-mad office, it's important for a corporate man to have broad interests, even an appreciation of trendy movies. You have to be able to talk to wives after all.

He is well rounded and grounded — ideal corner office material. Beside him his top-of-the-range machine will be purring, the chrome warming rack for extra space full of Wedgwood plates, and a total of 22,000 BTUS firing up in unison. His cold beer in the iced cup holder, his clean-shaven reflection is caught in the glare of the gourmet double wall hood by the setting evening sun. He is not wearing socks. The sales figures have beaten all targets. He is more than a safe pair of hands. DIY Declan is a winner. He is achieving. The Attainometer is registering top marks. He is moving up. The gazebo reinforces everything. It is perfect for surveying spreadsheets on long summer evenings — the boss can sense this without asking. Declan is on the right track, the sun is warm, the grill is A Class, the steaks are juicy, everyone's glass is full. Paradise in Deckland.

Chapter 13
Deckland Awakes

Aleksei Stakhanov was a Russian worker who mined 102 tons of coal in less than six hours (fourteen times his quota) in 1935. He was made a hero for Soviet workers and an eponymous movement was set up by the Kremlin to celebrate the hard work and incredible productivity of individual workers. Brigades of Stakhanovites were set up in every Soviet factory. These were the new Soviet men, the image that every Soviet schoolchild should aspire to.

Decklanders are our suburban Stakhanovites who commute, who put in long hours, who work overtime, who pay tax and pay the wages of talk radio hosts. Car advertising is directed at them. They are the reason Ireland's economic statistics look so impressive. In the same way as the efforts of good communists like Stakhanov drove the Soviet five-year plans, our good corporate citizens, the Decklanders, drive Ireland's world-beating productivity record. Irish Decklanders are the most productive workers in the world. Forget the Chinese, Japanese or Americans, people like DIY Declan and the Kells Angels wipe the floor with them. Ireland's productivity growth in the period 1995–2005 has been nearly twice that of our nearest competitor, Finland, and nearly four times that of the EU fifteen.[1]

Decklanders make Ireland the most profitable place for US multinationals in the world. Their sweat pays the bonus and Augusta green-fees of the corporate dullards who thrive in many American corporations. You know the 'Bottom-Line Brads' whom you see in Lexus advertisements — the corporate men who couldn't find anyone's box, let alone think outside it. While they are in Ireland for their three-year posting, they live in spotless bachelor pads, paid for by the firm, and high-five each other on quarterly result day. Their stock is rising. They take the business news on CNN seriously and their ambition is to ring the opening bell on Wall Street. If you are ever unlucky enough to sit beside one on a flight, pretend you are French. They are afraid of the French. French people are subversive. Talking to French people contravenes the Homeland Security Act. The minute you see the penny loafers, the Brookes Brothers suits and the trousers that are slightly too short, grab your special pre-packed copy of *Le Monde* and pout. Yet these are the very corporate apparatchiks who benefit from the enormous drive and energy of Irish Decklanders. These are the guys who use Concierge Ireland to do their shopping, send their wife flowers, pick up their dry-cleaning and queue for tickets. Concierge Ireland's business is rocketing. They are the corporate aristocracy.

And what about the Decklanders who drop their kids to crèches at 7 am and pick them up at 7.30 pm? What about our Stakhanovites, in their €400,000 houses with the 98% mortgages, in Sallins, Kells, Blessington, Gorey and further afield? What's in it for them? Well let's go and have a look, let's see Deckland as it wakes up.

STAR DRIVE

With 50% of its readers under thirty-five, the *Irish Daily Star* is the place to find Deckland. The *Star* has 25% of the 19–34 age group market. The Pope's Children read the *Star*. Out in the BabyBelt, all across Deckland, the *Star* is the paper of choice. So let's go out with the drivers who deliver the *Star* in the middle of the night to get an idea of where the Decklanders are living, where they are shopping, what they are doing in the mornings and how they are living.

The Stillorgan Road at 3 am is teeming with plastered teenage girls spilling out of the themed Aussie nightclub doing very passable Ukrainian hooker impressions — lots of cleavage, fishnets and calf-stretching stilettos. Staggering around, squealing at each other from across the road, these south-Dublin JAPS (Jarred Annabels Princesses) wave dementedly at taxis. Most drivers pull in but quite a few speed up, pointing apologetically but unconvincingly at their taxi-sign as if to say, 'Sorry love, you're not getting into my cab but I haven't the heart to tell you so I'll pretend I'm pre-booked.' That unfortunate girl's reading on the vomitometer was obviously too high.

3.05 am TERENURE

The first thing you notice pulling up to the *Star*'s printing works is the flickering red light of the synagogue's security system. It is a sad sign of the times in multicultural Ireland, that Ireland's oldest ethnic minority — the ones who aren't covered in Metro Éireann — feel obliged to defend their primary place of worship so tightly. You don't notice it during the day, but at night it is clear that security has been beefed up dramatically with high walls, security gates and the constant flicker of cctv cameras.

Beside it, the printing works is going at full throttle. Everywhere is noise. A giant conveyor belt repetitively fires out thousands of copies, hot off the press. There are Nissan forklifts everywhere, swivelling and swerving around silently. Pallets are stacked haphazardly and enormous, half-ton rolls of Swedish *kvarnsvenden* paper are pushed into position where they are gobbled up by giant kba, Man Roland or Rockwell Tribune printers. (If you want to see where the might of German engineering goes, check out the machines in places like this at night, all marked Mannheim, Regensburg or Treptow.) The printers use only four colours — yellow, magenta, cyan and black — to press the newspaper copy and spew out 8,000 metres of today's *Star* per roll. This is transferred immediately to an array of Ford Transits, Fiat Ducatos, Citroen Relays and Merc Sprinters. Cork go, Dundalk go, Limerick go, Galway go. With exact precision, the likes of which you don't expect here in Ireland, the papers are on their way out to the BabyBelt, the Decklanders and beyond.

This year, the fastest growing destinations for the *Star* were counties Longford which is up 30%, Westmeath 27%, Louth 29% and Wexford 31%. The BabyBelt is bursting at the seams and our night-owl van drivers are the first to pick this up. The finest leading indicators of social change are not the economic institutes, the government or academic agencies, but Ireland's late-night van drivers. If you want to get a vision of what the country will look like in 2016 — 100 years after the Rising — get down to Terenure in the middle of the night. The clock is ticking.

3.15 am — Three transits head out towards Longford and Sligo, two red Citroens go south to Wexford. Everyone wants their papers in the morning. It is the only certainty. In the past a bowl of cereal was a must but not anymore. Nutri-grain bars in the car seat have replaced snap, crackle and pop at the table. But the paper is still essential, so it must be out before dawn. The timekeeper is happy this morning, everything running smoothly despite the complication of an inserted flyer. Tonight's is a Permanent TSB first year's free interest mortgage product. Flyers can ruin an entire print run and hold up the vans. The timekeeper hates flyers in the same way as the van drivers hate CDS or book giveaways which are forever falling out, forcing the driver to stop and stuff his deliveries himself. This costs time and time is everything in this game. *Ireland on Sunday*, or Golden Discs as the drivers call it, is the worst culprit. 'They'd give away hand-jobs if they could,' says one of the security lads.

The security office is a shrine to Celtic, Jordan and the Dubs — their pictures are plastered all over the walls. Security portacabins are the last refuge of the ageing Irish Teddy Boy. This is where you'll find them; in their early sixties, puckered bulbous noses from far too much stout, resting on thick moustaches. Receding hair swept back with enough oil to fry a pair of batter burgers, and a barely decipherable duck's arse — a sad reminder of past glory. Tonight our Teddy wears steel-capped boots but you know he'd love to be sporting his finest brothel-creepers, jiving in the Arcadia in Rialto or flicking proudly through his Frank Chisum back catalogue. He drags hard on his Major and whistles 'Boulavogue' through the exhaled smoke. He's worried about the Belfast run getting its 16,000 *Daily Express* to East Belfast on time. 'The Billys will have nothing to read over their Ulster fry this morning,' he chortles.

The drivers are discussing tonight's 'swaps'. This is the secret barter currency of Ireland's nocturnal delivery men. It is a finely attuned exchange rate, sensitive to demand and supply. Tonight because of Punchestown the *Racing Post* is king. One *Racing Post* buys you two sliced pans, a couple of packets of scones and a few pints of milk. The *Star* and the *Mirror* get a pound of butter, two brown scones and a six pack of Yoplait and so on. The milkman swaps with the bread-man who swaps with the paper-man who swaps with the butcher who swaps with the fruit and veg man, who gets tea, coffee and eggs and swaps it back to the milkman. Goods are bartered all night. Typically the drivers arrive home to the missus before seven with the breakfast, dinner and tea under their arms in exchange for today's papers. Services are also bought. For example, the early traffic warden is involved. The only weak links in the chain are the cops who, according to van drivers, just take, tap their noses and swap nothing. Apart from the cops, the market is perfect, responding to daily demand and supply — a case study of it would be worthy of the Michael Smurfit Business School MBA.

Anyone who has ever worked at night will understand the deep, masonic bond that builds between your co-workers. To be up when everyone else is asleep, open when all else is closed, whistling when everyone else is snoring; to live in this back-to-front, upside-down world where black is white and night is day, creates an almost conspiratorial closeness. You pick this up immediately from working with the drivers. In the paper business it is even tighter because this profoundly anti-social life is reinforced by the fact that they only get one official night off, Christmas Eve. Christmas Day is the only day there are no papers. Christmas Eve is their night out and Dublin's paper van drivers — the men who bring you the news in the morning — can be found in McDowell's in Inchicore. This existence is not all that unusual. Two hundred thousand of us work shiftwork and 20% work at least one night per month.

4.30 am SUBURBAN SINUSITIS

Time to go: we jump into the cab, papers in the back. We are headed for Naas, the buckle of the BabyBelt, the capital of Deckland. The drivers stock up on water. There is no coffee or Red Bull here. These are seasoned sleep evaders. Their existence is a game of cat and mouse with sleep, and water is the only substance to keep them awake. Terry the driver is referred to fondly by the other drivers as the first refugee. He's Welsh. He has been doing the Naas run for eighteen years. Up until 1998 he had seven drops in Naas; now he has fifty-six. That signifies how much pressure the buckle of the BabyBelt is under. So many Spars, Centras, Maces, Essos and Maxols have sprung up in the past eight years on the road to Naas, all of them servicing segments of the enormous population growth. Deckland could easily be called Sparland.

Terry used to drive out as far as Edenderry as well as Lucan and Leixlip. Not now. He notched up a 187-mile round trip every night, but today traffic congestion and the mushrooming of shops and garages makes that impossible. It now takes four vans to do what one van did in 2000. The costs of congestion are rising exponentially. Other drivers wait in Portarlington, Tullamore and Abbyleix to pick up papers from the earlier Cork run that left Terenure at 2 am. No company can service those places from Dublin now — the early morning news would arrive in time for lunch. Back in 2000 Terry could do all his drops in Naas in fifteen minutes. Now it is one of the biggest markets in the country and it takes all morning. Everything has become clogged and congested. The BabyBelt is suffering from a bizarre form of suburban sinusitis. By 5.30 am the lights on the Naas roads inbound are beginning to merge. By 6.45 am it is a car park.

But it's still early now and the Ford Transit leaves the road blazing through Tallaght. The stopwatch is ticking. Deckland is stirring and we have to be there and gone before seven. The skeletal remains of Shamrock Rovers' dreams flit by on the left. The world looks different from the front of a White Van. I feel like texting a radio station. DJ Class A spins the discs on Raidió na Life but she doesn't do interactive. Through Killinarden now — the only place in Dublin that looks more desolate in the day than at night. A charred car smoulders. First drop is a Statoil Station in City West manned by a lone Chinese student who hardly looks up from his Playstation Portable. The dawn is breaking. Saggart, followed by Rathcoole and Kill, a couple of drops in each village — places which have bloated over the past half decade, where Chinese takeaways have taken over from agricultural credit unions at the cheaper end of town.

We move out onto the main artery — the constantly worked-on Naas Road. There are enormous yellow Caterpillar trucks everywhere. The earth has been gouged out on either side to make room for another lane. This is going to put all the road-side garages out of business but they don't care, not after the huge CPO payout. We drop at a bright Esso, reinforced glass smudged with fingerprints of tired drivers all night having to prop themselves up as they sign their Visa slips. Running on Empty? enquires the ad at the Esso-cum-Wimpey. Another Statoil, Mace and Spar, more drops, more hot-food counters, more immigrants pouring 20 kg drums of cold baked beans into giant lamp-heated casserole dishes, ahead of the breakfast rush. This is Deckland's Pantry — the Kitchen of the BabyBelt — offering deluxe breakfast rolls, potato wedges, hot panini and chicken wraps.

In the recent past when you drove on Ireland's roads, provincial towns and villages signalled their proximity by a local GAA club. These were usually a mile or so out of town. As a driver, you knew you were coming into New Ross, Athy, Stradbally, Athboy, Trim or Kells by the gates of the local St Enda's, St Brendan's or St Ciaran's. Today, towns announce themselves by huge roadside ads for housing developments called Ard na Rí or Ard na Gréine, maybe a drive-in McDonald's or out-of-town Lidl. Naas is signalled by the ubiquitous roadworks and hundreds of slightly askew traffic cones kicked around by a pair of drunks on the way home the night before, and of course the prestige (they are always prestige, luxury or exclusive) development, the Old Town Demesne. This half-built estate is Deckland in Excelsis. There is a Porsche Boxster outside the first house, surely parked by the developer? These are expensive houses, signalled on the outside by the curved drive, railway sleepers in the front borders and neutral tones. Inside, the island in the middle of the kitchen, hardwood flooring and maple deck reveal you are in €450,000 territory at least. The double-doored fridge is a real giveaway. The Demesne is waking up. You can almost feel the pressure from all those power-showers draining the Liffey in nearby Sallins.

We drop at the Statoil and move on. Tesco 24 hours in Naas is a hive of activity. Terry gets a few 'swaps' — sausages, rashers and a few eggs for two *Racing Posts* and a *Mirror*. At 5.50 am the petrol pumps at the Mace are full of red-eyed commuters filling up. Most of the Spars and Centras are located in the middle of labyrinthine estates which, like some ancient grammatical constructions, have various derivations of the same stem, so you have Morrel or Hazelmere (the stem) Gardens or Crescent, Park or Avenue, Close and Rise. All these houses look identical. The names are a giveaway. Anything built before 2000 is likely to have a posh English-sounding name like Hazelmere, Morrel or Berkely, those built afterwards will normally have Irish-sounding names like Carraig Grianán, Ard na Gréine or (incongruously) An Gorteen Mór — the enormous little field. The Centras are open by 6 am and extraordinarily only one petrol station in Naas is not open 24 hours. Naas is a 24/7 town whose population has risen by over 100% in ten years. In 1998 there were no taxis in Naas. There are now 98. In Naas town itself, Terry used to have 10 drops in 2001. He now has 27.

The Naas Road is backed up nearly to Newbridge. Looking down from over the flyover, as far as the eye can see, is one long queue, about four miles long of chrome and metal, shining in the morning sun, drivers on the phone, texting each other, work, radio stations, their lovers or sales managers. These people may have been on the road already for thirty minutes and 'Morning Ireland' has not even started. Given the evidence from the BabyBelt, the programme should be called 'Mid-Morning Ireland' or even 'Coffee-Morning Ireland'. It's five to seven and there is a queue of anxious mothers in 4x4s, all blonde highlights, sensible navy suits and GHD-straightened hair waiting with Destiny's Child — their little genius — outside Little Harvard, Naas's finest crèche. Little Harvard? Need I say more about the Expectocracy? Little Harvard does breakfast and dressing, so the kids are just dropped in the peejays. Mummy hopes she's packed the bags properly. Her new Nissan Terrano dwarfs the 98 D Punto of the foreign carers who look after her children — she is in a different league to those who mind her kids. Her highlights are Toni & Guy, theirs out of a bottle; she is Chablis, they're Blossom Hill; her Brazilian is by appointment, theirs is home made; she is rich, they are getting by. Yet by her own admission, theirs is the most important job in society, which explains (a) why she'd never do it and (b) why she gets paid multiples of their combined salaries. A procession of super-sized Ford Galaxys, Renault Meganes and Volvo XC 70s disgorges designer-clad Destiny's Children out into Little Harvard where the Attainometer has been on since dawn.

Mummy would love it if this nursery operated a web cam so she could log on to see her darling's progress during the day from her office. One similar hothouse offers the following:

> *Continuous interaction is encouraged to ensure that children enjoy a normal and natural upbringing and develop close bonds with our staff and their peers. Stimulating and exciting activities for inquisitive and active young minds such as Irish dancing, music, speech and drama, French, Irish and arts and crafts, with specialised teachers, are introduced at every age level. Computers and other modern visual training materials are also used. Term plans are issued to parents and progress reports provided bi-monthly. During the school holidays, children will enjoy a specially designed programme to suit their ages and interests.*

You can never start too early in the Expectocracy, and remember, the Attainometer is always on.

By 8 am the dynamic of the crèche changes. The mummies get older, look more weary and tired. There seems to be more car-equality now. Polos, Lupos, Mazdas and Mitsubishis arrive. Maybe the rich get first dibs at breakfast? Then you realise that this is the next wave of the same type of kids. The former were lucky, they saw their mummies at least fleetingly, shrieking over the Strawberry Alarm Clock, handing out nutri-grains. The next batch is being dropped by granny because mummy is up and gone before they are awake. These kids arrive clothed and fed, armed with Disney rucksacks and Barbie school bags, some time between eight and nine. Mummy is putting on her lipstick in the mirror just past Rathcoole. That's one good thing about the traffic: you've loads of time to get made up. She flicks stations, using the new gadget on the steering wheel as it would be far too much hassle to lean over and touch the buttons on the stereo. Her tummy rumbles. Daddy meanwhile has little idea what it feels like to drop the daughter in the crèche, squeeze in a hard day's work before rushing back to the crèche and being a good mother at bedtime. Daddy is having his first conference call of the day, before catching the early-afternoon flight to Heathrow for a suppliers' meeting in Staines. He'll be back on the 9 pm tonight. Granny tidies up and switches on Radio One.

Deckland is at work. The Stakhanovites are toiling away, ensuring that Ireland comes out top of the list in the tables at the back of *The Economist* magazine. This makes great copy for politicians, the IDA, stockbrokers and bores like 'Bottom-line Brad'. We've never had it so good.

Chapter 14
Destiny's Child in Deckland

– *Welcome to the Riga Ghetto, Sir.*

This is how Janis the manager of the Texaco in Lucan describes this place. Other than Jaquinder from the Punjab, all the workers at 6.45 am on a Saturday morning are from the Baltics.

– *What about Irish workers? Where are they?*

– *They don't work, they just spend.*

Janis has been here five years and his view is that there are two types of people in this country: the workers and the Irish. The immigrants are the workers and the locals are only good at blowing cash. His right-hand man Fjodor is also from Riga. They run the place like clockwork. Behind the hot-food counter — the haute cuisine of Deckland — three Baltic girls flick through *Heat* magazine and chat away to each other in their common language, Russian. Elana and Christina are Lithuanians and Alla is Latvian. They snigger as the last of the wiry, arseless ravers space in, pupils dilated, head to toe in full hoody, tracksuit and Diadora runners garb, looking for bottles of water and smokes in tens.

– *Sorry, only twenties.*

– *For fuck's sake.*

Elana and Alla have been here for just under a year. Both are students. Christina, who looks younger, has a five-year-old son Ignas with her who is very happy at the local national school. Normally she works 3 pm to 11 pm and her husband drives for Tesco all night. They don't see much of each other, but it saves on the childcare bills. Her parents are also here working in another garage cum shopping emporium cum fast food joint, suitably titled 'On The Run', which feeds, informs and refuels the legions of worker bees that make up the 'fast move nation'. So there are three generations of this Lithuanian family depending on the Irish commuters for a living. They have a target of two more years when they will have the €30,000 for a place in Kaunus — their home town. Christina is going home for a week in June. The girls all have typical Slavic faces, sallow skin, deep photogenic green eyes, set wide apart which suggests that they are in fact Russian, not Baltic in origin, grandchildren of the scattered victims of Stalin's paranoid whims.

Christina is tired this morning. She has been doing back-to-back shifts because it is little Ignas's birthday today. Christina didn't allow for the First Holy Communion upsetting her plans. Despite being notionally Catholics, Lithuanians don't do communions Irish-style. Come to think of it, nobody does communions like the Irish. She, like all mothers, wanted to give her little boy the best birthday ever. He had never seen a bouncy castle before last year when she promised him on the way home on the bus that he could have an even bigger one for his next birthday. Ignas never forgot it and reminded her of it every night before he went to sleep. This would not only make his day, but it would show their neighbours in Celbridge that they too could afford a big day in the back garden. More importantly they could take photos and email them back home to Kaunus that afternoon to the begrudging, doubting Thomases who didn't believe that they had their own house with a front and back garden in the West. Photos on the net are the 21st-century version of the 'Letter from America'.

Christina's problem was that she only tried to book in late March, giving her, she thought, plenty of time — nearly two months. But all the bouncy castles in the BabyBelt were booked ages ago, sucked up in the big suburban communion frenzy. She felt awful, the way only proud immigrant mothers can. She rang around like a demented dervish using up all the credit in her phone, twice. Finally, an unscrupulous bouncy castle dealer claiming to be from Carlow (you can't tell for definite these days with mobiles), where young families constitute over 30% of all households, making it one of the richest bouncy castle fiefdoms in the kingdom, heard the distress in her voice. He shamelessly involved her in a bidding war against another distraught mother who had also missed the bouncy castle boat. Christina ended up paying €260 for a Spiderman castle which should have cost €160. As a result, she has worked three double shifts this week, but the castle will be delivered this morning before Mass and the invaluable photos will be on the net by 1.30 pm. She has arrived.

Didvis, another Latvian, has just moved from Thurles where he was picking mushrooms. He shares a one-bedroom place with two others. The other girls live together, along with a 20-year-old Estonian, Laura, who is breezily counting thousands of euros from the till. She dropped out of economics in university but intends to go back when she has made some cash and seen a bit of the world. For now, €7.65 an hour, free food and a view of the N4 will do just fine.

– *Why Ireland?*

Because their mates came here first, it is easy to get a job and Dublin is plastered all over Russian websites as the place to come to. Dublin, according to a Eurostat Survey,[1] has the reputation of second easiest city in Europe out of thirty for immigrants to get a job. News travels fast. The CSO estimates that by 2020, a quarter of a million more new immigrants will be living in Dublin. That is 25% of today's population. It also forecasts that 120,000 Dubliners will leave the city during the same period. These east Europeans are obviously the first wave.

The place is packed at 7.15 am. Ella is doing a roaring trade in Breakfast Rolls, Big Breakfasts and hot ham and cheese baguettes. The national diabetic epidemic comes closer with every hung-over mouthful — 14% of the male population obese and counting. The fizz of Lucozade bottles being opened by red-eyed, early-shift Guards resonates through the shop. In the early morning, carbonated sugar is the 'fast move nation's' drink of choice.

– *What are the Irish like?*

When they are sober they are lovely, very polite and considerate. When they are drunk and need soakage after the clubs shut they are awful, very rude and very demanding. Also they don't eat very well, things tend to dribble and they talk with their mouths full. They are also violent in a messy, drunk way. But in general they are a good bunch and pretty fair. The girls hate working the night shift but do it for the money.

It's 7.20 am. The first-communion Dads arrive. You can tell them by the deranged look in their eyes, the two twelve-packs of Hula

Hoops under each arm, fag in the mouth, laden down with fizzy drinks. Now it is obvious how this nation spends €721 million a year on soft drinks — it is the currency of choice for blackmailing tweenies. It buys peace in a house of pesterers. Today is Communion Saturday in the middle of May and the BabyBelt is up to high doh. I grab my Robert Roberts coffee and leave a Nigerian haggling over the price of a Jumbo carvery roll. The Slavs were never good at hiding their racism and, unfortunately, those lovely, wide, green eyes turn rather narrow at the prospect of serving an African.

Three miles away in Celbridge — deep in one of the fastest growing towns in the BabyBelt — Bouncy Castle Brendan packs up the last bouncy castle in his red Ford Transit. Brendan used to be in the taxi business, but deregulation, competition from weekend drivers and congestion all made it impossible to earn a proper crust.

From the look of his square mock-Georgian house, he's making a fine living. Brendan is a good bloke, the type that lays patios in his garden. There are three railway sleepers, about to be put to good use in his driveway. His is a detached corner house, an original show-house in Sylvan Court, an up-market Deckland estate just outside Celbridge. It was described as the talk of the town in 1999 when, as the IAVI website of that year gushed:

> traditional city developers like Cosgrave builders moved out to Celbridge in Kildare with a £20 million scheme of just 96 houses, and their Sylvan Court development saw four-beds priced from £189,000 and five-beds from £237,000.

Locals thought they were mad. But recently, just up the road a similarly sized site (just the empty site) went for €77 million. This puts Cosgrave's £20 million into perspective. Or does it? Anyway, today the houses sell for €500,000 to €700,000, so Brendan and his neighbours feel rich. In fact, they are extremely *asset* rich. Most of them will have close to €400,000 in untapped equity in their houses and they are taking advantage of equity releases for cars and second house loans. The estate is a shrine to new chrome and steel, cabriolets and Bluetooth technology. Almost every driveway has a top-of-the-range new car and, tellingly, they are all European makes. This is a give-away in the BabyBelt; while poor Decklanders prefer Asians, rich

Decklanders prefer blondes. Almost exclusively, they buy cars made in tolerant blonde northern European social democratic countries that opposed the war in Iraq. Ironically, these top-end 'axles of evil' now threaten the landscape for Destiny's Child — the heir and heiress of the BabyBelt. As well as basketball hoops in front gardens, hanging baskets, electric coach-lights in porches and fake Victorian free-standing street lights in 10 x 15 ft brick-paved driveways, rich Deckland is infested with speed bumps.

SPEED BUMP MOMS

The politics of speed bumps sheds some light on the dilemma for politicians posed by the BabyBelt. The arrival of speed ramps on a new estate typically follows months of lobbying the council by groups like 'Concerned Young Mothers for speed bumps'. The chronology of such groups is straightforward. Young Decklanders move into an estate; there is no adequate public transport so they all buy cars. They also use their cars as status symbols, so the cars like the children on the estate get bigger every year and the average height and weight of both rises in tandem. The second child arrives, followed closely by a kitchen extension. The value of the houses goes up and up. This allows the Decklanders to release equity for a bigger car, which is usually justified for reasons of safety. After all, if you are to spend three hours a day in the car it may as well be a safe one. Eventually, the cars outgrow the children rather than the other way around. Soon the suvs become so big that there is a lethal blind spot just under the bull bars where the petite drivers simply can't see a stroller, even the now favoured double-height new articulated super-stroller.

Safety anxiety sets in and it gives way to panic following a story from somewhere in England relayed on TV3's 5.30 news about how a mother ran over her own child in her enormous suv. She was coming back from work. She had had a row with that sleaze from accounts and was distracted. She was trying to get home early to make sure the eldest wasn't the last left in the crèche at 7 pm. She hates being the last. His little face, all his friends gone, the carers impatiently tidying up getting ready for tomorrow — another long day in an English Deckland — and he is crying, 'Where's my mummy?' She was speeding, but that's understandable. She knew nothing until she felt the little bump under the wheels.

Back in the TV studio, the early-evening news producer knows her audience: fear sells. 'Don't smile, empathise,' is the message from the control room which gets relayed into the presenter's earpiece as she turns from camera two — the 'happy' camera where they do stories about people overcoming cancer, families reuniting after twenty years apart or news about celebrities' shoes — to camera four, the 'sad' camera. With the same mechanical ease as a remote control turns down the sound on a stereo, the presenter fazes out her normal sparkling ivory smile. Her legendary smile which won her the *Woman's Own* 'Smile of the Year' last year is courtesy of a new one-hour whitening product on the market — Britesmile — which works instantly. You don't even have to give up coffee temporarily which, for the diet-obsessed presenter, would be a nightmare. For weeks on end, nothing but strong *Illy* espresso passes her collagen-enhanced lips. Almost tearful, she delivers the tragic news about mother and child from England which the producer only stumbled upon by accident on the news wires yesterday. It hits the spot. The producer is ecstatic, she can almost feel the ratings and her career rise — they should have led with that story rather than the mind-numbing stuff about the European constitution. After all, what's the golden ratings rule she learnt on her stint at WSPN Milwaukee — 'If it bleeds, it leads.'

The stay-at-home mums are aghast. Bon Jovi ringtones sound out, texts beep and phones ring. Fear grips the BabyBelt. Greed and fear are the dominant emotions of Decklanders. And in the same way as the greed is insatiable, the fear is largely irrational. There is probably more chance of being attacked by a great white shark in Brittas than driving over your own child at your own driveway, but the story resonates. They can all imagine the awfulness of the little bump, and because of the new Corrs CD blaring and the blind spot under the bull bars, the mother, in her hermetically sealed chariot, didn't hear, feel or see a thing.

This tragedy galvanises the 'Concerned Young Mothers for speed bumps' campaign. The speed bump moms get going. Within days, there are councillors from every party eyeballing the road, measuring out imaginary bumps and promising landscape features so as not to detract from the Arcadian suburban bliss of up-market Deckland. Speed bump moms expose the great new dilemma for the politicians. In last year's by-election, less than 30% of the BabyBelt voted. As far as they are concerned, the government can't do anything for them except leave them alone. Speed bump moms vote for the right to opt out, pay low taxes and drive Ford Galaxys. Then a tragedy occurs and they clamber for politicians to do something. But wait a minute, what are the politicians expected to do, protect the speed bump moms from themselves in their large SUVs? This is the nub of the politics of Deckland. It is single-issue land. The BabyBelt only gets political when a single issue like a school, a speed ramp, an access road or a landfill encroaches on its little nirvana. This makes the BabyBelt almost ungovernable and because it is growing faster than any other area of the country, it poses a serious dilemma for the political system.

In the last election, there were reports of canvassers getting lost in the new estates, not being able to pin down issues and having no idea of who was who. In addition, as most people were not home before 7 pm, it made the process of canvassing difficult because there simply was not enough time to rap on all the doors before dark. A cynic might argue that this is the reason for the move now to post codes. The political marketers realise that if they are to win the suburbs they have to start by knowing who lives where exactly, and the quickest and most definitive way of doing this is via post codes.

The political contrast between the BabyBelt and the BoringBelt couldn't be more stark. The BoringBelt is old Ireland, the established 1960s and 1970s suburbs of Cork, Dublin, Galway and Limerick. These people vote; turn-out in these areas is always above 60%. Dún Laoghaire is the fulcrum of the BoringBelt. In the 1980s this was the former hotbed of radicalism. The constituency voted for divorce, abortion and any liberal campaign. But things have gone quiet. Back then they would have voted for free leather gimp outfits, replete with whips, chains, manacles and throat chokers, with a few poppers thrown in, for every consenting adult. Today there are no secondary schools in the town, there are no local children and the evangelical church is the fastest growing in the town. Those children who remain live in houses so expensive that their parents send them to rarefied fee-paying schools where they can mix with their own from adjacent suburbs. The BoringBelt is old and rich and its schools are closing, as against the BabyBelt which is coming down with children, bursting at the seams and pregnant with incipient social problems. In contrast, last year, the biggest civic issue in formerly radical Dún Laoghaire concerned the future of the golf club.

COMMUNIONOMICS

Bouncy Castle Brendan is getting agitated. He has three vans out this morning and the lads have already started dropping. They are jammed today, fifty-four castles to deliver and the trick is to get out on the road to the furthest destinations first and work your way back in. By 7.45 am he passes Edenderry out to 'Budland'. Budland is the most incongruous province of the BabyBelt. Brendan has noticed in the years in the bouncy business that the social topology of his areas has changed dramatically. Up until a few years ago, the clientele got rougher as you drove from Celbridge towards Dublin to places like Clondalkin and Ballyfermot. Now, the opposite is the case. The estates far out past Edenderry and Port Laoise are much dodgier. This is where a new class is settling. This is 'Budland' where, as they said in 'Cheers', 'Everybody knows your name' and your name is Bud.

He hates dropping to Budland because although money is usually no object and they cough up straight away in cash, they tend not to have any idea of the diameters of their postage-stamp back gardens and he usually has to try out at least three castles before he gets one that fits. Also the parents get very messy, usually drinking since early afternoon, and by the time he calls to collect around 9 pm, they are hammered and using the castle themselves, leaping around like Sumo trampolineists. The combination of the booze, spliff and windburn from having been sitting outside all day on their decks can make them a bit narky. Brendan usually takes two lads from the GAA club, Paul and his brother Michael McGettigan, with him for his night runs to Budland. These lads were Irish amateur boxing champions in the 1990s, Tyrone's answer to the Ukrainian Klitchko brothers. They can look after themselves, and the northern accent with its vague associated hint of the 'Ra helps enormously, he finds. His conversations in Budland typically go along the following lines:

8.30 am arrive	– *Alright, Bud.*
8.36 am measure the garden	– *Sorted, Bud.*
8.45 am castle up and inflated	– *Deadly, Bud.*
8.55 am mention pick up time	– *Sound, Bud.*
9.05 pm knock on door to collect	– *Are you serious, Bud?*
9.09 pm move to unplug machine	– *Don't even fucking think about it, Bud.*
9.16 pm square up with one of the Buds	– *I'm not messin', Bud.*

9.18 pm McGettigans appear from the van – *Chill out, Bud. Take
your fucking castle.*

But Budlanders are good clients, there's usually lots of repeat
business and they always pay in advance and never remember the
altercations from the time before. They are also the only ones who
have bouncy castles for first birthday parties.

There are a few standard sizes. The Maxwell House of Bouncy
Castles is the 14 x 12 ft without slide which costs €120 per day. A step
up is the Nescafé Alta Rica model, the 15 x 15 ft retailing at €130.
A souped-up version of this with slides will knock you back €150.
Then we are into the Bewley's Café latte end of the market, with the
18 x 18 ft saloon model at €170 per day. Finally, we get into double-
espresso of bouncy castles territory with the bespoke Giant Giraffe or
Pirate Ship retailing at €220. Brendan noticed that there is less price
resistance the lower down you go on the social pecking order. The
more overlooked the back garden, the more likely they are to accept
any price. They simply have to have it. Of course, there is a
communion day premium on all the above castles of between 30%
and 50%.

On average, Brendan's season is six months, from March to
September. That's twenty-four weekends which together with a few
corporate mid-week hires makes about fifty-two days a year. And the
key is to get as many of his castles hired each day.

He is lucky to be based in Kildare because two factors have ensured
that communions in Kildare, Meath and surrounding counties to the
west take place on Saturdays and Sundays, as opposed to just
Saturdays in Dublin. The first factor is that the BabyBelt is full of
young children and therefore there are not enough churches to go
around, and the second factor is the size of the churches. In Dublin in
the 1960s and 1970s, because church attendance was as high as 96%,
large estates came with large churches. The Church worked together
with the developers and bought land adjacent to the estates where
huge suburban churches sprang up. Today, mass attendance amongst
young families in the BabyBelt has fallen to well below 50% and the
Church no longer builds churches. It also knows that, after an initial
flurry, almost all of the little girls and boys who make their
communions will not be at Mass. So while the churches in Dublin are
large cavernous affairs where half a dozen communions take place on
any Saturday, the churches in former country villages that have seen

their populations rocket cannot cope with the once-off communion rush.

For us, communions are no big deal. They are part of May. But it must look strange if you have never seen a first communion before: the sight of dozens of little girls dressed up in white frilly dresses, tiaras, dainty shoes and veils, accompanied into a packed church by dozens of little boys kitted out like miniature Nickys from Westlife. Many years ago, a foreign friend of mine on first seeing little girls in full communion garb, thought that the form of Catholicism here was so traditional that we must also be in the child bride business.

As noted, Mass attendance has fallen progressively, but the communion business has flourished. It appears that the less privately observant we are, the more publicly ostentatious our expression of religion becomes. While this begins at over-the-top baptisms (christening parties in the Four Seasons are not unheard of), the first communion frenzy remains the exemplar.

Every May, the BabyBelt turns into a bonanza for people like bouncy castle vendors, parasol-floggers and three-star hotel owners who cash in on the chicken and chips circuit. Indeed, if you have children whose birthdays fall in May, the chances of getting a bouncy castle for the day at a decent price are slim, as Christina the Lithuanian found out.

The great Irish communion splash-out has been the subject of much debate on the airwaves, largely because poor people tend to spend more than rich (and in the extreme get into debt). But it has ever been thus. The bourgeoisie love to complain about the fecklessness of the poor. It makes them feel more virtuous.

This vignette of Irish society consists of a fusion of the two aspects of the lives of the Pope's Children that both John Paul and Benedict have emphasised. One of the key messages of the Catholic Church has been that individualism and consumerism are not healthy. The Church urges us to be more spiritual and community-driven. However, the communion frenzy allows us to be both: we can be *communitaire* by celebrating together, while at the same time we can compete in the consumer arena by allowing our kids to out-parasol each other on the big day.

Communions are serving a number of disparate roles, which is why the ritual is so fascinating. First, a big splash for the communion allows absentee parents — who are guilty about not seeing the children all week — to give something back. So they splash out. The second role for a communion is to get family and friends together, because the stresses of mortgage, sales targets and commuting mean that you never get to see your friends. So a communion, far from being a religious event, acts as the catalyst to an afternoon session with old mates. Third, the communion is a chance to show off. This is typically driven by mothers and passed on to daughters, who in turn will pass it on to their own daughters. Communions are fashion statements.

If you don't believe me, just explore the website of the thoroughly fashionable 'Off the Rails' show. The section on communion makeovers for eight-year-olds is quite the eye-opener. There is an eight-year-old girl modelling dresses from Clerys, Baby Bambino and Little Angels. Let's take for example the offering from Baby Bambino, which tells us that 'at Baby Bambino in Clarendon Street, Dublin, they go for something a little less traditional'. Maria Fusco suggests buying separates which can be worn again. They don't do any of the accessories such as veils, tiaras and socks. 'A basic linen dress can go from €90 up to €450. For this model they chose a linen jacket with silk organza skirt and two feathers in her hair.'

So there you have it. The great communion frenzy is upon us, with child models, fake tan ads, highlights for eight-year-olds, bouncy castles, parasols and Chicken à la King. Destiny's Child's communion is a flamboyant affair — all big hats, bright colours, bespoke tailoring, swanky dresses, pomp and ceremony. Communions sum up modern religion for many thousands of young Irish parents caught in the no-man's land between being good parents and being good career employees, while genuflecting to tradition. If you want to get a glimpse of modern Ireland, forget politics, commentary or current affairs — just go to a communion.

For Bouncy Castle Brendan, who frankly doesn't really care about what the communion frenzy tells us about the country, what is important is that this religious, demographic and economic conundrum is a commercial godsend. Because the BabyBelt churches can't cope with the one-off rush, it means he gets two days' business at the busiest time of the year, and by recycling the castles he makes more cash.

And the cash is extremely good. The workhorse of Bouncy Castles is the standard 14 x 14 ft. He buys these in the UK for €1,100 and rents them out for €120 a day. If he gets fifty-two days of this it is €6,240 per season. Typically he can get five seasons per castle, so you are looking at just over €30,000 cash generated. Take wages, insurance and costs out of that and the profit margin is still significant. Brendan coyly says his margins are above 60%. Let's say that his capacity is forty castles which rent for an average of €150 per day. That's €6,000 per full day. Multiplied by fifty-two days in the season he makes €312,000 per year for only working weekends for half the year! Nice work. Obviously he will not be at full capacity all the time, but nor would he have bought so much stock if he wasn't working close to full throttle.

The moral of the story is that there's buckets of money to be made from the Pope's Children, and the bouncy castle sellers are at the cutting edge. Not only is the bouncy castle market driven by pester power, so that Brendan does not so much have *customers* as *agitators*, but a second factor driving the market is bouncy castle envy, where parents are trying to out-bouncy castle each other.

This is down to our old friends, greed and fear, again. The fear comes from the parents' fear of rejection. They are on a guilt trip and fear that because they reject their children every morning when they drop a clinging, crying infant to a crèche, their rapidly growing-up children will reject them. How does 'speed bump mom' who is putting in a fifty-hour week in Hewlett Packard make it up to her children?

What better way to make up to little Chloe? Knackered, overworked speed bump moms display their own 'good parenting' badge (so important these days) via the lavishness of their eight-year-old's communion party. The 'no bouncy castle is big enough for her communion party' syndrome comes into its own. This combination of fear, guilt and lavishness can be termed 'bouncy castle syndrome', and it afflicts many back gardens in the BabyBelt.

Another part of the similar but slightly different trend is 'bouncy castle envy' which leads, in Brendan's experience, to changes in orders usually phoned in on a Monday morning when people have seen a neighbour's bouncy castle the previous Saturday and ring to make sure that their one is just as big if not bigger. He is regularly asked whether he does marquees. This usually follows an uber-Deckland communion where the parents attain super stratospheric status by hiring their own marquee — a bouncy castle for adults. This serves to ratchet up bouncy castle envy. After all, the Attainometer is always on in Deckland.

This is the Midnight at the Olympia approach to economics at work, leading to a type of suburban bouncy castle arms race. Brendan doesn't mind. He's in clover.

The last call
But the clock is ticking as Brendan roars down the N4. It's 8.45 am and all the castles have to be dropped, set up and in place before Mass at 10.30. He calls the lads; they are ahead of schedule and on their way back. They have a few drops on the northside out in Swords, but they should easily be in Joel's on the Naas Road by 12.30 for lunch as they are religiously every Saturday.

By 10 am Bouncy Castle Brendan is on the road back to Celbridge, twelve drops, one to go. He checks today in his big black eircom diary which is an incomprehensible jigsaw of mobile numbers, first names, addresses scrubbed out and scribbles. It would defeat CIA code breakers. Only he knows what everything means. The next one is some girl with a foreign sounding last name.

He swings into the maze that is Old Mill Town. He's looking for the Demesne, 128 The Demesne to be precise. The skyline is a sea of satellite dishes. We are in Skyland. Each house is an identical box cut in two. There are over 600 of them. The boxes are indistinguishable from each other at first blush, down to the identical holes which are in precisely the same place in the masonry in the downstairs loos where the developers couldn't have been bothered fixing a door stopper to prevent the fake brass handles from taking lumps out of the chalky plasterboard. But on closer inspection the social pecking order of Deckland is evident. There are tell-tale signs about who is on the way up and who is on the way down, who is passing through and who is a lifer.

Gardens are a dead giveaway. First, they tell you that there are many more investors — 21st-century absentee landlords — than owner occupiers. Overgrown, untended lawns mean renters. But Brendan has noticed that the owner occupiers seem to exist in clusters in these huge estates. They tend their little merkinish lawns beautifully. The neater the lawn, the greater the amount of the take-home wage taken up by the mortgage. And a renter with an overgrown lawn in a cluster of owner occupiers will be immediately frozen out. At Christmas this little cluster will do its best to crash the national grid with a lightshow unrivalled since Kiss played the RDS. There will be reindeers prancing around on the slates, Santas climbing into blocked-up chimneys, sleighs deposited on the front lawn and plastic elves holding helpful signs declaring 'Lapland 10 miles' on the painted half-barrel at the bottom of the lawn. There are only two man-made things that can be seen from the moon with the naked eye: the Great Wall of China and Celbridge at Christmas.

The renters are more likely to have something on blocks in the drive. Owners have hybrid petunias and other overly bright red flowers in overblown hanging baskets that look as if they are going to take the entire supporting outside beam with them when watered. Owners all have names for their houses, announced by little painted aluminium plaques available from €15 with ludicrous names like Deep Well, Four Winds or Levantine. The saints used to be very popular but they have been relegated. So too have patriots from the names of estates. For a place where Sinn Féin hopes to make significant inroads, Deckland displays a deep form of Anglophilia which is evident in the names of estates. An interesting case in point has been the airbrushing of all patriots from the newly renamed Ballymun Towers. So Pearse, Plunkett and Connolly Towers have been airbrushed out, to be renamed by the rustic home-counties sounding Orchard Square, Marewood Crescent and Barnwell Drive. These sound more like the surnames of Cromwell's NCOs than Irish heroes.

Porches reveal a lot about the inhabitants. Porches are to a house what a mouth is to a face. Everyone wants full, bud-like lips, white straight teeth and a wide smile, but most of us get none of the above. However, through a combination of expensive dentistry, a bit of cosmetic and lip gloss we can get there. Similarly, the porch is crucial in Deckland. Any extension at all, particularly a jutting-out mock Georgian portico affair, with plastic supporting Corinthian columns, is a true sign of people on the way up. They won't be here long: next stop Knocklyon. Likewise, any wrought-iron feature or supports for climbing creepers — all these improvement features signify a couple under social starters orders. Any ceramic animals or birds, particularly eagles, anywhere close to the porch are also a giveaway of social desperation.

Renters' porches, on the other hand, are festooned with Apache pizza, the Peking Kitchen and the Bombay Pantry flyers as well as the odd milk carton and empty Silk Cut box which have blown in from the overflowing bin that someone has forgot to put out for three weeks. These people have pre-paid mobile phones. This is one of the most acute social indicators in Deckland along with scratch card dependence. If you see a mum buying phone credit and playing the lotto regularly, she is either very poor or very rich. Most aspiring Decklanders will not pre-pay. It sends out all the wrong signals.

Brendan goes round the back of every house, past the punctured footballs, the rusting Barbie bikes and discarded third-birthday presents. Around the back on the deck he can tell a lot about the people. Those with wooden garden furniture will haggle over the prices. Those with white plastic sets of four chairs, a table with broken parasol and rusting clasp will pay straight away. The more like Tip Head the garden looks, the more cash available in the house. The neater, more classy looking and anything vaguely resembling a water feature, means no ready cash but lots of pride. These are the type of people who ask for tasteful bouncy castles.

A young renter from Monaghan in a souped-up Opel Astra, weighed down at the back by a huge boom box with accompanying mega-base bin, screeches by, Eminem blasting out, vibrating windows all around Old Mill Demesne. Bouncy Castle Brendan's heart sinks because it has not been unknown for bouncy castles to be hired for 21sts and they always come back in a terrible state with rips, tears and cigarette burns. But the boy racer speeds up, pulls a handbrake turn, screeches left and revs on down into the bowels of Old Mill Dale.

Brendan presses the bell. An Abba ring-tone — very promising, thinks Brendan. Decklanders who spend on such frivolous gadgets usually pay up in advance. A beautiful woman answers the door. Christina has had some sleep. She knocked off from the Texaco at half seven and has had about two hours' kip. Tinny Russian music blares out from the kitchen and there is a 42-in. plasma screen over the fireplace in the living-room. There are gadgets everywhere and remote controls, little bits of ancillary technology placed precisely in a row underneath the plasma screen which is showing a robust game of Bulgarian ice hockey. Little Ignas, dressed up like a Tsar for his fifth birthday, is so engrossed in his x Box that he doesn't even notice the bouncy castle being lugged through the house. The place is spotless even if the mock Victorian dado rail looks out of place in such futuristic surroundings. Christina takes out a digital camcorder to record the arrival of the bouncy castle in the same way as her parents once recorded the take-off of Soyuz 17 from the TV.

This is a big moment for her. The Shrek bouncy castle is up. Her neighbours can see that they are people of stature. Ignas is thrilled and already catapulting himself around. The photos are on the Net and the doubting compatriots negated. All Brendan hears as he packs up the Transit is the whir of synchronised electric toothbrushes before they leave for the church. It's 10.19 am in Deckland, the sun is out and another expectant day in the life of the BabyBelt unfolds.

Chapter 15

Deckland Dines Out

Joels looks more like a Nissan sales showroom, in keeping with the Naas Road topography, than a restaurant. It has ceiling-to-floor glass windows. You half expect a new silver four-door, top-of-the-range Almera to be suspended from the ceiling, rotating invitingly. Inside, Joels is a little bit of Hawaii on the N7. The colours are Honolulu art deco, lots of yellow and sky-blue which sit incongruously in the plant-hire and Caterpillar-truck surroundings of the Red Cow roundabout. But not quite as out of place as the fake palm trees with embedded flashing Christmas lights which spring up inside Joels. All we need now is a couple of Polynesians shaking their touches in grass skirts.

Joels is uber-Deckland, the BabyBelt's diner of choice. It is nestled on the busiest road in Ireland, a stone's throw from that feat of modern engineering — the forsaken Red Cow roundabout — the watch-word for all Deckland's commuting nightmares. Incidentally only in Ireland with our property fetish could a developer, building a block of apartments directly overlooking Ireland's equivalent of spaghetti junction, get away with trumpeting that vista as *spectacular panoramic views*! But that's the spiel in the brochure for the ludicrously entitled Hillview complex. 'Traffic view', 'snarl view' or maybe just plain, simple, honest 'motorway view' would be more apt. Its sister block, which looks directly onto the M50, is called Highgrove. Now correct me if I am wrong, but isn't a grove a wood, an orchard or a copse, or maybe even a cluster of trees? The closest thing to a grove around here is Woodies DIY garden centre.

Bouncy Castle Brendan pulls up beside the rows of Mitsubishi Galants, Izusus, Pathfinders, Camrys, Corollas and Mazda Premacys. The car park guard nods, clocks the reg and goes back to his *Star*. Brendan peels himself out of the Ford Transit, shirt sticking to the seat. He breathes in that familiar smell and fills his lungs with the essence of deep fat fryer which is blasted out into the West Dublin air by two gigantic, sticky extraction fans.

The place is awash with communion parties, eight-year-olds in shiny fabrics and the GDP of a small African nation in cash in their little matching pearl handbags.

But Brendan's not complaining. Communions are his livelihood and he's here to discuss business with one of the lads who drove for him this morning. Harry is a good skin. He sells and fits plasma screens and Bose home entertainment systems. He has known Brendan for years and helps him out when he's swamped. Harry doesn't do it for the cash alone; the bouncy castle work gives him a chance to see his market from a different angle. Market research he calls it.

Harry used to install Sky dishes, but over the past three years he has been doing full home entertainment fit-outs. He is making out like a bandit with his home entertainment systems — €18,000 each and he has bookings until October. Christmas will be mad. He needs to keep reinvesting the cash to avoid paying tax so he bought two houses off-the-plans in Budapest last week. He hasn't been there, but he has heard it is very sophisticated. He is in Joels with his sister, whose eldest, Hayley, made her communion today. His sister works for one of the big mobile phone companies. Her commission is based on revenue per user. And given that Irish mobile users spend an average of about €570 per year on mobiles as opposed to €360 in Germany and France, she is doing well. We talk even more than the Spaniards, who pride themselves on having a young, chatty population, yet their mobile bill averages about 60 per cent of its Irish equivalent. Because we are a nation of phone addicts, her substantial April bonus went on a new Cherokee jeep. She is the Donatella Versace of the mobile phone business, all peroxide hair, plunging necklines and tit tape. She sits in the middle of the booth, surrounded by friends and family.

Despite doing well at the phone company, she is making even more cash from her nixer. Together with her old school pal, Michelle —

whose son Dwayne with his freshly highlighted tips was also welcomed into the Catholic Church today — she set up a ringtone-selling franchise. She offers over 2,000 different ringtones over the web at €5 each. This is a big business that can be leveraged in a few interesting ways. For example, Donatella can trace the age of her clients and build a database based on the ringtones they choose. Although technically illegal, she sells this database on to her other brother John Paul, who runs a security and home alarm firm. He employs a couple of Russian girls on commission who 'give great phone' and don't mind cold calling to offer deals. Donatella gets fantastic 'pay as you go' phone deals for them as well, so it hardly costs John Paul a penny. The database is useful because anyone with a Toto, Bon Jovi or Guns 'n' Roses ringtone is highly likely to live in a new estate in the BabyBelt. It's an age thing — a late 1980s or early 1990s teenager is likely to be a first-time buyer in 2004. First-time house buyer also means first-time alarm buyer, which suits John Paul. It also fits Harry's bill because alarms and plasma screens go together.

But Harry and Donatella have their eyes set on the real prize. They set up Ireland's first ringtone chart. Like the old singles chart of Top of the Pops fame, the new chart ranks ringtones according to their weekly sales. Harry plans to set up a reality ringtone competition — people text the ringtone they most love or hate to a special premium number so Harry can then have his own chart.

The reality game will involve benchmarking his chart against the real ringtone chart each week. Whoever guesses both the real number one and the most hated number one will get a free phone upgrade and a Blackberry, courtesy of Donatella. Harry pockets all the money from the premium rates. In addition, after a chat with his friend Wayo, who runs an online spread-betting company, he believes he can offer another premium rate line offering buy/sell spread points on the difference between the real ringtone weekly sales winner and his own weekly competition winner. The full-on nation is gambling on anything these days and Wayo's sure the demand is there.

Donatella's boyfriend, Gary, used to work in the alarm business with John Paul but now he runs a team of bouncers who do security for concerts. This summer will be the best ever as there are more concerts in Ireland this summer than almost anywhere else in Europe — Bob Dylan, Kraftwork, Nick Cave, The Streets, Britney Spears and Madonna. What's more, the promoters are suggesting that there is no price sensitivity for tickets. Prices have gone through the roof, but people continue to buy. We spend more per head on concert tickets than any other country in Europe. Scan the entertainment pages of any newspaper this weekend if you doubt the bonanza in live entertainment. Ireland's Oxegen generation are in party mood and Gary is, not for the first-time, cashing in.

Gary is busy until next February but should make his big money on crowd control at the summer's big outdoor events where he can charge double time. It is a good sideline, because the bottom has apparently fallen out of the clubbing market in the past year, where Gary used to make a bit of money on the doors trying to separate the dealers from the ravers. He can spot a dealer at five miles because he used to deal a bit on the side himself, making good money selling ecstasy during the 1990s, but he's clean now. Back then, when the kids were taking four or five pills on a Friday night, Gary was red hot, earning a fortune. He spent his dirty money on seven apartments in Dublin 1, took advantage of the last amnesty and is now a respectable short-term corporate-let landlord.

He doesn't smoke or drink, plays water polo regularly, and his only vice is handling counterfeit Dublin jerseys outside Croke Park on championship Sundays. He believes his mother spent so much in Arnott's on Communion outfits for his seven brothers and sisters that it is only fair to take a bit back now.

Twenty years on, it seems that every communion in Deckland is in Joels for lunch. The place is rocking. Brendan settles into his booth, just under the framed prints of dolphins. Ruth, his 'server', comes to the table with jugs of iced-water and a smile as wide as the Grand Canyon. She has been on some happy server course that only Americans can take seriously — but she has taken it in. 'Ruth', like almost everyone else working the floor, is Chinese.

Joels' menu would make a cardiologist weep. It is a homage to hardened arteries, diabetes, kidney failure and out-sized polyester Real Madrid strips. Everything is deep fried, 'topped' and 'smothered'. The loaded potato wedges are described as 'golden fried potato wedges topped with diced smoked bacon and smothered in melted cheese'. You can almost feel your capillaries clogging as you entertain the 'shallow fried, breaded brie cheese' or the nachos 'topped with melted cheese and served with chips and sour cream dips' or what about the deep fried mushrooms, barbequed chicken wings or let's just have the whole lot together, with what is called a 'table sample' at €14.75 which gives you a bit of everything — deep fried mushrooms, fried onions and wedges together, served with various (unspecified) dips. Joels serves Black Tower at €17.50.

Apart from an almost fruit and vegetable free zone, one of the first things you'll notice about Joels is that everything on the main course is weighed and specifically designed to super-size the eater. You can have the 8-oz breast of chicken with banana and pineapple fritters and grilled bacon. Joels' mini grill could feed three fully grown All Black prop-forwards — 'two sausages, two rashers, a 6-oz burger, topped with an egg, grilled sautéd mushrooms and a tomato'. Just in case you want to see how much stuff you can ingest in one sitting, try the large mixed grill which was obviously invented by the type of people who believe that the blue whale just simply isn't big enough. For €15.50 you are offered a 'large southern breast of chicken, three sausages, two rashers and a half-pounder topped with an egg and a grilled tomato'. If you are feeling particularly peckish you can attempt the 16-oz T-bone steak which is actually heavier than Ruth the Chinese waitress. Tastefully, the menu states that they 'just took the horns and hooves off this one'.

All the burgers of which there are five varieties, smothered and topped with all classes of gooey sauces, can be doubled for just €1.75. Bizarrely, the three pasta dishes, standard carbonara, linguini, primavera, all have the rather inexplicable option of coming with, wait for it, a breast of chicken for just €2 extra! Why? It is amazing that anyone actually fits through the door on the way out. Joels is the culinary equivalent of Hotel California. They claim, because of BSE presumably, that all the meat is heifer beef, but it's not the mad cows at the Red Cow that should concern us, it's the little elephants poured into their communion dresses. After a quick glance at this fare, it is hardly surprisingly that Destiny's Child has a weight problem.

According to the national taskforce on obesity,[1] 27% of eleven-year-old Irish boys and 29% of Irish girls are overweight and little Irish girls from five to eight are ballooning much quicker than boys. One in three is overweight. We go from toddlers to waddlers in a shockingly short period. And, most worryingly, 11% of Irish seven-year-old girls are obese. Like everything else in Ireland there has been a great blurring in fatness. In most countries, rural people are less likely to be obese than city-slickers. Not in Ireland, where there are

slob culchies and slob Dubs and the level of overall obesity is the same
for both groups at 14%. This is an extraordinary figure and deeply
ironic in a country for whom famine and the memory of the famine
is supposed to be part of our identity.

The prevalence of obesity in our children is making them unhappy,
with one in five of our eleven-year-olds saying that they are
dissatisfied with their weight. This figure rises dramatically, to over
one in three by the time the girls are thirteen. Twenty per cent of our
fifth-class girls say they are on diets, while in a recent survey of Dublin
schoolgirls one in five of them said that smoking was part of their
dieting strategy. As for exercise, well it's not surprising they are dieting
because they are not getting out. Decklanders slob around the house.
Ireland has the highest proportion of houses with Sony Playstations,
at an amazing 41%, while levels of DVD and video rental are three
times higher per head here than in Britain.[2]

So if they are not dieting, watching TV, glued to the Playstation or
smoking, they are eating, gorging and expanding. This carry-on is
now being blamed for the dramatic rise in diabetes in Ireland
according to the Diabetes Federation of Ireland:

> Diabetes is the leading cause of cardiovascular disease, kidney failure
> and neuropathy which affects at least half of all people with diabetes.
> Heart disease accounts for 50% of all deaths among diabetes patients
> in Europe. There are currently 200,000 Irish people diagnosed with
> diabetes, while a further 100,000 have diabetes but are unaware that
> they have the condition. Diabetes treatment currently accounts for an
> estimated 10% of the total healthcare budget in Ireland, costing the
> Exchequer approximately €444m annually. It is predicted that the
> incidence of diabetes in Ireland will continue to grow and will have
> doubled by 2010.

If that figure of €444 million sounds big, let me put it in context for
you. We spend more each year on the following nine diabetes-
inducing, refined sugar-based products: Coke, Tayto, 7UP, Club soft
drinks, Dairy Milk, Kit-Kats, Mars Bars, Maltesers and Cadbury's
Roses! Seeing the big picture? Diabetes is Deckland's disease of the
future.[3]

Back in Joels, Brendan and the communion cortege are tucking in.
The service is Milwaukee attentive, 'servers' buzzing around, every

detail seen to. You can buy Joels gift vouchers — the perfect Christmas gift. And, written in the type of script that ambassadors use when inviting politicians to garden parties, is a comment form which asks you to grade food, service and value. The loos are called rest rooms and the doors seem appropriately wider than the average for heroic eaters. And for the young man on a date in Joels, 'vend a scent' dispenses men's cologne for €1. As Deckland prefers cash, there is an ATM in the corner of the restaurant.

Donatella, Harry and Bouncy Castle Brendan are discussing a new venture which involves a three-in-one package giving Decklanders a full entertainment suite. Plasma screens are where the money is, so they have to come up with a plan that ensures Decklanders buy their plasma screens off Harry. Why not offer them a full entertainment and security package? New Decklanders are obsessed with two things; top of the range gadgets and robbers. So they have come up with a plan to offer a screen, alarm and a free bouncy castle for the kid's birthday and special occasions. They will use pester power as the battering ram. What Kells Angel could refuse Destiny's Child and what Destiny's Child could refuse a free bouncy castle?

From travelling around, they have figured out that most owners of plasma screens have children of bouncy castle age and they know their mobile numbers from Donatellas's ringtone database, while Harry's experience installing satellite dishes will be crucial.

In fact nothing maps the growth of Deckland like the growth of Sky. Drive around the new estates of Ireland and the first thing you notice are the Sky dishes. These are the telegraph poles of the 21st century — ubiquitous signs of globalisation and disposable income. Rupert Murdoch has turned suburban Ireland into Skyland. On 1 Jaunary 1999 Sky Digital Ireland had 70,000 customers. In the past six years that figure has risen by 500%.[4] Today there are 355,000 which, coincidentally, is just about equal to the number of new houses built over the same period. They are still experiencing double-digit growth. And while Sky's penetration of the total market is 26%, in the BabyBelt the figure is as high as 40%, revealing two factors: the first is globalisation and the demand for the ninety-six-channel package which is clearly necessary for all young families, the second is that the BabyBelt is stretching so far so quickly that the technological infrastructure such as broadband can't keep up, so the satellite option is the only one they have.

Sky knows where the BabyBelt will extend even before it is built because it does deals with developers to rig up an estate even before the first sod on the site is turned. Where there are sites, there are satellite dishes. Interestingly, ninety years after the 1916 Rising, much of suburban Ireland and England is identical. Because of globalisation, global brands and global sports, the habits of Irish and English Skylanders are almost the same. TV watching has not escaped the great blurring. For example, the pay per view rates for English Premiership soccer are practically identical for Ireland and England. The average revenue per user is €550 per annum here, the same as in England. The number switching off in each country is 9.9% and, more tellingly from a cultural perspective, the ninety-six packages offered to Irish and English punters are exactly the same. Ironically, for Sinn Féin which is targeting the BabyBelt in elections, Skyland is more British today, with more British influences engaging the average commuter every day, than was ever the case when they ruled us!

For Donatella, Harry and Bouncy Castle Brendan, none of this matters. They, like the majority of Decklanders, don't vote. They see an opportunity to become the Rupert Murdochs of the plasma screen world and they are going to go for it. Onwards, upwards and outwards — the motto of Deckland.

Chapter 16

Seducing Breakfast Roll Man

It is early on a damp Friday morning. The traffic is, as always, endless. The head is a bit sore. The few pints last night didn't help. He shouldn't have gone to Diva Nightclub in the Red Cow Complex (I bet you didn't know there was such a micro-conurbation) with the lads but one of the chippies was leaving so he had to turn up. Anyway, it was Diva Party Night and all the drinks were €2 until midnight.

She looked like something out of Girls Aloud, and because of the sunken dance-floor he could check her out all night without having to commit early. It was designed for pulling. Her hair was razor straight, a bit too much fake tan around the ankles, but he didn't see that until later and by then he wasn't complaining. She was good in bed too, not bad for an eighteen-year-old, a bit young for a Hollywood but. She said she was doing a secretarial but he figured she was still in school. He's twenty-four — 'that's almost statutory, mate,' he chuckled to himself.

He had to scarper early, not only to be on site by eight, but he didn't want to meet her Ma. Waking up her sister who shared the room to make her move and sleep downstairs at half-two, was bad enough. She said her Ma wouldn't mind, but all the same there are still some rules. He took her number but she said she wouldn't have credit 'til later. He might call her, see how the day goes.

Breakfast Roll Man needed food, a bottle of Lucozade and a few solpos and he'd be fine. Jesus, where was he? She must have lived miles away and he shouldn't have driven. The first drag of his squashed Johnny Blue which he had just spent ages straightening out, made him shiver a bit, but now he is where he has wanted to be for the past twenty excruciating minutes, at the hot food counter of EuroSpar. Chicken drumsticks, chicken wings, hot panini sandwiches, a pizza or Danish. Will he try something else? No, fuck it. It was no time for culinary adventure at ten past seven on a Friday morning with a raging hangover, three hours' kip and a clinging wan who wanted to introduce you to her nuclear family. Anyway, the usual was only €3.39.

    – A full breakfast roll please, love.

    – Wha' ya want?

    – Sausage, rasher, hash brown, black pudding, tomato, egg and mushroom.

He is dazed, staring at the side of the hot food counter supplied by Martin Food Equipment, Dundalk, watching the condensation dribble onto the congealed oven plate of solid scrambled egg. Cuisine de France ads are everywhere. He bets the French baguette and smelly cheese merchants never expected black and white pudding smothered in brown sauce dripping over their poncey baguettes.

    – That's the lot?

    – No, The Star, 20 Blue, two bottles of Lucozade, a pack of Solpos, a six pack of Actimel and a Twix, please.

His mobile goes. He knew that ring-tone was cat. Oasis covers. What was he thinking about? Two lads smirk in the queue behind him. Switch it off.

    – Thanks.

    – See youz fucks on site.

He climbs back into his jeep. Life is sweet. Sweeter had they not sold United to Glazer but he reckoned that if Glazer was smart, which he was, why would he have any interest in standing over the decline of the club? Anyway, one of the lads on the site yesterday had made the good point that all clubs go into decline. Look what happened to Liverpool and it was only a matter of time before United went the same way, Glazer or no Glazer. Breakfast Roll Man was Liverpool through and through until they got so poor he slipped allegiances to United. His brother never forgave him and his Dad brought it up during family rows, saying it pointed to a deep weakness of character, a profound and enduring absence of loyalty. And look where loyalty got his father. Twenty years at Dunlops getting paid piss, followed by a decade on the rock 'n' roll.

He checks his tool belt, dusts off his jeans which had been in the back all night. You can't get into clubs in your work stuff, so most of the lads carry a spare set of clothes — usually stuffed into a Centra plastic bag — on Thursdays and Fridays. He pulls on his hard toed boots and Columbia fleece over the heavy check shirt and T-shirt. He calls the lads. They are on their way in the contractor's minibus from Navan. It's been a good week. Breakfast Roll Man has three lads working for him and two other apprentices. They're all from Ballincollig in Cork originally but now only get home for the Munster final. They're scattered all over Kildare and Meath. That's where the work is. Houses and rents are fairly cheap too and this particular gaffer likes them. He's from Togher, 'Bar's country, and usually looks after them.

Breakfast Roll Man wouldn't mind a job in Dublin for the buzz and a chance to see that Argentinian au pair again. Maybe he'll work in Spencer Dock in the summer, but he's not well in down there. Anyway, why move now? He's cleaning up here. He took home over €100K last year, has his gaff in Inchicore and the apartment in Alicante and he's just signed on a place in Florida off-the-plans. It'll have guaranteed rental income for three years and after that he's sure it will be easy to flog. The bank gave him interest only so it'll wipe its face. Alicante is vacant most of the time, no-one can move anything down there, but it only cost him €59K and he hardly sees that coming out of the account each month. He's been down once in two years and the brother and his mates went down for his 21st and wrecked the place.

He sticks on the Gorillaz, puts her into second and throws on his Hiviz vest because it's still cold even in May. He hates that about the site, the cold and the filth. When he hears civil servants complaining about pay he wonders if they would work in these conditions. It is the Irish version of the New Orleans Superdome. Someone should do a programme about the conditions on Irish sites. There's no safety. The toilets are always blocked or broken. There is no running water. Lads are shitting everywhere, the smell is atrocious and the place is degrading. There is rubbish everywhere and fellas are risking death every day. The problem is the buildings are going up so quickly, there is hardly any time to think, let alone plan the site.

Not only are the sites going up quickly but the developers are so keen to get rid of them that soon after the showhouse goes up the team is cut in half and they are on to the next job, leaving the people who have paid their deposits waiting years for completion. This is because once the deposits are in, the developer can bank the site and move on. He has to move on or else he will face a huge tax bill on profits so he rolls over the development and ploughs cash into the next place. Also with such a demand for lads, a good developer has to keep his crews working even in fallow periods. No-one wants to be hiring fresh outfits these days.

The site is announced by a huge sign: 'Gorteen Heights — an ideal family base, only €315,000 interest paid for the first year'. Below the sign, scurrying about like ants, is a sea of bright luminous yellow. Hundreds of Breakfast Roll Men in their identical bright yellow Hiviz bibs, white hard hats, and hair matted by sweat and the constant dust, red fleeces and gingham shirts, scuffed Timberlands and frayed jeans, tool belts hanging down like a scruffy straight version of Village People. One in eight of the Irish workforce gets up every day to work in the construction industry. Breakfast Roll Men are the pumping heart of the economy. They take home on average €45,000 per year. They are now building more houses in Ireland than the Germans were building just after the war as part of their all-out national effort to rebuild the country. The building industry has trebled in size since 1995. This explains Breakfast Roll Man's apartment in Florida. The construction industry has made Dermot Desmond even richer with its insatiable demand for Celtic away strips.

At lunchtime he's back at the hot food counter. The blood sugar levels have plummeted again, he needs soakage — lasagne, authentic pizzas, chicken wings, beef stroganoff, chicken Thai curry, southern fried chicken in a burger bap or barbeque ribs smothered in a hot, spicy Chinese sauce, or he could go for the second breakfast roll of the day. But this time he pitches for chicken in a bap, a few more bottles of Lucozade and a Red Bull. The same Chinese girl with the Helen name tag who was smiling at seven this morning is still there, hair tied up in a net, under a Spar visor, pristine uniform, the same inscrutable eyes and that Chinese way of covering her mouth when she giggles.

From the standard, ubiquitous CCTV camera, unbeknownst to himself, Breakfast Roll Man is being watched. He is part of the Spar generation — a shopper with no loyalty who wants convenience, wants it now, close at hand and wants it in the car. Why do you think

Irish garages which were once petrol stations and then newsagents are now Mandarin-speaking twenty-four-hour restaurants with names like Night and Day? This is the new face of suburban Ireland and Breakfast Roll Man is its chief architect, head financier, town planner and designer.

He and his generation are driving the enormous profits in Ireland's fastest-growing retail sector — the convenience store market. If An Taisce wants to know what the Irish suburban landscape is going to look like, they should talk to the carpenters, sparks and plumbers of the country rather than academics, environmental correspondents, local politicians and tasteful tree surgeons. Napoleon once said that an army marches on its stomach. Well, the Irish BabyBelt marches on the hung-over Ned Kellys of its tradesmen, craving instant hot-food, Lucozade and Twixes. These lads will have a bigger impact on the landscape and streetscape of Ireland than any government taskforce, EU environmental directive or regional plan.

Hot-food-to-go sales increased by 50–60% in Ireland in 2004. The big retailers now say that this is where the cash is and may account for 20% of their entire profits next year. Breakfast Roll Man lies in the fault-line between the discount stores of Lidl and Aldi, the big players like Tesco and the smaller stores like Spar and Centra. Their corporate strategies overlap inside his head. Their planning teams are looking for sites in the suburbs where he lives and their marketing questionnaires respond to his answers. Nothing will be done without his imprimatur and yet he is unaware of this.

He has no idea that every time he chooses a Southern Fried Chicken Bap over a Breakfast Roll, it signals a chain of events and calculations, forecasts and projections made at head office which will decide what will be the next big thing in the stores. Every time he buys a packet of smokes, petrol and Maxim, he is being slotted into a category, every time he picks up a girl, gets two hours' sleep and bolts from a suburban house like a burglar before dawn, his movements are being tracked.

In response to Breakfast Roll Man, the retailers have sent out special SWAT teams to the US to see what the future will hold. They know they can't beat the discount stores on price, but they know too that our hero and his mates have so many crisp fifties in their wallets that money isn't the issue. How will we seduce Breakfast Roll Man? The shops try to tempt him at every turn. For example, when he gets home tonight, the EuroSpar in Inchicore will be his temptress. It is built just under his block of apartments. (Actually, for those in the property game, there is a strong argument to suggest that the best leading indicators of urban gentrification are Spars and Centras. Their planning departments scour the city every day looking for new sites which are determined by population density and the right demographic — singletons and young couples living together — who also happen to be the best renters. If you see a Spar sign beneath the dusty hoarding on the ground floor of a half-built apartment block in any town or city, you know you have your anchor tenant who has done all your research for you. As long as the market is going up, your place over the Spar will go up more than most.)

Eurospar doesn't have a door. They call it a portal. The lights in Eurospar will be gently dimmed for the evening. The aim is to light the product, not the shop. Breakfast Roll Man can have a coffee in the Starbucks-like café area in the front, with papers and copies of *Loaded* strewn around casually. He can log on, if he wants. When he feels like shopping, he will first encounter an Arcadian vision of abundant fruit in rustic boxes, overflowing with apples, grapes and bananas. Eve wouldn't be out of place here. All is calm, unobtrusive and bountiful. Above all the fruit and veg displays are large portraits of the suppliers — wholesome fruit farmers from north Dublin under the slogan 'A passion for goodness'. This is to appeal to Breakfast Roll Man's possible health concerns. What could be more natural than local produce, locally served? The signs are early-20th-century hand-written in chalk-effect plastic boards, to give the impression of an old-world cavernous fruit market down by the docks somewhere. He can almost hear the steamers. Nostalgia sells, it comforts and soothes. He has been here before. This place is part of his family tree. He is not shopping: he is experiencing. Looking across over this 21st-century Garden of Eden, beyond the crates spilling over with avocados and pears, he sees an old print of the 1950's legendary St Patrick's Athletic team — all grainy black and white, short back 'n' sides and brown stitched leather ball. This was an innocent time, when shopping was local, everyone knew each other, the tenements were full of characters and everyone looked out for the other. Just beside it is a picture of the last tram which left the Tramyard in 1959. The image is clear. Eurospar is part of local history and local history is Eurospar. Jim Sheridan couldn't have made it up.

Breakfast Roll Man isn't the best in the kitchen so he makes for the chef, kitted out in full white chef's battle fatigue, fully equipped knives, skewers and the sense of purpose of Gordon Ramsay. If you didn't know better, you might expect him to unveil a Michelin three-star, gourmet dinner. But this is the hot-food counter of the Spar in Inchicore.

– *What does Sir fancy this evening*? says the Polish chef, showing the enthusiasm of a new starter. *We have three types of* BBQ *chicken in three sizes, stuffed chicken, breaded chicken nuggets or southern fried chicken portions, all come with suggested wine.*

– *Chicken nuggets.*

Breakfast Roll Man swivels around the detergent and household goods aisle, past the three girls in Bank of Ireland uniforms who are comparing moisturisers. This makes him think, for the first time since this morning, of Karen, Carol, Claire? What was her name, his schoolgirl from Ratoath? Maybe the four missed calls were from her. Who cares?

He arrives at the off-licence. The floor changes from supermarket tiles to knotted, hardwood planks, sprinkled with effect sawdust. The lights are softer and the dog-eared map of the Andalusian wine region is a reassuringly faded yellow. Above the wines there is a ship's galley effect with authentic-looking port boxes and the 'New World Wine of the Week', a rich Australian Merlot, can be sampled, while sitting on upturned old wine crates marked Santiago de Chile. The special offer case of the week sits on original wooden Guinness barrels from St James's Gate. The cross-merchandising is implicit. In order to maximise sales per metre, there are bottle openers, lemons, mixers and Alka Seltzer, Panadol and Disprin in the off-licence.

Subconsciously, Breakfast Roll Man grabs a couple of packets of Panadol as well as two bottles of the Merlot and makes for the checkout but gets side-tracked by the smell of fresh bread into the bakery and the cute Italian girl. He saw something on Channel 4 the other night about eating too much sliced pan bloating his bag. And as he couldn't be bothered going to the gym maybe he should eat some of this other stuff instead. Giovanna introduces herself and proceeds to offer him a Pecan Raisin Oval or a Rosemary Olive Oil Round. Maybe he wants a Sesame Seed Baguette or just a Sourdough Loaf? Breakfast Roll Man began to glaze over. What about a sliced pan, he thinks to himself, but goes for one of them, he can't remember which one. The Russian cashier tells him to have a nice day which at half eight at night is a bit hopeful — she must have learned it on her corporate meet-and-greet course — and it was probably the extent of her English. She gives him €100 cash-back and smiles to reveal her uneven teeth like headstones in an ancient church yard. The communists were not big on braces. Off he goes to watch the UEFA Cup final on his new 42-in. plasma screen which he bought last week. Bliss: soccer, food, wine and bed. Maybe he'll call Karen later after all.

At the door he brushes past a group of five Chinese students. Helen tries to catch his eye, but he doesn't see her and they all look the same to him anyway. She has just finished her twelve-hour shift at Spar. Her legs are tired from standing, but she has left Dublin and is back in China the minute she sits into the minibus which ferries about forty Chinese students from their work on the Navan Road back to their three flats in Inchicore. Breakfast Roll Man had no idea that they live in the same block, Kilmainham Heights in the Tramyard. But then again there are 400 apartments in the complex. They are the first of four huge developments going up, which will ensure that the complexion of the area will change dramatically over the coming years.

Helen has been living and working in Ireland for eighteen months. She is twenty-three, but looks younger. She comes from Dalian, one of the most prosperous cities in China. The biggest star in Dublin's Chinaland, Oliver Wang, also comes from there. On the way back to Inchicore in the van, they listen to Oliver Wang's 'Voice of Chinatown' talk radio programme on Anna Livia. Oliver, a camp, effete and very stylish gay man with an Irish boyfriend, is a godsend. His programme broadcasts to an audience of around 40,000 Dublin Chinese every week. That's a considerably bigger audience than many celebrity broadcasters, yet it is almost exclusively Chinese. Oliver Wang's other programme at the weekends is a must. The 'Voice of China' tells Helen everything she needs to know, what's going on, what the rate of pay should be, what's the story with visas, who are the best employers, how to send money home cheaply, where to get the best internet and phone prices and most crucially where to find a job or an apartment. What's more, because Oliver is from her city, it's like a girl from Dundalk having access to LMFM in Beijing. Comforting.

Back home, she went to private schools, where she excelled in mathematics, science and foreign languages, primarily English. She has already attended university, obtaining not only a bachelor's degree but a Master's too. Hers are the most educated hands ever to fill a breakfast roll.

She herself is upper-middle-class in China, the one and only child of well-to-do, Communist Party card-carrying parents who have invested their life savings and those of their parents to send their 'little empress' (real name Liang Liang) to learn English in Dublin, Ireland.

This support notwithstanding, 'Helen' must work at Spar far above the twenty-hours-a-week permitted by her student visa, so as to be able to pay her way in rip-off Ireland (where the minimum wage is now a whole €7.65 per hour, and Spar doesn't go much above this). Officially she attends an English-language school in town (Quick Learn Language School) for full-time tuition, but in fact she rarely attends as she is too busy working and making money. But that's okay, because Tom, the former Department of Justice official who saw an opportunity with the arrival of the first refugees in 1998 and who runs the school, always gives students Certificates of Attendance required by his mates at the Department of Justice just so long as the €5,000 fees are paid on time. Tom is on a five-year career break on full pension.

Helen has considered using a fake certificate of attendance the next time she applies for her visa renewal, as friends of hers have got away with it, but then she read on an internet bulletin board that the department has been cracking down.

She lives in Inchicore above Breakfast Roll Man, in a two-bedroom flat that she shares with eight other Chinese, including her boyfriend — if her parents knew she had a boyfriend, let alone that she was living with him, they would have a major knicker-fit and would probably make her come home immediately. That's one of the advantages of living in Ireland. In China a respectable girl isn't even seen holding hands with a boy. They found the flat through an ad in the *Shining Emerald* newspaper and a few of the flatmates came through an ad on the notice board in the Asia Market.

She doesn't mind sharing with eight others — it provides company, just like when she shared a dorm room with twenty other girls at university in China — and it makes the rent affordable (€1,500 per month, divided by nine people). And at least here they have plenty of hot and cold water whenever they want it, adjustable central heating and no prurient dorm supervisors — they've never had it so good.

They cook and eat communally as much as their varied work schedules allow — the rest of her flatmates work in petrol stations, cafés, bars, and other convenience shops. Communal eating and drinking is a big deal for them.

They spend a fair amount of time in these hole-in-the-wall Internet café joints, where they get special rates between 10 pm–8 am — maybe €10 for the whole night, which they use for emailing and instant-messaging each other and friends back home, and participating for hours on end in role-playing games.

Most of the boys also love to gamble, both online and with other Chinese in Dublin — they would now be the main customers in the arcades around the city, and a growing segment for the casinos such as the Merrion Club too. In fact, problems associated with gambling are the main reason that the Chinese community would come to the attention of the Irish authorities.

Their main social outlets are eating in other Chinese friends' apartments and maybe singing a little karaoke, or watching pirated DVDs of movies not yet out in the US (they saw the 'new' *Star Wars* movie last December), and going to the UCG cinema on Parnell Street — they have four UCG Unlimited Cards between the nine of them (€15.99/month unlimited movies) and they use them a lot.

For special occasions like birthdays and Chinese New Year, they will go to a restaurant together. The etiquette here is crazy — who sits where, who chooses the food, who pours the drinks, and most of all who gets to pay the bill. And of course they get the secret menu and probably a private room.

Helen shops mostly in Aldi or Lidl or travels to the northside to discount places there — you know the type of Moore Street shops that come and go. She also has a discount arrangement with the Spar she works in, and her flatmate who works in a Chinese restaurant brings home buckets of free food. She'll occasionally go to the Asia Market or similar places on Camden Street for something from home when she feels down, like after she found out that her boyfriend had been two-timing her with one of her roommates. But the Asia Market is very expensive so it's only for special occasions. Helen and her flatmates also buy foodstuff in bulk through some connection to the restaurant trade, and of course her parents send over as many treats from home as they can.

What does she think of de paddies? Outside of work, and the

occasional racist taunt from school kids on the street, she actually doesn't have too much contact with any of the natives. She has never been invited to an Irish person's home, and has only been inside a pub once — what a bizarre sight. She doesn't really mind the Irish, so long as they leave her alone. They don't seem like bad people, and their country's economy is certainly doing very well, just as China's is beginning to.

And she is used to seeing construction workers everywhere, just like home — the only difference is that in Ireland the builders wear security gear, and seem to have lots and lots of cold hard cash in their pockets — many of them simply leave the change behind when they buy their breakfast roll and a copy of the *Star*, which makes up about 10% of her wage.

She likes the openness and the freedom enjoyed by Irish people to live their lives as they want to. But she also sees the downsides of such freedom: endemic shoplifting in the Spar by young kids, all that porn on the top shelf, so much drunkenness and the random violence outside the Spar and on the streets at night.

She will stay in Ireland for another year or two, and maybe try to get a qualification first — one or two of her friends are studying for business degrees from Griffith College. But eventually she will go home to China, as all her friends intend to as well, to live in one of the big cities, and use her English-language skills and foreign experience to land a job that has been outsourced to China from the West, probably Ireland.

We are cannibalising ourselves by educating and hosting the very people who will eventually take our jobs — and in the great blurring we don't even notice.

Chapter 17

Opposition to Deckland

THE SEVEN DEADLY SINS

Are we living through terrible times, losing ourselves in gluttony, greed and lust worthy of Dante's *Inferno*? Or have the past five years been a financial liberation for hundreds of thousands of Irish people — the first generation not to suffer under the depression of economic under-achievement? The jury is very much out.

Listening to media comment on the economy, it would be easy not only to be pessimistic, but also a bit confused. The charges against the Expectocracy are significant. This is what they say. People are working long hours only to feel less secure in their jobs. We are having children but we never see them. We have outsourced parenting often to understaffed crèches and will reap a vicious harvest of depraved youth. We have more golf courses than children's playgrounds. We are buying houses but are pinned to our collars. No-one has control over his own life anymore. The corporation is subjugating the family. Rural Ireland is being destroyed by one-off housing or rural Ireland is being destroyed by not enough one-off housing. Banks are lying and ripping us off, yet we continue to get into even greater debt. Our spiritual values have disappeared and all we do is shop to ease the problems of life with vacuous retail therapy. The future is Tesco. Ireland is losing its soul. We are obsessed by money. The environment is being destroyed. We can't trust our water or our food. We don't know our neighbours. We are becoming atomised. Nobody talks any

more. Our teenagers are drunken, fornicating yobs. Come to think of
it, our thirtysomethings are drunken, fornicating yobs. The health
service is in ruins and getting worse. Standards are slipping. Suicides,
depression and hedonism are rampant. Oil is running out. There are
dark forces behind the media, playing us like violins. The end is nigh.

This type of carry-on is familiar to any of us who read the papers,
listen to the radio or watch TV. Our commentary has become infused
with Endism. We might call it the Liveline School of Futurology.
Depending on who you are listening to, Ireland and the Irish can
resemble the damned in Dante's *Inferno*. We have succumbed to the
Seven Deadly Sins and Joe Duffy is our Dante.

On the other hand, survey after survey roundly refutes the
horsemen of the apocalypse view. On the contrary, the Irish are
amongst the most happy in Europe. It is the best place to live in the
EU, according to international research from the *Economist*. Over 70%
of us are happy with our standard of living. Four out of every five are
content with our personal relationships. We have the *craic*. Sure
everyone loves us. Far from not talking to each other, 72% of us know
and speak to our neighbours regularly. As opposed to being not
spiritual, nine out of ten Irish people believe in God, while nearly a
quarter of us think reincarnation is likely. Over three-quarters of us
are happy with our families and over 80% consider ourselves very
healthy.

We are amongst the richest people in Europe and are building assets
for the next generation at a rate not seen anywhere since the great
American expansion of the 1950s. We are taking more holidays abroad
then ever. We are living longer than any generation before us. We
spend more on cat food than on Third-World debt forgiveness. Yes, so
we are a bit frivolous, but that's our prerogative. We are at work in
greater numbers than ever before. Only one in ten of us is worried
about losing our job next year as opposed to one in four for the EU
average. After working all day 18% of us are too tired to do housework,
but 40% of Spaniards feel similarly wrecked in the evening. In Europe,
only the French are more fulfilled in their lives. We are the fourth most
trusting people in Europe, suggesting that people are generally well
intentioned, honest and straight up. Only 4% of Irish people, the
second lowest in the EU, say that they are having difficulty making ends
meet.[1] In contrast to the Liveline School of Futurology, 85% of us are
either optimistic or very optimistic about the future.[2] All of us agree

that we've the best football fans in the world.

So what are we to make of these two very contrasting views of Irish daily life, our psychology and the state of the nation? One view suggests that the end is nigh and the other that the future has never looked so bright. One view says we are all close to depression and the other contends that we are ecstatically happy. How can we explain such bi-polar analysis? Why does the world of the Pope's Children, the Kells Angels, Destiny's Child and DIY Declan seem so confused? Why does the Irish Expectocracy mean so many different things to so many people and why are these views so heartfelt? To get a handle on this we should try to examine how the opposition to Deckland sees itself. How do those who reject Deckland, its cash, its flashness, its values and its optimism regard themselves?

THE REJECTIONIST CACOPHONY

In Ireland, the coalition against Deckland, Destiny's Child, the Expectocracy, its bouncy castles and plasma screens, is a disparate and unusually diverse alliance. The coalition is driven by pessimism. It fears that we are running up a cultural, economic, environmental, social, political, familial, religious, musical or religious cul de sac. Endism reigns. Take your pick of possible Armageddons.

In his study of pessimism in Britain *Up the down Escalator* Charles Leadbetter portrays those who reject progress as a diverse coalition united by what they are against more than what they are for. In Ireland, we see similar developments, the rejectionists come in all shapes and sizes, right and left, revolutionaries and reactionaries, religious cultists and cultural commentators.[3] We can add to this group, Hibernian nationalists and global cosmopolitans, traditionalists and visionaries, Sinn Féiners and Fine Gaelers, environmentalists, corporatists, young crusties and old fogies.

The speed of societal change is generating such heat that arguments are being turned on their heads, entrenched positions are melting away and old foes are falling into each others' arms. Old-fashioned right-wingers say we are losing our identity, moving away from the family, the community and the Church and are replacing these solid foundations with the spurious gratification of consumerism, brands and money. Similarly, old-fashioned left-wingers state we are losing the strong, humane sense of ourselves, as our communities are being atomised by greedy landlords, our family life is being torn apart by corporations, we are losing our concern for the poor, the state bureaucracy has allowed avarice to replace planning and we are melting the bonds between the various classes, all for the spurious gratification of consumerism, brands and money. Old right and old left are fusing together.

In turn, the greedy landlords say we are being undone by stodgy bureaucrats, while the stodgy bureaucrats say the greedy landlords are the real enemy. Corporations say that by giving a livelihood to the family they are helping to keep them together; psychologists claim the opposite and contend that stress is gnawing away at the fabric of the family. Traditionalists claim that commuting is killing the Kells Angels, yet overlook the fact that the Kells Angels are the first Irish generation for centuries who are able to actually live in the same country as their parents if they choose to.

Secular urban trade unionists worry about the destruction of the food chain by large superstores that are industrialising the food process and thus endangering our health and the jobs of workers. Yet their former enemies, the rural Catholic fundamentalists, also believe that farmers are being eliminated by the same forces. Pro-choice left-wingers worry that we are losing our sovereignty; so too do the anti-abortion Christians. Ivana Bacik meets Dana and both speak of the threat that is the European constitution.

The common ground for all these forces is that we are losing some core values that make us Irish. Liberal, EU-loving, social democrat commentators see American-style consumerism as the enemy, while American-style Christians see European social democratic secularism as the great Satan. Both feel that people are losing their identities or balance. The old see the young as the problem. The young see the old as out-of-touch. If you are a European-style liberal, you see our young being corrupted by American advertising but if you are an old-style Catholic, you see European sexual decadence preying on our young.

The Sandymount sophisticate sees a lack of planning and the car ruining the land, while the Castleisland culchie sees too much planning and the lack of transport ruining local communities. Sinn Féin see rampaging globalisers such as managers at Intel ruining the work force, while the rampaging globalising Intel managers see Sinn Féin's economics ruining the opportunities for the work force.

Protesters as diverse as the 'reclaim the streets' merchants and the St Thérèse of Lisieux processionists seek common ground in opening

204 The Pope's Children

up the streets to marches, campaigners and religious observants. Virulently anti-clerical Socialist Workers Party activists and virulently anti-socialist conservative Church leaders lead the anti-globalisation protests. Everything is blurred.

Bottom-up lobby groups believe that the government is ignoring democracy and is being driven by marketing suits, while the government believe that single-issue lobby-groups advised by cynical PR firms have hi-jacked democracy. The politicians believe that the media have too much power, while the media contend they are muzzled by libel laws. The entrepreneurs think there is too much red tape and the red-tapers believe there is too much freedom. Conservatives are worried about the pace of immigration. So too are liberals. Liberals believe the place will lose in its generous sense of itself if we don't allow enough immigrants in, while conservatives contend that the place will lose its generous sense of itself if we do. Moralists say the family is being destroyed by creeping liberal agendas such as divorce and cohabitation, while liberals say the family's space is being privatised by large corporations who control TV, DVD and Playstations. To the liberals, hard work is ruining the family by robbing parents of their time with their children, resulting in over-tired TV dinner families plonked in front of reality TV programmes. On the other hand, traditionalists see hard work as the saviour of the family, instilling values, mores and discipline to children at a young age. Old-fashioned anti-clerical liberals see money as the root of all evil but so too do the Ten Commandment Catholics for whom money is a false god.

The common theme between all these disparate forces is that the headlong pursuit for individual happiness is destroying the community and leading to a selfish and degenerate nation. Romantic Ireland, in both cases, is dead and gone; it's with O'Leary in the grave. But by flying us all over Europe for half nothing it's O'Leary who is ruining Irish tourism, and by flying half of Europe in here he is turning us into a theme park!

And theme park is a description that both traditional Hibernian conservatives and New-Age, cosmopolitan liberals constantly use to describe the country. Ireland has become a plastic-Paddy, Fáilte Ireland cardboard cut-out of out-sized jolly green giants, Guinness ads and fake signs to Skibbereen in pre-packed, take-away Irish pubs. There is nothing real here. We are fabrication.

All these disparate groups are searching for the authentic Ireland.

The Gweedore-based, Irish-speaking, fáinne-wearing, Provo-loving teetotaller and the suburban, cliché-ridden, dreadlocked, tattooed, pot-smoking Crusty are finally at one. Both are seeking out the real Ireland. Both think the outside forces of marketing, branding, consumerism, secularism and other big things have robbed us of something precious whether it is our smallness, our uniqueness, our Irishness, our pagan mysticism or our Catholic clarity. We are becoming all the same, a homogenised bloc of brand managers' fodder, we have become degenerate, we are nothing. No, we are worse than nothing.

Joe Duffy was right all along: the place is going to the dogs and all we can do is ring Joe and moan. The seven deadly sins have infected us. We are greedy, proud, angry, slothful, gluttonous, envious and lustful. Ireland is set to burn in an all-encompassing consumerist inferno.

Given all the opposing views to the present Expectocracy and the fact that so many believe it is going to end in tears, it might be useful to examine some of the most conspicuous dissenters from the present regime. In the next few pages we will examine four powerful groups of people who feel Deckland is doomed and with it the soul of Ireland. These are the Rural Nostalgists, the Carrot Juice Contrarians, the Economic Enquirers and the Confused Cosmopolitans.

THE RURAL NOSTALGISTS

Every year, in the thoroughly modern, Internet-savvy town of Ennis, the Ceifin Conference hosts its annual bash. The organiser is Fr Harry Bohan. Harry is an excellent man, tall and robust with a shock of thick grey hair, who speaks from the heart and for ordinary people. He also has the extra local kudos of having managed the Clare hurlers before they won anything so he has paid his dues. He is heavily involved in rural resettlement and believes passionately that Ireland is waltzing into an economic, moral and social cul de sac which will scar not just the face, but the soul of the nation. He regards what is going on in his county as a microcosm of what is occurring throughout the country and he does not like it. We have heard the charges before, but they are worth reiterating — over-development, rampant consumerism, environmental vandalism, alcohol dependency, resulting mental illness and the huge stress being put on young families on average incomes by the cost of housing, child care and keeping up appearances. Each year, Fr Harry draws together top-notch speakers who try to articulate, tease out and confront these problems and offer certain solutions.

The conference, like all others, has a well-known chairperson and the usual combination of commentators, academics and business people as well as grass-roots activists sitting on a panel, taking questions from the floor and giving their own pitch. For each speaker, it's a chance to shine. For budding intellectuals it is the beginning of a process that will hopefully culminate in the holy grail of the commentariat, John Bowman's 'Questions and Answers' and possibly a weekly column. Panellists may have a single transferable speech slightly doctored to take into account the different audience or they may be unveiling a new thesis on its maiden outing, but the key is to get into a national newspaper — so say something provocative. The surroundings are pleasant and with ample EU funding for the chattering classes, there might even be a fee in it. Ultimately, this is an opportunity to network and have the customary rake of pints after the gig while you nod sagaciously with some big thinker or other.

Unlike other gabfests, the Ceifin conference attendees are different. They are good people, interested in the state of the nation. However, they are drawn from the 'it's just not right' brigade, heavily rural with an ample sprinkling of nuns and priests and farmers' representatives. The atmosphere is more Brussels sprouts than mange touts. Also represented are environmentalists, language revivalists, old-style liberation theologians and the few remaining Quakers in the country. While they are debating the future, it is hard not to draw the conclusion that many would actually like to go back to the past. They seem to yearn for the certainty of the old days when Ireland was poor, pious, pretty and protected. They appear to lament the passing of Church dominance, but most of all, they miss order and predictability. They are probably the last generation to wear headscarves. They applaud speakers who ask rhetorically whether in this headlong dash to the future, we are forgetting something.

The hall nods in unison — like synchronised North Korean children — when panellists allege there is too much freedom, or paraphrase Paul McCartney with 'money can't buy me love' speeches. In general, there is an undercurrent that the forces building up outside and inside the country are propelling us off on the track that can only lead to chaos. Immigration, globalisation, money sloshing around the globe, Islam, Rupert Murdoch and Roman Abramovich are all conspiring to change the nation and no-one seems to have a plan, a vision or an answer. For many in the audience, the future is bleak in an alien, indescribable way. Our children don't see their children and have to outsource parenting to crèches and child-minders. The old world of the stay-at-home mothers and the manly fathers going out to work, providing for all, has passed and they do not like it. What they see most of all is the lack of a guiding hand or the gentle nudge of a greater force on the tiller. They see grand conspiracies, orchestrated by a political or social elite, miles away, which are affecting their lives. They feel remote.

In general, they have a microscopic rather than telescopic view and regard all that is small, local and Irish as good. In contrast things that are big, urban and foreign are bad. So tiny one-off houses using local timber, built by lads from the village, is good whereas a large development financed by outside builders, using Lithuanian carpenters and sold off-the-plans by a city estate agent, is bad.

Rural nostalgists go to Mass. They voted against divorce and against abortion and for the citizenship referendum. They want to conserve Ireland the way it is and not change further because, possibly rightly, they see a false nirvana in the economics, politics and philosophy of Deckland. The rural nostalgist buys the RTÉ *Guide*. Despite being nationalist, the rural nostalgists have no truck with Sinn Féin and deify St John Hume. Today they couldn't tell you who runs the SDLP. They remain, despite Fr Harry's ecumenicist leanings, rather sceptical of Protestants and think Ratzinger was the logical choice. They are evenly split between Fianna Fáil and Fine Gael. They supported Mary McAleese in the first Presidential election and guessed she was speaking the truth when she compared Northern Protestants to Nazis. They have elderly cousins in the US. Some know the geography of Boston better than Dublin. Daniel O'Donnell and Count John McCormack are their stars.

Rural nostalgists live in houses with Sacred Hearts, concrete blocks in the drive and garage extensions. They talk to Joe and lap up *VIP* magazine in the doctor's surgery. The rural nostalgists are pure Hibernians and many have difficulty with the opening up of Croke Park to foreign games, particularly soccer. They see consumerism and increased indebtedness as a one-way ticket to national degeneration, and believe that the country is being run by a far-off elite in Dublin, Brussels or Washington. They want the country to slow down and they bristle when Mary Harney describes the Irish as a good workforce. The rural nostalgists assert that the nation cannot be reduced to a workforce and think we have lost the plot, the inimical liberal agenda has won and it is time for the country to go back to traditional values with nation, Church and family at the core.

THE CARROT JUICE CONTRARIANS

The flyers are up in the farmers' market. The goatees are agitated. It's time to reclaim the streets. Indymedia types have their camcorders on stand-by. It's time to fight the power and the enemy is Monsanto — a company so large that it owns the environment, the trees, the very DNA that makes up our ecosystem. The Rathmines Chapter is ready. So too are the ageing right-on pundits with their Nicaragua Libre slogans and quotes from Daniel Ortega (before he joined Pizza Hut's payroll). The fun-day kicks off at two and the debate will be the focal point. On hand will be face painters, street performers, comedians who couldn't fill Vicar Street and the gap-year jugglers. The venue is the Ark in Temple Bar — a children's centre in the least child-friendly city centre in Europe.

These are scruffy people. The younger ones don't like shaving. The older ones wear T-shirts far too late in life and have been fighting the power for so many years they fail to see that by now they are pretty powerful themselves. Let's call them Carrot Juice Contrarians. Fair-trade is the issue and Tesco — the fastest growing supermarket in the land — is the enemy. The Carrot Juice Contrarians claim that big business wants to take ownership of our food chain, revealing a horrific vista where commerce owns science. It is time to protest. The theme of the debate is 'Will Globalisation poison our planet for our children?' There is no dissent.

After the debate, various Green and Labour politicians will walk — cutely hand-in-hand like school children afraid of the traffic — up to the Dáil and drop in a signed petition saying no to genetically modified food. All sorts are there. There are bike couriers in dreads. Young girls in tie-dye T-shirts and the dreaded bongo player. The son of a bank manager from Trees Road in Mount Merrion is there, stripped to the waist, puffing into a didgeridoo. There are lots of skinny lads on bikes blowing whistles. The authentic crepe factory (quite a shameless marketing pitch) is doing a roaring trade. Instead of toffee apples, the kids have carrot sticks. The organic lovers are there fingering bulbous spuds, the more gnarled and swollen the better. Women who have gone grey early carry children in home-slings which on closer inspection have the Authentic Africa brand. The look is dungarees, flat shoes and wrist straps. Every stitch of clothing comes with a 'sweat-shop free' label.

There are Palestinian flags everywhere. Wrong continent maybe? And what about the Star of David nestling into that Swastika flag — oh right, so all this Monsanto stuff is aligned with the Palestinian cause is a large Jewish plot with the help of former Nazis? Surely not? The first speaker, a brilliant columnist and polemicist since the 1970s in overly tight jeans, stirs the crowd with a rousing speech about international solidarity, one world and our social responsibility. Together with the usual targets of banks, lawyers, America and Nikes, the new Pope receives a broadside for his aversion to rubbers even in Liberia. (Everyone overlooks the fact that he is the Pope after all, not the brand manager of MTV. It's such a terrible shame the Pope is so Catholic, don't you agree?) As it does in East Belfast, Pope-bashing gets a special cheer, particularly from those in the audience above fifty who are all terribly internationalist and profoundly anti-clerical. They are for some reason the generation that seems to know more about South America and the Spanish Civil War than north Dublin and our Civil War. They are the 1970s made flesh and poured into a kaftan.

Fair-trade Frank, a veteran of every protest since Carnsore Point, smiles wider at black children than white ones for some reason and seems to understand Bedouin nomads better than Ballinasloe Travellers. His CD collection is an altar to world music and Killing Joke. John Kelly is his touchstone for musical cool. He was in the Green Party but finds the idea of a leader or even a rotating chairman difficult to digest. Speaking of digestion, he is single-handedly trying to kick-start his appendix — a victim of Darwinian selection — back to life with an exclusive diet of yams, roots and fibres. Fair-trade Frank is a citizen of the earth. His world is a united colours of Benetton canvas where all can co-exist. He suspects that the Korean restaurants on Parnell Street have one menu for us and a second much better and cheaper one for themselves upstairs but he can't quite believe it. He loves the new Moore Street with all its hair-straightening shops, boiled fish heads and cheap phone shops — so much more exotic than Seán McDermott Street old wans.

For Fair-trade Frank, Deckland and the Expectocracy is a ticking time-bomb. The degradation of the environment is emblematic of the selfishness of Irish people. The fact that we spend almost twice as much on fizzy drinks than development aid evidences our enfeebled morality. We are like an overweight man cannibalising our own life support system. Diversity is being steamrolled and we are ethically culpable. He is a fantastic man for figures. Did you know that the population of the earth has risen fourfold in the past hundred years? Or that industrial production has devoured four-fifths of our resources?

In fact Fair-trade Frank, despite calling himself a humanist in arguments about religion, is actually the opposite — he is a self-hating human. We are the problem: there are too many of us, devouring too much, killing the ecosystem, felling trees and making species extinct. According to Frank we are in the midst of a biological holocaust where species are being wiped out at a rate of 27,000 per year or three every hour. It is all our fault as we look on, sanitised by a diet of tax-cuts, low-interest rates, car finance plans and reality TV. Wake up, smell the Fair-trade coffee, the Expectocrats are a zombie tribe marching over the cliff, pushed by the stick of keeping up with the Smurfits and pulled by the carrot of air miles and Tesco club card points.

THE ECONOMIC ENQUIRERS

Every October, the great and good of the Irish economics profession meet at the annual Irish Economic Association bash in the salubrious surroundings of the Park Hotel in Kenmare. The economists, statisticians, government advisors and financial journalists meet up in the foyer of the hotel on Friday afternoon and promptly head for the bar which they leave on Sunday night. In between there are a variety of papers delivered mainly by academics to hung-over other academics. The bash is jovial and good fun. Nobody takes it too seriously. Years ago it was a bit of a jobs fair with smart public servants hoping to get jobs at the brokers firms. It was here that Dermot Desmond first spotted Michael Buckley. These days are gone, but like all symposiums it gives the biggest peacock on the block the opportunity to show off his or her feathers. For others it's the opportunity for a drunken letch and for most it's just a chance to get away, have a drink and discuss the issues of the day.

One of the constant topics is about how long the boom will last and whether it will end in bust. Ireland has been proving the sceptics wrong for years now. Given that I am one of the high priests of the sceptical enquirers, I am well placed to rehearse these arguments. The basic contention is that nothing goes up forever and that the Expectocracy is fuelled by an unsustainable tsunami of other people's money, driving up property prices which can only fall at some stage. We are living in a bubble and that can only burst. According to the sceptic, those who cannot see this are either wilfully blind or Machiavellian because of their vested interests.

The sceptics see a tragic end for the Expectocracy via the 'inevitability of economics' which will see a fall in house and property prices in general. Another fear of the sceptics is that the boom is flattering to deceive. They contend that history is repeating itself and that we are simply in our version of a gold rush. A feature of the original gold rushes — particularly those of the late 19th century in California, South Africa and Australia — was that, in the mania to be involved in gold at all costs, other businesses were sacrificed, not intentionally, but as a result of the gold industry sucking in all the best cash and the best people. The reason is very simple: the returns from gold were so much more than in other businesses that all ventures were benchmarked against the precious metal.

Why bother with carpentry, tanning or teaching if you could try your hand at gold prospecting? Why invest in agriculture, industry or shipping when you could punt on a gold mine?

It is interesting to look at the diaries of the man who first found gold in the Sacramento River in California, Johann Sutter. Looking back, he said that, because of gold: 'All my plans came to naught. One after another my best people disappeared in the direction of the gold fields; only the sick and crippled stayed behind.' He was lamenting the fact that his real project was to expand his farm, bakery and sawmill business but, on discovery of gold, his men and investors left him so they could speculate, hoping to strike it rich overnight. In the event, only very few did so. But so extreme was the mania, that even the schools in San Francisco had to close because teachers and then pupils headed off into the hills to prospect.

The crucial point is that the impact of gold for the rest of the economy was deleterious because, while it made some people very rich, it starved many other businesses of money and people.

Fast-forward to Ireland in 2005, and it is clear that we are in the grip of a frenzy much like a gold rush. Land has replaced gold. Quite apart from the social dislocation arising from astronomical land prices, the economical enquirers contend that a real problem for our society is that so much of our cash and debts are being funnelled into this most unproductive and speculation-prone of assets.

The dilemma for a society that allows itself to be swept up in speculation fever is the pernicious impact that 'frenzy greed' has on all other businesses. Instead of building a long-term business with customers, branding, employees and cash-flow, the lure of the easy money in land speculation is far too attractive.

In Ireland, say the sceptics, we are experiencing the same dilemma California faced in 1849. Back then, real businesses were judged not against benchmarks such as profitability, robustness and market share, but rather against the absurd capital gain promised in gold.

The subtext really was that if you weren't into gold in some way, you were a bit of an eejit. Similarly, in modern Ireland the same type of mentality applies: if you aren't in land, many regard you as a bit of a simpleton. Land is, after all, where the action is.

Because of all our eggs being in one basket, the sceptical enquirers postulate that when the bust comes, it will be vicious in its severity and broad in its effects, economically, financially and emotionally. The problem with the economic enquirers is that although their logic appears to make sense, they have been wrong in their predictions for several years. Maybe now that the Shinners have gone all cuddly, the enquirers may adopt the clenched-fist pose of 'Tiochfaidh ár lá'.

THE CONFUSED COSMOPOLITANS

Suburban sprawl, super-sized McDonald's, obesity, out-of-town shopping centres, suvs, second homes and 'You're a Star' — is this what the 1970s and 1980s liberal Cosmopolitans fought for? Where are the bicycle lanes, the trams, the state-provided childcare, the rent control and the harmonious districts where docker and doctor live side by side? Where are the environmentalists with their concern for the common good, the recycling centres or the leavening taxes to pay for a state-of-the-art health service? Where is the sense of the common good? Where is the sacrifice for the 'good of the country'? How come Dublin's Left Bank quickly became a Vomitarium full of tanked-up local lads in Man United away strips, pissing in Frank McDonald's doorway? Was it not meant to be populated by sensitive Kierkegaard-reading types, living in tranquil award-winning, solar-powered apartment blocks? In short, how come Ireland today looks more like Denver than Denmark? Trade-off Triona who works for the Arts Council is so confused that she's thinking of becoming a life coach.[4]

She was at the vanguard of the 1970s and 1980s cosmopolitan movement which fought against the Church, censorship, the theocracy and its lackeys, the cute hoors in the Fianna Fáil Party. She was with her mates, the feminists, left-leaning academics, trade unionists, anti-clerics, the Georgian Society, people who could quote Bob Dylan's *Blood on the Tracks* and who loved the civilising impact of the EU. They wrapped themselves in the secular European social democratic flag and imitated the politics that had won out on the continent some decades previously. They were the liberal agenda. The cosmopolitans were enlightened, sophisticated and well-heeled. Their enemies, the Hibernians, were atavistic, sheltered and flat-footed. And the cosmopolitans won.

Their victory over old Hibernian Ireland was supposed to usher in a suite of ideas where equality went with divorces, where contraception and shiny A&E departments went hand in hand, where adult personal morality was the handmaiden of mature civic responsibility, where our children would all be free to learn at whatever pace they chose. Theirs would be an Ireland of the public realm, where clean, cosmopolitan children's playgrounds would spawn a new Irish man — almost indistinguishable from other EU citizens. Schools would be mixed. We would be a society of compromisers, a community that 'traded-off' individual desires for the greater good. We would be open, tolerant, socially aware, engaged with our communities, free of the Church and loyal to the new, efficient, secular state. In short, we would be Denmark, happy with ourselves but not preening, proud but not nationalist, rich not greedy, tasteful not bawdy, Hunter's Hotel not the Four Seasons, Channel 4 not Sky. Trade-off Triona saw us as law-abiding, socially sensitive, social democrats on bicycles in summer, car-pooling in winter.

Instead we got commuters and wedding planners, *VIP* magazine and holiday homes. We got vast swathes of jerry-built suburban estates where people don't even know what their neighbours look like, let alone their names. We got desperately unsporty housewives in sports utility vehicles dropping over-tested children to 'yoga-with-French' classes. We got privatised crèches with aspirant names like Little Harvard and golf-obsessed Mc-dads wedded to low taxes, large cars, overdrafts and infused with a singular and very individual desire to 'trade up' rather than 'trade off'.

The disappointment of old liberal Ireland is palpable because their victory looks predestined. In 1990, their champion Mary Robinson was in the Big House, the Church was getting a hammering, divorce and gay rights were on the cards, everything was running in the right direction. They even managed to spin the fall of the Soviet Union — a place some of them had a sneaking admiration for — as a victory for European social democratic values. They were republicans in the old French intellectual style, not like those gutties from the Ardoyne. And by 1995, with the ceasefire in place, the IRA would indeed run away. It was only a matter of time before Dublin turned into Copenhagen and Ireland turned into Denmark with high taxes and no religion. But what happened? Where did all these SUVs, Hermes bags and Cerrutti suits come from? Who conceived of the Ice Bar? What happened?

Terms like peasants, vulgarity, inanity and shallowness are thrown about in the editorial pages of our papers. There's lots of tut-tutting about traffic, commuting and the rape of the countryside on the editorial page, yet the money-spinning property supplement is cheer-leading the very suburban estates that create this problem for the editorial writers.

And this blurring of the lines is a feature of our country that the confused cosmopolitans with their weakness for science over spirituality, order over flexibility, rules over discretion, set menu over *à la carte*, cannot deal with. Amongst the confused cosmopolitans there is a lack of empathy. Despite all rhetoric about liberalism and tolerance they are very intolerant of dissent to their creed. They want the world to work in a pre-ordained fashion with a benign state orchestrating from the top, with a clear mandate, a clear set of rules and objectives and a clear way of executing this grand plan, politically, socially and economically. They get confused by disorder, spontaneity and prevarication. They wanted straight lines, but they got squiggles. They wanted European but they got mid-Atlantic; they wanted controlled freedom and they got chaos; they wanted intellectual clarity and they got a hodgepodge. How could they have snatched defeat out of the jaws of victory? To answer this question, we have to take a bit of altitude, rise above the day-to-day posturing and regard the changes in Irish society as a continuum rather than an end point.

Chapter 18
The HiCo Emerges

THE GREAT DEBATE: HIBERNIAN VERSUS COSMOPOLITAN
The wonderful thing about us Irish is our weakness for our own propaganda, our willingness to believe that our national dilemmas are unique and our reluctance to accept that the same questions have been asked in almost every country at various stages in history. This misconception leads us to offer empathy to every downtrodden, ethnic-cleansed, beaten-up race in the world. We are the only race that can shamelessly side with Jews and Palestinians, Croats and Serbs, Tutsis and Hutus. We can convince ourselves that we feel their pain even if we have actually spent most of the previous two years watching Sky Sports and the closest we have come to ethnic conflict is hurling abuse at Dutchmen playing for Glasgow Rangers.

Like many countries, peoples and races, the patriot versus cosmopolitan debate has dominated our national thinking since Independence. Let's not get bogged down here, not least because people's rearview mirrors tend to get a bit fogged up. But it can be helpful to characterise, in very broad brush strokes, the recent history of Irish ideas about ourselves and the world as a long struggle between Hibernians on the one hand and Cosmopolitans on the other.

The term Hibernians is best known in the guise of the Order of Hibernians which first emerged in 1565 as a defender of the Catholic faith in Ireland. In 1562, the Lord Lieutenant, a man called Thomas Radcliffe, prohibited all monks and priests from Dublin — a pretty sectarian move even for the time. The Irish Catholic noblemen under Rory O'Moore responded by setting up the Hibernians to protect and hide priests and to defend themselves from the Tudor monarch Elizabeth the First who vowed to exterminate the Irish Catholics by the use of 'dungeon, fire and sword'. The spirit of these old Hibernians was behind the later setting up of the Ancient Order of Hibernians, which was established in 1836 in New York to defend the interests of Irish Catholics both at home and abroad.

The first *Hibernians* were the font from which flowed various subsequent Catholic nationalist organisations, from the 'White Boys' and the 'Ribbon men' to the 'Terry-Alts' and the 'Fenians'.

For our purposes the term *Hibernians* refers to those Irish people who regard themselves as Irish first, expressed by the Catholic religion, Irish culture, history and language.

On the other hand there are the *Cosmopolitans*, who are those people born on the island who regard themselves first as citizens of the world and secondly as Irish. Their definition of Irishness is fluid and hard to pin-down. They are the type of people that unselfconsciously call themselves European first and Irish second. They have always looked abroad for answers. Some traced their intellectual lineage back to Greece and Diogenes the Cynic, but many simply wanted to get away from what they saw as a claustrophobic hegemony and imbibe other ideas.

Looking back over the past hundred years since James Joyce (who for many was the supreme Irish cosmopolitan) penned *Ulysses*, it is helpful to regard our country's cultural history as a long battle between the Hibernians and the Cosmopolitans. For many years, positions were entrenched and exclusive. If you were a Hibernian you were unlikely to accept any of the Cosmopolitan agenda and vice versa. Hibernians regarded Cosmopolitans as fancy Dan dilettantes who were anti all things Irish. The Cosmopolitans on the other hand saw the Hibernians as a backward, suspicious, insular force that needed to be overthrown. Both saw the other as a retarding influence. There was also a class element to it. Cosmopolitans were metropolitans and tended to be better educated. In fact, the more Cosmopolitan you were the more likely you were to have a letter or two after your name and appear in *The Irish Times* marriage announcements.

It is a history that can be broken down into three distinct time periods, each one shorter than the last.

The fifty-year period from 1916 to 1966 was the age of Hibernian hegemony when the Church and the state were practically indistinguishable and this was a Catholic nationalist country in almost all aspects. This was the period of building the nation and forging an identity which was Catholic, rural, poor, anti-imperialist and where practicable, Gaelic in language, sport and culture. If these objectives were a bit hazy and not well formed, the project certainly knew what it wasn't, and that was English or British. It is fair to say now that behind all the bluster, it was a deeply paranoid and insecure state of mind, but it would have been difficult to expect much more openness after a traumatic previous hundred years. Books were banned, moral rectitude was paramount and the religious orders ran the education and health systems. The constitution reflected this and the aspirations of the country seemed to put piety above much else. Our politics was dominated by de Valera and his mates who had fought the War of Independence and they were, in the main, deeply traditional Catholics. The economy under-achieved in almost every area because of what can be termed economic kosherism — a strict diet of protectionism and self-sufficient rhetoric. When compared with other small European countries, our economic record was appalling and, tellingly, one in every two people born in the twenty-six counties emigrated! As a result the population continued to decline until the mid-1960s.

By 1966, when the rest of the world was experiencing the Beatles, weed and Woodstock, Ireland had both the oldest and youngest population in Europe. The huge chunk in the middle had emigrated mainly to the UK, the US or Canada. The Hibernian hegemony had been corroded by its own internal inconsistencies and by economic failure. Symbolically, it seemed to end with the final act of gratuitous Hibernianism when Nelson Pillar was blown up in Dublin on 9 March 1966, so he couldn't piss down on our Easter parade to mark the fiftieth anniversary of the Rising.

For many it was an oppressive period. For others it was a liberation from colonialism. The rules were strict but at least they were ours. There seemed to be determination to stem the cosmopolitan tide washing over the rest of the western world but this was/is not exceptional by any means. Most newly independent countries go through this pattern and it is repeated today for example in the new countries of the former Yugoslavia, where nationalism, Church adherence and an exaggerated fear of the former enemy tends to make up the cultural background noise.

Just after the fiftieth anniversary of the Rising came the cosmopolitan counter-revolution and this lasted more or less for thirty years from 1966 to 1996. Most of today's opinion makers, politicians and industrialists are products of this cosmopolitan counter-revolution which is still deeply rooted in the politics of the 1970s. The two defining battles of the age were over sex and guns, but ironically it was money that really settled the argument.

However, throughout the early 1970s the cosmopolitan liberal agenda began to take hold, with the McGee Supreme Court case allowing married couples to import condoms — amazing as it seems today, that was only thirty years ago. Ireland joined the thoroughly cosmopolitan EEC in 1973 and one of our only cosmopolitan politicians, Seán MacBride, won the Nobel Peace Prize the following year. Eamon de Valera, the grand wizard of Hibernianism, died in 1975. But if the Cosmopolitans thought they were on the pig's back, the Pope's visit in 1979 showed them what the Hibernians could muster at the drop of a mitre.

Throughout the summer of 1979, a pitched Hibernian versus Cosmopolitan battle raged for the attention of the country. On the pure, Catholic, Hibernian side were the preparations, both spiritually and physically, for the Pope's visit. This was to be the high point for Catholic Ireland, the clerical icing on the constitutional cake. For enthusiasts, the Pope's visit would act as a catalyst, a recruiting agent for another generation of staunch Hibernian Catholics in the face of the Cosmopolitan revolution which had swept Europe and was waiting, menacingly, at the gate. It would be Borodino, Stalingrad and the Battle of Clontarf all rolled into one and the good staunch defenders would repel the foreign foes and march on to victory.

But snapping away at the Pope's heels, pouring bilious scorn on old, Hibernian Ireland was the main man of the summer, the utterly decadent, cosmopolitan Bob Geldof who had been at number 1 in the UK — the first Irish band ever — for eight weeks with 'I Don't Like Mondays'. The cosmopolitan Geldof (he even had a foreign name) was the hippest man in Ireland and dominated the airwaves, particularly pirate radio, that set the 1979 agenda.

In 1979 the battle lines were drawn between the Hibernians and the

Cosmopolitans around these two charismatic figures. The older, established Hibernian forces gathered around the Pope, hoping that his presence would stem the tide against what they saw as dangerous, anti-Catholic outside influences acting against them. The younger, upstart Cosmopolitan army rallied around Geldof.

The Pope came and went and Geldof changed his focus, but throughout the 1980s the sex debate raged and the country seemed split in a cultural civil war. But the facts on the ground told a different story, with a huge increase in single mothers on the one hand and a massive fall in the overall birth rates on the other, but in the Dáil, on the airwaves and at local level the set piece public battles continued. On the one side you had the liberal cosmopolitans rallying around the figure of Garret the Good. Pitted against them were the forces of Hibernianism championed by their rather unlikely poster boy, Charlie Haughey.

The stakes were raised over abortion in 1983 when the country voted overwhelmingly to insert an anti-abortion amendment into the constitution. A few years later I remember phoning home from New York in the summer of 1986, assuming that a divorce referendum would have passed, to be told it had been stoutly defeated. But this victory proved pyrrhic — a sort of high water mark for Hibernianism. In 1990 the country elected its President, Mary Robinson, the Archangel of Irish cosmopolitanism.

A number of things undermined the Hibernian case, particularly the widespread revulsion at IRA atrocities. One of the central myths of Hibernianism had always been the heroic nature of the national struggle. But if part of that legacy was killing babies in Belfast, many concluded we wanted none of it. So although the original exposure of anti-Catholic discrimination and the Troubles, bolstered by national sympathy for the hunger strikers in 1980, gave a shot in the arm to Hibernianism, ultimately the overall impact of Northern nationalism was to strengthen the cosmopolitan counter-revolution in Ireland. Hibernianism became associated with a vicious nihilistic sectarian war and the vast majority of us ran a mile from it. It also defined Hibernianism as a negative violent force that could only express itself in opposition to what it wasn't rather than celebrating what it was.

While the traditional economics of Hibernianism was a type of financial kosherism, involving the banning of certain goods and viewing imported Curlywurlys as a threat to the old order, the economics of most Cosmopolitans actually wasn't cosmopolitan at all in the strictest sense. It was socialist in the Scandinavian sense. Irish Cosmopolitans constantly held up Scandinavia as the model for what would be achieved here when the Hibernians were finally routed. In the cosmopolitan nirvana, Ireland would be a secular north European state, with paternity leave, comprehensive social welfare and trams. Loads of trams. Sometimes listening to Cosmopolitans eulogise trams, you can't help get the feeling that a virulent strain of engineering fetishism runs though them. Cosmopolitan Ireland will be right-on, politically correct and nice to Travellers. Our emigrants will suddenly be called a Diaspora and the British Council will have a casting say on our national school curriculum. All immigrants will be welcomed like drunk horny girls on a stag night and no-one will live in bedsits. That was the promise of cosmopolitanism. When the editorial writers of the liberal media would finally take their rightful place at the cabinet table, Ireland would resemble one large ESRI report. We would become just like Denmark. By 1990 this United Colours of Benetton future was very much on the cards.

Hibernianism was about to receive two blows from which it had no right to expect to recover. The three central pillars of Hibernianism were Catholicism, nationalism and the GAA, all central to the creed. Language, literature, traditional music and other unique expressions of Irish culture are supported by the stability of these three pillars. In the 1990s, the Irish people rejected two of them — Catholicism and nationalism. One would have expected Hibernianism to have been holed below the water line.

From the early 1990s to the end of the decade, sex scandals, cover-ups and obfuscation damaged the credibility of the Catholic Church. Mass attendance fell rapidly, vocations dropped precipitously and the halo slipped, revealing incompetent men, out of touch and out of their depth. Although this had been coming since the Pope's visit which was the beginning of the end, few could have imagined how disastrous a decade the 1990s were to be for the Catholic Church. The decade ended with the Church hiding paedophiles while threatening poor victims of predatory priests with senior counsel.

Then, in 1998, the Irish people voted overwhelmingly to drop articles 2 and 3 of the constitution. These articles were the legal basis for the desired all-Ireland state, claiming jurisdiction over the whole island — including the North. This was dropped overnight without a whimper. Partition was accepted and the British majority in the north-east of the country was told that they had won. 95% of people in this supposed nationalist Ireland voted for this. Overnight, the so-called core value of reunification disappeared — it was airbrushed out of history like one of Stalin's lieutenants, by the Belfast Agreement. Hibernianism as the dominant cultural force on this Ireland looked spent.

On top of all this, there was an economic counter-revolution. In the late 1990s although not understood at the time, a much more potent victory for Cosmopolitanism was achieved. Ireland decided to abandon the most outward sign of economic nationalism, the Irish currency, and adopt the Euro in its place. This is the financial equivalent of scrapping the national soccer team and picking a European first eleven instead. It has had by far the biggest ramifications of any of the cosmopolitan victories on people's lives here, but back then and even today it is not always fully appreciated.

Thus by 1999, the cosmopolitan counter-revolution was over. They had won the battle with Hibernianism on three crucial fronts — religious, nationalist and financial. The war was over. Cosmopolitan ideas and concerns could now dominate the ruling elite in Ireland. They could, with the vindictiveness of true ideologues, pick off one by one the old Hibernian strongholds.

But something happened while they had been away at the European Court of Justice, the UN, the WTO and the EU Commission. They had taken their eye off the ball and the country they had just inherited didn't look like Denmark. It looked, smelled and felt much more like Denver. How could that have occurred and what was going on?

Chapter 19
The New Elite

The late 1990s saw the emergence of a new class of Irish people who instead of being one or the other, either Hibernian or Cosmopolitan, took the best elements of each, blending them into one identity. A new tribe has emerged in the Ireland of the 21st century that is a healthy and unique mixture of the old Hibernian and the new Cosmopolitan — the HibernianCosmopolitans or HiCos for short.[1] The HiCo class is both a counterpoint to the materialism of Deckland and a perfect synthesis of the two sides of the old argument that defined Irishness.

Unbeknownst to us, we have seen the central tenets of Greek philosophy play themselves out here where the thesis (Hibernianism) was opposed by the antithesis (cosmopolitanism), leading ultimately to the fusion of the best parts of both, the synthesis (Hiberno-cosmopolitans). In *Bobos in Paradise* David Brooks, looking at similar trends in the US between the old implacable enemies the Bohemians and the Bourgeoisie, explains how they have come together to create a new upper class, the BoBos. The HiCos are an Irish version of a similar phenomenon.

So while the starting point is totally different, based as it is on historical Irish nationalistic battles, the end point is disturbingly similar, so much so that in certain areas it's hard to know where Connecticut ends and Ireland begins.

The new Irish elite are the most educated Irish tribe ever. They have done very well in the past ten years. They have driven the economy and, more importantly, the image of this island. They are like nothing that has gone before. The HiCos are the aristocracy of the Pope's Children.

You will start to see them all around you. When you look for them you will notice them everywhere, you will hear them in cafés in Schull, drinking macchiato and talking about the simple beauty of the Cape Clear people. In Westport, in whole-food shops, sipping smoothies before doing Croagh Patrick; or in the English Market in Cork, insisting on local cheeses and real sausages. Although they might work in the cosmopolitan world, their children have their names down for Gaelscoileanna. While they might watch the Lions in New Zealand, they celebrate hurling like no other sport. They eat ethnic food, yet drink in bars called Solas and Anseo.

They first came to life in the mid-1990s, just as the cosmopolitan-counter-revolution was marching to victory. Commentators were talking (although not in the following terms) about Deckland and the Kells Angels, money, cars, jobs, house prices and immigrants, but there was something even more interesting just bubbling away beneath the surface.

There was a fundamental shift in our culture that could not be ascribed to money, immigration or politics. Something seismic was happening. For example, the traditionally liberal area with the highest yes vote in the 1995 divorce referendum — Dún Laoghaire — now has the fastest growing evangelical Christian church in the country. Meanwhile, the town with the highest no vote — Macroom in Cork — is now full of health-food shops, holistic pagan festivals and hemp outlets. What was happening? Old conservative Ireland has become a magnet for pagan New-Age travellers and old liberal Ireland is brimming with evangelical Christians!

Irish-speaking Raidió na Life is the trendiest radio station in Dublin featuring young women spinning discs under names like DJ Class A while late-night Raidió na Gaeltachta features hard-core hip-hop, topped and tailed *as Gaeilge*. The Irish language is cool, enrolments for courses in Irish language diplomas are full, Gael Linn is bursting at the seams yet Chinese is the lingua franca of Moore Street. Old-fashioned black pudding has replaced new fusion blackened cod on menus. Graphic designers have dropped Verdana for Celtic script. Fionn Mac Cool is back in the children's books business, having lost out to Pooh Bear years ago. Despite all the talk about post-Catholic Ireland, pilgrimages to Lough Derg are up for the first time in a decade and the Pope's death led to authentic national mourning. Numbers attending evangelical Christian churches are up 1,000% in ten years and 78% of these people are born in Ireland, having converted from Catholicism. On the other hand, Síle na Gigs are back in fashion, the pagan site of Tara is now a national issue and GUBU — named after the resolutely heterosexual Charles Haughey — is one of Dublin's gayest bars. Old certainties have been challenged. The traditional Irish hipster reaction of dropping everything native for the imported version has been turned on its head. What is going on?

Was it just the appearance of TG4 and Gráinne Seoige that made the Irish language attractive? Could Hector have shot to prominence twenty years ago? When did names like Oisín and Aoife rocket up the top-ten lists of children's names? When did the trendiest clubs in Dublin change their names from the Las Vegas-sounding Pink Elephant, to Connemara inflected RíRá? And speaking of Gráinne, when indeed did these raven-haired beauties emerge from the Gaeltacht to pout on the news?

Why did the GAA and particularly hurling — long associated with the antithesis of progress and sophistication — become hip? Even in the early 1990s the GAA was about Christian Brothers, the national anthem and red-faced lads kicking forty shades out of each other. When did it mutate into slick Guinness ads, corporate sponsorship and cute girls in county jerseys?

And what about Gaelscoileanna? Back in the 1980s, the few Gaelscoileanna that existed were the preserve of children of linguistic campaigners, national schoolteachers and on-the-run-Provos, as well as the odd member of the Free-State aristocracy who could trace their roots back to the foundation of the state.

Today, Gaelscoileanna are sprouting up everywhere. There is at least one Gaelscoil in every county and there are over thirty in Dublin. Most parents who are sending their kids to these schools at best achieved pass Irish in the Leaving Cert and are from English-speaking families who went to English-speaking schools. Now these same parents are clamouring to get their kids into Scoileanna Lan-Gaeilge.

When exactly did Irish and references to Celtic mythology infect the language of business and marketing, from satellite soccer on

Setanta Sports, to bottled water Uisce, to weiss beer Breo? Think of the growth in alternative medicine. How many of these courses have websites called Croí Nua or Spiorad Difriúil, *nó mar sin de*? We now have 'yoga through Irish for the under-10s'. This is the perfect fusion of the ancient East of Goa and the ancient West of Ireland.

The elevation of all things Hibernian is recent. In the 1970s and 1980s, only imported things were cool. So, for example, the dreadfully insecure expression 'Ireland's answer to' was the prefix used to describe almost every endeavour from show bands to architects as if we ourselves had no form of self-expression. It appeared to be accepted that all we could do was imitate. All this has changed and now Irish traditions, and indeed the country itself, is seen as a precious resource — a brimming and inspirational font.

In a country that has become incredibly globalised over the recent years, this change might seem counter-intuitive. Many street protesters and No Logo supporters believe that globalisation will inevitably lead to the dominance of the English language and a genetic Anglo-American culture symbolised by Nike, Starbucks, John Grisham and Walt Disney. In Ireland, something different is occurring.

Irish traditional music has never been more popular in the face of massive saturation of global MTV music culture. Pagan Irish Christian names are now *de rigueur* and far from seeing a diminution of Hibernian culture, it is on the rise. People who used to be one thing are now another. Old-fashioned nationalists are now cosmopolitan and former cosmopolitans are mixing it with the provincials. The Hibernian is Cosmopolitan and the Cosmopolitan is Hibernian.

A symbolic representation of the pragmatic fusion that has occurred over the past few years is the blurring of the positions of the two champions of Hibernianism and Cosmopolitanism from 1979. Back then, the year most of the Pope's Children were conceived, the Pope and Bob Geldof were polar opposites. But by the time he died this year, the views of Pope John Paul the Second and his old arch-rival Sir Bob Geldof the First had, on many crucial issues, merged together. Both were literally and metaphorically be-knighted by their fans, both adopted saint-like characteristics and on issues as varied as Third-World debt, food relief, western capitalism, the role of the USA and the war in Iraq, their views were indistinguishable. They managed to meet somewhere in the middle like a pair of *à la carte* nibblers.

Their fusion is the story of the HiCo and isn't it interesting that in the year Pope John Paul died, not only are his children coming to dominate the Irish landscape but his nemesis Bob Geldof entertained running for the position of President of Ireland? Yet again, the Hibernian is Cosmopolitan and the Cosmopolitan is Hibernian.

The HiCos cherry pick from each suite of beliefs. Concerned about the environment and the land, unlike the Carrot Juice Contrarians, they are prepared to entertain the heresy of nuclear power as part of the solution. Like the confused cosmopolitans, they are *communitaire* and believe that Ireland is a society, but unlike Trade-off Triona, they do not trust the state to gel the society together. They are politically savvy, but do not vote in great numbers. They are secular in nature, but Christian at baptisms. Like Fair-trade Frank, the HiCo wants to 'make poverty history' but in contrast, the HiCo thinks that free trade rather than fair-trade is the answer. HiCos are European by culture and have been to the odd Lars Von Trier movie, but are American by inclination. Unlike the remote economic enquirers, they understand popular culture, but know their Dow Jones from their Bridget Jones. Like the rural nostalgists they too want to preserve the best of our past but they realise that you can't turn the clock back.

HiCos see no conflict between celebrating Irishness while simultaneously being part of the New World Order. Unlike the Decklanders, they have no problem rejecting American consumerism but do not, like the confused cosmopolitans, see this as a justification for anti-Americanism. In short the HiCos see the us state department as more than the PR wing of McDonald's. HiCos are European without being obsessively so.

They see alliances where others see inconsistencies. They see no conflict between being an artist and an entrepreneur or a good business person and a good socially-engaged citizen. They vote for lower taxes, but regard tax exiles as immoral. They are Catholics as long as they are allowed to take out the bits that are not nice to girls. They believe in clean air and more roads. They understand the problems of personal debt but do not want to opt out. They will celebrate an inter-county hurling victory on a Sunday and be in a New York corporate headquarters the following Tuesday signing a mega-deal. They are Paddies after all. The crucial distinction is that they are the first generation of Hibernians for whom the cosmopolitan world offers opportunities rather than alternatives. HiCos are not new, but in the past they had to go to Chicago, Sydney or Paris to feel liberated. Now they can live at home, free from the strict rules that drove them out in the past. Unlike previous generations, they see cosmopolitanism, not as the antithesis to Hibernianism, but rather the perfect platform from which Hibernianism can be relaunched. Instead of having a strict diet of beliefs, influences and ideas, they are a promiscuous marriage of all sorts. HiCos are a fusion, the hybrid offspring of the great blurring.

To explain the emergence of the new elite, we have to delve a little deeper into economics which created the Decklanders and gave rise to the HiCos. Interestingly, in the traditional debate over what it means to be Irish, the role of economics has always been underplayed. It explains the pyrrhic victory of the cosmopolitan counter-revolutionaries who dreamt of Denmark but woke up after their long war, in a place resembling Denver, full of 4x4s, gated communities and HiCos. It's time to rectify that oversight.

ANCESTRAL VOICES

The emergence of the HiCos owes much to globalisation. According to survey after survey, the country is now more middle class, better educated and happier than ever. This means we can now discriminate in a variety of areas. For the first time ever, the Irish are rich enough to stand on our own feet and take a look at not just our culture but that of others as well. We can pick and choose what suits us. The overwhelmingly suffocating inferiority complex — the handmaiden of economic under-achievement — has lifted.

In the past, the major driver of the jettisoning of Irish or indeed any minority culture and language was economic. English language, English mores, English thinking and the British Empire were the dominant linguistic, commercial and geographical entities. Why hold on to something that was perceived as a failure? This more than anything drove the Irish language and the culture to the margins. Today the very same process is making it accessible again. When the economy is booming, people can indulge in exploring their own culture. The corollary is when unemployment is close to 20% and emigration is high, there are more important fish to fry than culture.

We can see a significant positive correlation between interest in the culture and the performance of the economy. From the mid-1990s, demand for Gaelscoileanna, GAA and traditional music increased dramatically with national income.

A factor associated with globalisation has been a rejection, in certain quarters, of mass-produced, branded generic goods. Across the globe, in response to an age of abundance, many people are reacting to the perceived false and disposable nature of much of our material world with a renewed interest in the authentic, the ancient and the historic. In Ireland this reaction has been amplified by the unprecedented possibility of associating Irishness with material success. In a growing economy, there is room for everything and everybody, which helps explain why Hibernian culture and cosmopolitan culture live side by side so easily in Ireland for the first time. In short, Hibernianism is no longer for losers.

Far from drowning that which makes you different in a sea of bland, fake, generic consumerist product, globalisation allows difference to thrive. The difference is the key; this is where the value is and it is what people are striving for. The reaction to rampant consumerism has been a 'keeping it real' backlash. Hibernian culture fits this 'real' bill. Full-on consumerism is very Deckland. When everything is accessible, the inaccessible becomes valuable.

The HibernoCosmopolitan or HiCo handbook is the Irish chapter of a global lifestyle manifesto which seeks out authentic experiences. As searching for the authentic is a reaction to abundance, Ireland had first to be swamped in a gluttonous sea of frivolous luxury goods before the hunt for the genuine and the unique could begin. The revival of Gaelscoileanna, traditional music and Celtic mythology could not have happened without the Brown Thomas charge card. The HiCos needed to see, feel and smell Deckland in all its full-on incarnations before they could react against it. And in a political sense Deckland and its counter-reaction, HiCoism, would never have happened had we not mutated into the hybrid nation of Ameropeans — half American, half European. This allowed us in a narrow economic sense to be good global corporate citizens, happy to take the best of Europe and the best of the US. The domestic cultural implication of such global economic licentiousness was the fusion of the two warring tribes that had knocked each other and the rest of us senseless for eight decades.

Of course, some stalwarts remain and we get Hibernian fundamentalists who rail against the degeneration of the morals of young people, while cosmopolitan fundamentalists react to the Pope's death with an apathetic shrug of the shoulders. These fundamentalists have yet to grasp that most of the rest of us are somewhere in the middle.

EMIGRANT VOICES

The emergence of the HiCo has been greatly bolstered by two other developments related to the booming economy. The first is the return of our 1980s emigrants and the second has been immigration.

Walk into any office, bar, shop in Ireland and you will see them — the Leaving Cert classes of the late-1980s — Ireland's nomads, just back. In the office, it is likely that returned emigrants are doing well and they will ultimately make up a significant proportion of the top brass. They have arrived home in their thousands over the past few years. While most of the attention is directed at immigrants, a much overlooked story is the returned emigrants, who tend to come home quietly and get on with it. They have been changed by their experiences abroad and they will change this place as a result.

They are the most cosmopolitan Irish generation ever — equally at home in Beacon Hill and Hill 16 — and their experience is global. In fact, they are the epitome of globalisation. Had it not been for globalisation they could never have left this country in the first place and nor could they have returned. It was both their safety valve in the late 1980s and 1990s and the key that subsequently unlocked the door in the last five years. They are the human face of economic figures which reveal that Ireland is the second most globalised country in the world. These people are modern, tolerant and open to change. They have had a huge influence on the economy but not yet on the politics of the country. We should not underestimate the role that their contacts, networks and personal friendships, particularly in the US, have played in driving foreign investment here.

If modernity can be described as the ability to change, take on board new impulses and ideas, blend them with the old and take change in your stride, then we can fairly describe Ireland as a very modern place. In fact, sometimes we fail to see that Ireland is a truly modern country.

Take these returned emigrants who have worked and lived abroad. They constitute 20% of the workforce in their thirties and forties. This is an extraordinary figure when you think that only one in twenty

Americans even has a passport.[2] So one in five (of this age group of) Irish workers has worked abroad, taking in different cultures, learning new tricks and thriving in an alien culture. I doubt that the corresponding figure for France or Germany is even close to 3%, if that. This nomadic tribe plugs us into the global economy like no other and makes us ideally placed to take advantage of the opportunities that globalisation affords.

These nomads are extremely well educated. Initially, they were likely to have been twice as educated as those who stayed put. This implies that Ireland, up until recently, was sending out an emigrant aristocracy who left Ireland not just because there was nothing here, but also because they wanted to get on, see new things and create a career for themselves that they could not have aspired to here. While there was a brain drain back then, they have come home even more educated than when they left, with more experience. As a result the men are getting paid more and promoted faster than those who stayed at home. In another interesting finding, men who said they left for career purposes get paid 5% more than those who left just to see the world. So being driven pays. However, it is worrying to see that women who have come home, even with all this extra experience, do not get paid more than those who stayed. So emigration is good for the boys, not the girls.

Although the estimates vary, about 200,000 returned emigrants have come back in the past ten years and their cosmopolitan outlook has played a role in our acceptance of change and immigrants. When they were away, they cultivated an acute sense of Irishness. Most of them returned with a stylised view of Hibernia. Because being Irish served them very well abroad they had got used to hamming it up, but behind the stage-Paddy performances, many began asking questions about their identity. What makes me different? It must be more than USA '94, U2 and Riverdance. In addition to these searching questions, many came back to educate their children in the Ireland they had invented in their heads. So, the Irish language and Hibernianism featured strongly. Maybe they were just fed up with being called English, but for whatever reason, they arrived back with a stronger sense of Irishness than they had originally taken away.

While emigration heightened a sense of Irishness in returned migrants, immigration has also contributed. The more multicultural the country has become and the more Irish people hear other languages on the streets and other cultures flourishing under our noses, the more we ask about ourselves. What have we left behind? Who are we? Are we just a province of the USA? Are we simply Boston with bad weather? There must be more to our nation than simply an enviable GDP figure and as the Tánaiste said 'a good workforce'. Does that do justice to us? Are we just friendly football fans poured into the jerseys of a Scottish team? Is there more to us than a property boom, second houses in Spain and heroic drinking?

For many, there is something else — a fusion of the old and the new, domestic and foreign, Hibernian and Cosmopolitan. For others, being a HiCo is not so much what you are as what you are not. And they are defiantly not Decklanders. Some HiCos are the new snobs who look condescendingly at the *noveaux riches* of Deckland and throw up age-old barriers of appreciation over possession, learning over money and discrimination over abundance. As befits the great blurring, HiCos can be left or right wing, rural or urban, young or old, boy or girl, rich or poor.

To recap: four factors have brought us to where we are. First, when things are going well you can afford to think about culture and ask the 'who are we' question from a position of strength, not weakness. Second, the reaction against bland global consumer culture has elevated the value of the things that make us different. Third, when everyone is lumped together in the middle and when status is fluid, the old, educated middle classes — sensing that their patch is being invaded — throw up barriers such as education, cultivations or appreciations, which are distinct from possessions which can be easily bought. This serves to keep the merely moneyed, rather than the actually cultured, out. Finally, our educated Diaspora have come home with more Cosmopolitan experience and yet more Hibernian dreams than any earlier generation. Let's now examine the HiCos in one of their most telling habitats — their children's schools.

Chapter 20

The Early Years —
Gaelscoileanna

I turned to see which uber-HiCo was referring to the FBI one second and breaking into Irish the next. There he was, head stuck in a perfect Celtic Tiger position, phone wedged between the left shoulder and the ear, propped up by a corpulent collar — our Minister for Justice, dropping his child to school. Great!

    – What! The FBI!
    – Dia duit!
    – The FBI! My god!
    – Maidin, le cúnamh dé!

One hundred years ago, the perfect image of the Irish was a doodeen-smoking, seaweed-picking, bare-footed peasant, smiling in bewilderment for some well-meaning English anthropologist who had just measured the circumference of his cranium. In 2006 a perfect snapshot of the Irish is of a man in an expensive, ill-fitting suit, hands-full, driving or maybe carrying a child distractedly, barking orders down a mobile on an English-owned network. The phone is jammed awkwardly between the shoulder and ear, right eyebrow raised to avoid crashing. The recent dramatic increase in the demand for massages, osteopathy and chiropractors for stiff, apparently stress-related, necks owes a lot to the impact of the mobile phone on Irish shoulders.

This morning's perfect snapshot was Michael McDowell, our Minister for Justice and a middle-aged, neo-liberal HiCo. The

Minister was being walked by his dog — an overweight, cuddly-looking black terrier — not very Rottweiller. Holding his right hand was his young child who was daydreaming as his distracted father discussed homeland security with his advisers at half eight on a Friday morning. We were outside the gates of two Gaelscoileanna on Oakley Road in Ranelagh — the hypotenuse of the D6 HiCo triangle. The Minister joined the ranks of other accomplished HiCos dropping their bilingual kids off at Scoil Bhríde and Lios na nÓg.

Scoil Bhríde is the grand old dame of Gaelscoileanna, having been originally set up in 1917 by Louise Gavan Duffy in St Stephen's Green. It moved to the grounds of Cullenswood House in Ranelagh in the 1960s and has, for years, been catering to the traditionally modest demand for Irish language education in the area. (As befits such an institution, a recent anniversary was celebrated in the presence of no less a person than Uachtarán na hÉireann.) The traditional Irish-speaking movement was structured a bit like a feuding sect of all creeds and persuasions with the common thread, the language.

Traditionally, children in Gaelscoileanna came from three broad sources. (1) They were the sons and daughters of the Irish-speaking aristocracy — a tiny minority of over-achievers, many of whom, like the Minister for Justice, can trace their roots back to the revolutionary movements of 1916. They are umbilically linked to the language revival movement and have always been conspicuous in the civil service, the law, academia and the arts. These Gaeilgeoiri aristocrats constituted a small, highly educated, cultural elite which emerged after the foundation of the state. Together with (2) the children of Gaeltacht people who moved to Dublin and (3) the *leanaí* of fáinne-wearing Gaeilgeoiri zealots, who can be termed the *cigire* class — the foot soldiers of de Valera's Ireland — these three groups of people formed the core of the Gaelscoil movement up until the late 1970s. What united these various strands (and there are many more sub sects) is an expression called '*ar son na cúise*' or 'for the cause'. This has nothing to do with the reunification cause and in fairness to the Gaeilgeoiri they were badly served by those who equated, willy-nilly, the language with the Provos. The *cúis* is the language and that is the objective. Like all minorities who are sometimes regarded as aliens in their own land, they will admit to being suspicious of outsiders. Like the Jews, who have the expression the 'righteous gentile' for some non-Jew who is on their side, the Gaeilgeoiri will describe someone as *báúil* if they feel that that person, while not one of them, is sympathetic to the cause.

Despite survey evidence showing that most people believe the Irish language is an integral part of being Irish, very few until recently took active steps to support the language. In fact the relationship between the majority and the minority was one of an uneasy standoff. For most people, Gaelscoileanna were out of bounds, in the same way as reservations were out of bounds for white non-Indian Americans. Rightly or wrongly there was a perception that the Gaelscoileanna were not particularly interested in embracing the *gnáth duine* nor was the *gnáth duine* particularly interested in what was going on inside. Over the past ten years in particular, the demand for Gaelscoileanna broke out of this reasonably narrow core group and extended quite dramatically into the mainstream middle classes.

As well as the general HiCo quest for authenticity, there were other factors that made people aware of and comfortable with their Irish heritage.

Riverdance in 1994 is our departure point. Moya Doherty had always loved Irish dancing and as a producer in RTÉ she had drawn sketches outlining what Irish dancing could look like. Her first drawings, jotted down on a piece of paper, showed a line of twenty or thirty tap-dancing feet in a long horizontal row across a stage. This was the *Riverdance* she imagined. Bill Whelan put music to it, combining in true HiCo fashion Irish traditional with authentic ethnic beats from Eastern Europe and Iberia. John McColgan re-mortgaged his house and choreographed it. Following the Eurovision interval performance, it was a free seven-minute video of that performance called *Riverdance for Rwanda*, combining Hibernian performance with cosmopolitan concern, that put *Riverdance* on the map. The following year, in January 1995, an inexperienced team opened twenty sell-out dates at the Point. (Whelan apparently was still writing the score a week before opening.) The rest is history.

By globalising Irish dancing and culture, packaging it and marketing it to a worldwide audience, *Riverdance* did something no-one had ever done before: it invented pop-trad. Pop-trad is what it says it is. Like pop-music, pop-art, pop-economics and pop anything, it brings its subject to the level of popular culture, where it is understandable, digestible and accessible. In the world of *Hello!* magazine, celebrity gossip and reality TV, pop-trad is the fusion of

Heat magazine and *Anois*. It spawned numerous imitators which is precisely what it was supposed to do, but even if it is not for the purists, it created the impression that this form of culture was exportable, commercial and bankable. Pop-trad fused the rhythm of Ballyvourney with the bottom line of Broadway. (The Riverdancers performed at the Grammys and Michael Flatley was mentioned in an episode of 'Friends'. The whole thing was lampooned in *Shrek* — it was that huge.)

Before *Riverdance*, the way had been paved by trad musicians in the 1970s and 1980s. To have pop anything you have to have the original article and they introduced traditional music to foreign markets initially. But the pop of *Riverdance* put it on a different level. There is little doubt that it made Irish dancing sexy, made Irish traditional culture attractive and made many thousands of Irish people who had an arm's-length relationship with the heritage, very proud of our culture. Traditionalists might not like it, but pop-trad in the guise of *Riverdance* helped the Hibernian revival movement enormously.

Another important factor was the cease-fire in the North. Arguably, this allowed Hibernian culture to break free from the stranglehold of Provisionalism. For as long as the Provos wrapped themselves in the flag, commandeered the culture and used it as a cover to kill people, there was a reasonable amount of suspicion towards the Irish language movement and its cradle, the Gaelscoileanna.

A third factor was the founding of TG4 which brought the Irish language to life. Overnight, young, assertive presenters emerged from the Connemara Gaeltacht, sending out a totally different message about the language. In the past the language was seen as backward, unattractive and forced. For many people it was something that, although we liked to think of it quaintly as part of a cultural package, we did not aspire to speak. The emergence of TG4 changed that perception somewhat. For the first time in generations, Irish people could imagine copping off *as Gaeilge*. Irish could be normal and aspirational.

For many HiCos, who are acutely aware of what their peers are doing, there was something different going on in the Gaelscoileanna. The fact that the Irish-speaking secondary schools, which are free, send more pupils to university than many fee-paying schools, indicates that there is something going on in Gaelscoileanna that money just cannot buy.

That something is participation. Parents in Gaelscoileanna get involved; they tend to be agitators rather than passive spectators. They are consulted, they are responsible, they feel ownership. And, it is as close as the HiCo parent can get to teaching without swapping their massive salaries for the modest teacher's one. More than anything else, it is that middle-class sense of ownership that drives them into the arms of the Gaelscoileanna. (The same is true in that other HiCo educational growth area, the multi-denominational sector, which places such stress on being parent controlled. In many cases multi-denominational schools are also parent founded.)

The Gaelscoileanna are a risk-free venture for HiCo parents. They can opt into the state sector, with all the psychological upside that has for the socially concerned world view, without jeopardising the educational prospects of little Saoirse. The aim of the HiCos is not to turn themselves into Gaeilgeoiri but to get the best for their family. As with everything they do, Gaelscoileanna allows them to pick the best bit from what the Hibernian menu has to offer and move on. It is an economic free lunch, spiced with the virtue of authenticity.

Gaelscoileanna are hip and much in demand. Gaelscoileanna and the multi-denominationals are the fastest growing sub-sector of schools in the country. From being perceived by many as being too nationalist, too Catholic and too atavistic as they were years ago, Gaelscoileanna are now the pinnacle of educated sophistication. People who send their children to Gaelscoileanna display great taste. They are erudite, refined and concerned. Twenty-first-century Gaelscoil parents are in a class of their own. They are both Cosmopolitan and Hibernian.

Many HiCo parents who now send their children to Gaelscoileanna were themselves middle-class Catholics who were sent to Protestant schools. Indeed, they are switching sides just as their parents did twenty years ago. Back then, liking Protestants was a sign of being sophisticated. Now, it's liking Gaeilgeoiri.

The growth has been phenomenal. When the Pope's Children were born there were only twenty-five Gaelscoileanna in Ireland. There are over two hundred today. This is an increase of over 900% when the school-going population was increasing by 20%. The number of children outside the Gaeltacht being educated in Irish has doubled since 1990 to just over 31,000. The majority of these new schools have been built in the past decade — the decade when the HiCos emerged as a separate educated elite.

Lios na nÓg, one of the new breed of Gaelscoileanna, opened just when the HiCo spirit was emerging ten years ago. It is a project school, non-denominational and liberal. In short, its proposition is a perfect HiCo fusion of language, old culture and tolerance — a sort of Countess Markievicz meets Greenpeace offering. What HiCo in his right mind could turn down such an authentic proposal?

Back in 1996, just when the economy was beginning to motor properly, the demand for places at Scoil Bhríde went through the roof with the result that many parents could not get their children into the school. They decided to set up their own in Cullenswood House itself which was just over the wall from Scoil Bhríde.

Cullenswood House is the cradle of the revolution. This is where Pádraig Pearse set up St Enda's — one of the first bilingual schools in the country — at the height of the first Gaelic Renaissance. Two signatories of the Proclamation taught in the school — Pearse was the headmaster and Thomas McDonagh the vice-principal. On its opening day on 7 September 1908 St Enda's was billed as 'a school for Catholic boys, promoting an Irish standpoint and atmosphere, modern languages taught on Direct method, special prominence given to science and "modern" subjects generally with careful attention to character building and moral training'. St Enda's played a significant role in the Irish language revival of the period and Pearse himself said that the years at St Enda's were the happiest of his life. This place is the holy of holies for the national movement. Here is where Pearse dreamed of an Irish-speaking, independent country and here is where urbane Irish middle-class Catholics, for the first time in two centuries, could express themselves educationally and linguistically in Irish.

For the HiCo, Lios na nÓg in Cullenswood House has it all. It is a restored old Georgian building (and in the HiCo architectural hierarchy little beats restored Georgian), yet it is the birthplace of the Republic; it is a project school, tolerant, cosmopolitan, non-denominational, yet, as everything is taught through Irish, it is pure Hibernian; it is suburban Ranelagh within a stone's throw of the HiCos' food emporium, Mortons, yet the principal is from rustic Ballyferriter in West Kerry, bringing with her the spirit and authenticity of the Atlantic seaboard.

The house was bequeathed to the state in 1960 by Pearse's sister and in what could only be described as a monument to the story of subsequent state indifference to national monuments of significance, it was turned into bed-sits and later fell into ruin. The house was rescued by a local group of enthusiasts. (Another HiCo trait is campaigning. They are always campaigning and preserving something. Whether it is the baths in Dún Laoghaire, the Hill of Tara or frog-spawn in Kinnegad, the HiCos are there with their banners, petitions and loudspeakers. HiCo coalitions are amongst the most eclectic in the country. It is not unusual to see feisty old ladies in full old cantankerous woman's rig-out — all purple hats and tartan shopping trolleys with Scotch terriers in matching tartan waistcoats — linked arm in arm with be-dreaded young Crusty in full bicycle courier chic, all tattoos, bolts through his extremities and day-glo cycling shorts.)

Lios na nÓg opened its doors to its first students in 1997. There were twenty-five in its first year and now there are 187 children. Lios na nÓg runs intercultural projects and has children from seven different countries. The experience is a world music melody played with a bodhrán and tin whistle. How more HiCo can you get?

Yummymummy arrives at the gate. She's a bit flustered. It took ages to get Sorcha and the twins dressed and today is green lunch day but there was nothing in the house apart from chocolate hobnobs. Luckily, Mortons open at eight. It's very busy in the HiCo triangle in the mornings, days are full, things have to be accomplished and how could anything be achieved if you are not up at the crack of dawn? Anyway, Gerry had to catch the red-eye to London at 6.45 so the whole house was up looking for his suit carrier. The children were tired by now and quite a handful in the back of the Freelander.

Like all good HiCo shops, Mortons has its notice board. That is one of the crucial differences between HiCo and Deckland shops. Deckland shops have notices telling you how much things are, what the sales price is and today's special offers. HiCo shops have community notice boards offering services which have nothing to do with the bottom line of the shop. Shopping isn't about profits, it's about experience and lifestyle. Nothing as vulgar as actually paying for stuff could ever be entertained.

The kids are playing football in the yard, speaking in Irish to each other. The parents are arriving now. Yummy has parked half way up Charleston Road so as to be able to partake in the walk to school initiative. She grabs Sorcha and the twins (the tell-tale sign of mid-thirties IVF) and rounds the corner into Oakley Road, bang on time — such synchronicity. This morning's been a triumph. It's 8.20 and classes begin in Lios na nÓg at 8.30 — half an hour before most schools. After all, HiCo parents, when they are not canvassing for better school facilities, books and relief teachers, are busy working, achieving, benchmarking and above all, creating.

Bizarrely, Irish is not heard. Not one parent speaks a full sentence to their child in Irish at the gate, but there are lots of gratuitous *sláns*, *dia duits* and the like. The *dia duit* sorority is a sight to behold — lots of mummies *dia duit*ing each other in the same way as black teenagers high-five each other in the ghetto. As soon as little Fiach is safely in the *doras* or through the *geata*, they then break into red-brick Ranelagh's finest nasal tones. But they are making a statement, and in this society authentic statements are crucial.

The difference between Scoil Bhríde and Lios na nÓg is significant. Scoil Bhríde mummies arrive in Range Rover Freelander jeeps as opposed to bikes and by foot. They have perfectly groomed hair, Riverview memberships and the whole vibe is upper professional. Scoil Bhríde is senior counsel, partners in law-firms, advertising executives and Mercs territory. You might be forgiven for thinking that the Leaving Cert points benefit of Irish alone is what is driving these parents. If so it is an acceptable, culturally far-sighted form of the Attainometer. Lios na nÓg is different. Pearse's direct descendants wear scarves, beads, wristbands, and cycle or drive 96D Mitsubishis. I also now know where the tall, skinny man who used to sell *In Dublin* outside Bewley's for many years is these days. He is dropping his daughter to school. It is more Celtic twilight than economic dawn.

Lios na nÓg wears sandals; Scoil Bhríde docksiders. While Scoil Bhríde is Minister for Justice territory, Lios na nÓg is non-conformist. Scoil Bhríde is Catholic and comes under the authority of the Archbishop of Dublin. Lios na nÓg is non-denominational and is run by a patrons' trust. Despite their differences, both schools are part of a greater movement: they are both Hibernian and Cosmopolitan.

The Lios na nÓg children all have little sweatshirts with happy suns smiling out from them and they skip into class. The atmosphere is very calm. Everything is good taste, far seeing and right on. The school has its own compost heap, all paper is recycled and a fatwa has been declared on Capri-suns and fizzy drinks. The greener lunch guidelines are enforced. Everyone is tolerant and well-educated.

This is where the HiCos send their children to school. It is the breeding ground for the new sophisticated elite.

Chapter 21
HiCo Habits

The HiCo has emerged from a deep appreciation of our culture and a well-intentioned quest for authenticity in a sea of the generic. For some, it is the end point of a journey that began with the question, 'Who are we?' For others, it is the logical next step in the development of the Irish national identity. For yet more, it is the rational culmination of their experiences as plugged-in workers, travellers, emigrants. Whether it is through their language, their children's schools or their own behaviour, this new, cultured elite are discerning, tasteful and authentic. HiCo-ism is that badge of uniqueness. However, for others it is plain snobbery and class indignation at what they see as a new oligarchy of the Decklanders. This is Marx's dictatorship of the proletariat — something that the HiCos vaguely supported when in college — except this time the proletariat has large overdrafts, credit cards and cheque books.

Recently an uber-HiCo friend of mine declared as a serious put-down to someone, 'He's a poor man with money.' This was a reference to a lack of taste, refinement and a voracious appetite for things, possessions, cars, second houses and stuff. This type of snobbery is central to the type of HiCo who does not like the fact that his status has been eroded by the great credit liberation.

Some of the old educated class feels threatened. They are being priced out of the housing market, being asked to up their game, being forced to open their clubs and bars to a new aspirant class that seems to have endless cash and limitless credit and that wants everything and wants it now. So a significant part of the HiCo counter-revolution is status protection. In an Expectocracy, where access to credit has meant that money no longer signifies class, other attributes such as appreciation, education, achievement, knowledge, subtle understanding and cultivation become badges of class distinction.

One of the easiest places to see this dichotomy between the cultured HiCo and the merely rich Decklander, is to examine the TV page of a newspaper any day. Television schedulers are a scientific bunch. They know who is watching, they understand the tastes and aspirations of their viewers and they tailor their programmes accordingly. With this in mind, look at the programme offerings of our two newest TV stations. TG4 is the ultimate HiCo product. Contrast that with TV3, the station that targets Deckland. In this case we are looking at the Sunday night (this is a random one in June of 2005) which is a big night for TV schedulers. At 7 pm TG4, after a news bulletin, kicks off with a history documentary about refugees from the Spanish Civil War and how they were tragically handed over by the French to the Gestapo and ended up in an Austrian concentration camp. TV3 shows repeats of 'Emmerdale' followed by repeats of 'Coronation Street'. TG4 goes straight for the high-brow history market which will only appeal to those with a grasp of the significance of both the Spanish Civil War and French collaboration with the Germans. In short, a cosmopolitan story narrated in Irish with English subtitles. TV3 goes straight for the bought-in English soap about a village in Yorkshire, followed by 'Coronation Street' set in Manchester. Both are repeats. This little story is not trying to make a value judgment about the merits of each offering, it just serves to underscore the marked difference in the target market of both stations and how that drives scheduling.

It is important to appreciate that nothing which comes out of English popular culture, from its football, tabloids, soap operas and DIY-fixated, Mondeo-driving, bitter-drinking middle Englanders, is remotely HiCo. French, Spanish or Italian popular culture is elevated by a judicious selection of those tasteful coffee blends, olive oils, wine or cuts of chorizo from authentic tapas bars. This type of stuff sends the HiCos into delirium. The continent is authentic and exotic. England is far too familiar to move the HiCo. That said, London is an exception because, with some justification, the HiCo sees London not as the capital of England but as a global metropolis on our doorstep. It is our Manhattan, and the HiCo can fly over grubby England physically, mentally and psychologically to get there. On the other hand, Decklanders refer to English football teams as 'we' — as in two Decklanders chatting about Arsenal versus Man United at the water cooler — 'We beat you last week.' Typically the Decklanders with the season tickets to Old Trafford are considerably wealthier than the HiCos on their cheap Ryanair flight to Stansted. The division is not in the wallet, rather in the mind.

At 8 pm TG4 shows an eclectic domestically produced comedy series followed by a piece of pure Hibernia — the actor and Irish language enthusiast Niall Tóibín reminiscing about his summer holidays in Youghal. By this stage TV3 is on to 'Heartbeat'. By 9 pm, TG4 has the ultimate HiCo programme, a cosmopolitan travel programme in Irish from Taiwan about its struggle with mainland China. Meanwhile, TV3 goes for an US romantic comedy. At 9.30 TG4 is back to a classic HiCo area, environmental degradation, with an investigative documentary tracing the environmental damage of Ireland's blight of illegal dumping. It is nearly midnight before TV3 broadcasts a programme with even an Irish accent on it. Meanwhile, the HiCo offering on TG4 has been given an authentic voice of the world through Irish eyes.

The television schedulers have achieved their aims. The educated elite have been armed with social ammunition that they can use at their next dinner party, while the Decklanders are sorted for a Corrie chat around the water cooler tomorrow morning.

The HiCo counter-revolution against the tyranny of sameness, generic products and mass production has thrown up some of the most unlikely heroes, such as recent deification of the common grocer. This is a serious turnaround when you think about how far the grocer has come in the past hundred years.

A century ago in W.B. Yeats's 'September 1913', the grocer was the enemy of romantic, dreamy Ireland. Yeats, 'the Arch-Poet', as Roy Foster referred to him in his biography, was the spiritual leader of the Gaelic League — the 20th-century version of today's HiCos. He saw the grabbing, greasy fingers of the small shopkeepers in Dublin as the enemy of Romantic Ireland.

> *What need you, being come to sense,*
> *But fumble in a greasy till*

And add the halfpence to the pence
And prayer to shivering prayer, until
You have dried the marrow from the bone?
For men were born to pray and save:
Romantic Ireland's dead and gone,
It's with O'Leary in the grave.

The grocer of middle Ireland, the local gombeen in a dirty white coat, overcharging for hairy bacon, butter and bread, is the stuff of Patrick McCabe novels. He was the solid backbone of the Fianna Fáil Party, the Legion of Mary and the local GAA club. In fact, the grocer was so central to the GAA that to this day the two umpires who determine whether a point is a score or a wide are dressed as 1950s grocers, replete with white coat and cap. Extraordinary. The grocer/umpire could be counted on. He was solid; he would uphold the establishment and keep the faith. For years, he was the face of the Irish petit bourgeoisie, the gombeen of the Irish centre-right. As such, the grocer/umpire was the enemy of the left-wing liberals, trade unionists, revolutionaries, romantic poets and anti-clerical radicals.

But go to any well-heeled town or suburb of the country and you will see the grocer up there with the farmers' marketers as the darling of the left and the environmental movement. The deification of the local grocer, in the eyes of the right-on anti-globalisation movement, has been quite remarkable. The grocer is seen as a local bulwark against the evils of hypermarkets and Tesco.

Overnight, the grocer has gone from gombeen zero to revolutionary hero. He will protect us against nasty E numbers, processed food and battery eggs. The grocer is now the heartbeat of the trendy upmarket suburbs with his rosemary and thyme sour dough organic breads and his flu-buster smoothies. Fashionably socially-aware mummies make a beeline for his organic carrots, his probiotic yoghurt and his Omega 3 oils. In short, the grocer is the home of a quiet, anti-Big Business counter-revolution. When Naomi Klein talks about consumers exercising their sovereignty and punishing Big Business, she is acting as a cheer leader for the new grocer.

So what has happened? Why would Yeats now see the local independent grocer as an ally rather than an enemy? Well it appears that two major economic factors have forced the change. On the one hand, the Tesco, Lidl and Dunnes of this world have slashed margins so much that local grocers could not survive against the out-of-town superstores, so they have had to change their game. The smarter ones have gone upmarket, offering quality at a price, rather than quantity at a discount.

By going upmarket and sourcing produce locally, the grocer has positioned himself nicely on the crest of a wellness wave. Many HiCos are now much more concerned about what they are putting in their bodies and the exercise they take. There has been a spiritual revolution where being right in the head and soul is seen by many as linked to what food we eat. This has led to a fusion where food meets apothecary, physical well-being and spiritual calm. The new uber-grocer is at that crossroads, open for business.

Our local uber-grocer sells Fair-trade coffee called Tiki, which goes under the slogan 'Tiki Coffee — A great deal for everyone without exploiting people or the planet'. Now what right-minded, socially conscious individual could fail to buy that stuff? Its package tells the story of the Indian farmers in Honduras who harvest the beans (sure that's a dinner party conversation all on its own). Remember, for the HiCo, shopping is political.

This is where the transition year on the Machu Picchu trail in Latin America meets Noam Chomsky — a delicious sweet spot for the bottom line of the new grocer. Because of this form of 'statement shopping', the grocer has become the darling of the right-on brigade. Editorials in liberal newspapers eulogise him, and academic conferences put him on their panels ahead of published social scientists. He is the new suburban Trotsky, the vanguard of a new counter-revolution. Who would've guessed that Romantic Ireland's 21st-century hero would be the once fumbling, greasy-tilled grocer? Not even O'Leary — but then again, he's dead and gone. But that's the great blurring for you. What was once Hibernian is now Cosmopolitan, what was once Cosmopolitan is now Hibernian.

Chapter 22

How to Spot a HiCo

HiCo SPIRITUAL
One of the major battle grounds of the 1980s and 1990s was the secular versus religious one. Many on the cosmopolitan side were fundamentalist secularists, while the Hibernian establishment on the Catholic Church side was composed of men who had trained in the pre-Vatican Two era and as such were traditional Catholics. So it's hardly surprising that both sides knocked the heads off each other.

In the end, the cosmopolitans probably had their most decisive victory of the era. Church attendance has fallen rapidly and the fall in vocations has been even more dramatic. In 1980, the year of the Pope's Children, there was not only a surge in fornication but also in abstinence, with 608 vocations. In 2004, that had plummeted to fifty-four; last year 428 clergy died and forty-seven left. So the clerical balance sheet is pointing to extinction in a matter of decades. We should be becoming like Denmark, a secular hinterland where religion is seen as a quaint reminder of the past, a bit like Raleigh Choppers.

But that has not happened. In the face of this secular onslaught, the very Hibernian concept of organised religion has not gone away, you know. In fact, there are signs that the decline in religious observance has halted. At least 2 million people still go to Mass every Sunday which is a huge figure. The Church itself is fighting back aggressively and employing tactics that are straight out of a cosmopolitan marketing course.

In May 2005, younger parishioners at St Andrew's Church in Westland Row, Dublin decided to market their Saturday night Mass by taking out ads in a Catholic newspaper, emailing potential customers and distributing fliers. They worked on the Mass itself, making it more interactive, and used text updates to remind people. The numbers attending jumped tenfold. The Church have now also issued a new stripped-down version of the catechism, which sounds more like a New-Age self-help book than the tenets of the Church. But it is working. Welcome to the leaner, stripped-down, authentic Catholic Church. Get ready for the ultimate New-Age religious vehicle — the Catholic Church unplugged.

And for those who still can't stomach the host, religion is also mutating into a fusion of New-Age spiritualism, mixed with Catholic ritual. This is another delicious reversal, because the early Irish Christians expropriated pagan rituals such as Christmas, Easter and Hallowe'en and moulded them into the calendar to make the new monotheistic religion more palatable to the formerly multi-theistic pagans. Now the reverse is happening. Formerly strict Christian rituals are being customised with New-Age pagan and spiritual sensibilities to make them more acceptable.

In reaction to consumerism and its ubiquity, many people are reaching for the spiritual. Indeed, many committed secularists of the 1980s who fought the Church on moral grounds are now so dismayed with the mass materialism of the Denver rather than Denmark outcome that they are urging people to 'tiptoe back to the churches'. A political need for some sort of anchor is melding with a spiritual yearning for some class of answer and is leading to a revival of religion in Ireland in various incarnations. In fact, to be religious in 2006 is to be radical, because it involves a rejection of all that is mainstream.

One of the most striking developments has been the rekindling of interest in a mystical, symbolic Catholicism. Let's call this Kabbalist Catholicism. It was evidenced in 2001 by the extraordinary turn-out of over a quarter of the country to see the travelling relics of St Thérèse of Lisieux. No-one was expecting such a turn-out. In fact, many of the Church's senior figures were against the idea. Kabbalist Catholicism is new in Ireland. Probably because we have so few canonised saints, we don't do relics. We do devotions but not relics. Yet this turn-out did suggest that something is overlooked by the secular commentariat and it is a yearning on the part of many to connect. Last year, there was record attendance at the Galway Novena, with crowds of 15,000 per day over nine days. Pilgrimages to Lough Derg and Croagh Patrick are both up significantly and the clergy are reporting that attendance at all sorts of ceremonies from throat blessing to Ash Wednesday ashes is also increasing, having plummeted dramatically in the late 1990s.

The return to religion entails nothing as simple as going to Mass in a large 1950s cathedral. No Whitehall church on a Sunday morning for the HiCo, but you do see him half way up Carrauntoohill at an open-air Mass celebrating the sunrise on Easter Sunday. Kabbalist Catholicism is a wonderful communion of Catholic ritual with spiritual New-Ageism where symbols are crucial.

Apart from the thoroughly pagan Macnas-led parade, the biggest exhibition in Dublin on St Patrick's Day 2005 was 'The Irish International Mind, Body, Spirit & Healing Arts Festival' held at the RDS. This was a spirituality fest of Newgrange proportions. The first workshop called 'Dancing the Rainbow' explored the 'power of dance to heal, create, replenish and energise ... deepen(ing) your ability to commune with your own creative process and saboteur within ... allowing you to discover the chakra system which is operating in your body and your life'. Take a HiCo who has been flirting around with the meaning of life for some time. Although he still holds down a job in the IFSC, he is becoming disillusioned. He wants more, he wants a connection and to be spiritually self-improved. And although he says he wants to be a better human, really he wants to feel better about himself. He'll take a voyage of self-discovery to put himself on a higher evolutionary plane to those tatty, materialist Decklanders who queue for tall lattes in Mocha Deck. It takes cultivation to stop and spend some time finding yourself. Ultimately, all this self engrossment becomes compulsive. The original spiritual self-absorption is said to be complemented by the physical so he takes up yoga, tai chi and falun dafa. This is the Jackie Skelly workout for people with bookshelves.

He glides through the crowds, barefoot, to a stall called 'Living with Crystal — An introduction to Atlantean Healing' which explores the 'diverse ways that you can work and live with crystal elixirs to create a healing sanctuary room. The crystals act as tools to assist healing for ourselves and sacred earth'. A little later, full of sanctity, he avoids the free lecture on 'Amma the hugging Saint' and relaxes with 'Celtic singer Seamus Byrne' who provides moments of 'self-exploration and inner healing to allow you to learn self-appreciation'. This is all about releasing the God within and all you need is a bit of self-appreciation, self-love. You are now walking on water, on a different level to the rest of the Pope's Children. You are a HiCo.

HiCos ON HOLLIERS

As well as spirituality, how a HiCo holidays reveals his elevated status. In 1980, the year the Pope's Children were born, the Dead Kennedys, a punk outfit from San Francisco, released 'Holidays in Cambodia'. Back then the whole idea of going to Cambodia without being armed to the teeth was terrifying. Today, twenty-five years later, HiCos, armed only with credit cards, are teeming into the former Killing Fields for a spot of genocide tourism.

HiCos don't really go on holiday, they travel. Deckland does holidays. The word 'holiday' suggests that there is a distinct break from what they do normally. It is time off, away from the mundane and the normal. Going on holidays implies that you are captured, tethered to some sort of existence which is not you. People who take holidays are wage slaves who live in two distinct worlds — the work world and the holiday world. For the HiCo, no such distinction exists. Travelling is an extension of their personalities, another experience that they have thought about for some time, merely a change of venue.

The most important attribute travelling can have is uniqueness. To be a proper HiCo your destination has to be undiscovered, untouched, unspoiled, unsullied, innocent, authentic, real and remote. This is the lexicon of the HiCo traveller. It helps if the country has a GDP less than Leitrim, for this allows them to trade 'value stories'. For the youngest HiCos, these tend to take the following form. Two HiCos meet at a bus station in Tanzania, unshaven, with their Guatemalan hemp rucksack slung over their shoulders. The look is distinct. You can spot it a mile off — 'gap year grunge'. And because they are both Paddies, unlike taciturn German travellers, they are actually dying for a chat and are the only white people for 200 miles, but they snub each other at first. (Never be too keen — a HiCo golden rule.) Eventually there's a tentative nod, and gap year BES introduces himself to gap year 3rd law, UCC.

– *Travelling on your own?*

– *Yep, more interesting.*

– *Staying where?*

– *You know how it is. Anywhere you can lie down, bush village mainly.*

– *There's a good hostel 50 miles north — €2 a night with shower.*

– *Fuck, that's a bit pricey.*

– *There's a trucker stop back about thirty miles — €1.30 a night.*

– *I was in one, a bit grotty, up in Malawi — amazing €0.78 per night.*

– *Jesus, that's not bad — there's one in Mozambique, a bit of a shack, full of hookers, demobbed soldiers and animals, not too far from that place, €0.25 per night, with breakfast.*

This conversation, as well as clearly driving the African tourism industry to the wall, reveals three essential HiCo traveller attributes. The first is deprivation chic. Extreme privation is absolutely vital for the real HiCo traveller. The traveller Misery Index ticks away all the time and the more adversity, the better. (Older HiCos and their families now go camping either to France or at home, where the elements are challenging. Remote cottages without electricity or running water score highly. Adversity on holiday is crucial so swimming in icy waters and cooking home-made sausages on a primitive fire, all rate highly. Not for them five hotels in Dubai even though they can afford them. That would be so Deckland.) The second theme the above chat reveals is the casual way in which both get in the fact that they have travelled overland through a variety of countries that are described nonchalantly as 'up the road' or 'further on'. This reveals adventure, time and curiosity. These 'gap year grungers' are on the road and determined to stake out their territory. They are independent travellers, on their own with a smugly self-deprecating but highly accomplished 'smidgen of Swahili'. The third aspect is proximity to danger. Demobbed militia and hookers in Africa: how much more authentic can you get from the lads who wouldn't go near Mayfield even in the daytime? For the HiCo the whiff of sulphur is another indispensable part of the trip.

Within a few minutes you will hear them eulogise the fantastic simplicity of the African and the fact that we are strangling him with our debt policies. The next minute they will be haggling with the African over the price of a beer, ensuring in their own little way that he stays firmly rooted in the Third World and reinforcing the view that all whites eventually screw the Africans.

Brooks noted in *Bobos in Paradise* that for the Bobo, holidays have to be hard work. When you look at the HiCo you see exactly the same traits. HiCos go to ramp up, focus, absorb and achieve, which leads to bizarre behaviour such as total kayaking — another HiCo favourite. It is difficult, dangerous and can only be done somewhere remote. In fact anything with 'total' preceding it will do. Total trekking, total diving, total white water rafting, total mountain biking and total heli-skiing are all quintessentially HiCo. Other extreme HiCos just run, pushing themselves through ultra-marathons for kicks. But it's all self-definitional, pushing you, the unique individual, through five pain barriers — what achievement.

Away from the thrills, spills and belly aches, the HiCo traveller also loves the complete opposite to adventure. He loves quiet simplicity — something that would prompt a Decklander to ask for his cash back. He is positively ecstatic at the sight of the unsophisticated Mediterranean boat builder, with plane in hand, working and reworking methodically the brow of an upturned fishing boat in an unspoilt dry dock on an inaccessible island off Croatia. He is a sucker for wizened farmers, gnarled old widows in black, savant peasants, and cheap putrid local brandy or home-made rosehip *loza* that even the old lads gave up drinking years ago. Whitewashed village squares, quiet and still at midday with a stopped clock and a bell tower, send him into rapture. Lazy stray cats, stretching in the sun, are a sign of simple sophistication, the type of erudition that we have lost. You see him immersed in the local culture, dancing and folklore. The 'rustic' locals regard him as a bit of an eejit, sitting out in the square when they are inside glued to WWF on the satellite dish that their son sent from Germany.

HiCo SHOPPING TROLLEYS
Shopping habits are a dead giveaway. Deckland is new, big and branded. HiCos' shopping rule is discernment. Items must have a story, be full of detail and, given the choice, small rather than large. Shopping is also political.

Money is never mentioned in HiCo shopping conversations. That is not to say that Deckland shops are cheap. They are not. Take Brown Thomas. This shop is uber-Deckland. No HiCo shops there. Everything from their Fendi bags to their Louis Vuitton luggage and Hermes range, screams brands, commercial sales forces and mass globalised advertising. These are the most inauthentic of products, and a poor HiCo would point out that rich Decklanders do not understand that there is a big difference between things being scarce due to expense and things being scarce due to taste. The HiCo will snub BTS for Jenny Vander any day. Unlike upscale Decklanders, HiCos do not queue for exclusive offerings, put their names on lists or go to opening days where they have to be seen to buy things.

It is not that HiCos do not spend money, they do, but not on luxuries. The crucial aspect of HiCo shopping is that they buy the same stuff as their parents bought in the 1980s, just better quality stuff. In contrast, Decklanders are constantly striving to buy gear that their parents could never have afforded, like Mercedes cars, top-of-the-range gadgets and jet skis. HiCos buy old cars, classics maybe, but definitely not 'top of the range'. In fact, they could not tell you what the 'range' starts at.

When they spend fortunes, it is on items that are regarded as functional. So, for example, speedboats are out but €800 Gaggia espresso machines are absolutely fine. Tag Heur watches are out, handmade Celtic torc brooches are in. But in general the golden rule of the HiCo shopper is one-downmanship. The shinier and newer anything is, the less valuable it is in the HiCo mind. They go to garden centres to buy new old-looking things. Recently, I heard three HiCo yummymummies gasp at a beautiful restoration furniture garden bench. It was faded, with the paint slightly stripped and peeling. This was bought flat packed but it looked ancient, and the older it looks, the better it is. This particularly goes for furniture. Anything that does not wash, heat or freeze needs to be original. If it washes, then it can be the most expensive wet room in the country. If it cools, it can be a Neff double-doored monster fridge or if it heats it can be a Cuisinière double oven with five monster burners.

A good place to observe this carry-on is in Avoca Handweavers. Even in the car park you can feel the tranquillity, the tastefulness and thoughtfulness. You are in a blissful place, where nothing is cheap and nasty; you are in Avoca heaven — the place where yummy HiCo mummies go when they die. The car park is an Arcadian vision of suburbia — all willows, beeches and strategically placed wheelbarrows replete with hoes, gloves, spades and shears. Endeavour is something the HiCos love, and no better place to be flexing your toned upper arms than in a Hibernian garden. The place is coming down with cream rhododendron.

Inside, it is a canvas of home-made ice cream shades, pinks, creams and pale greens. The entire proposition — from the books as you walk in, to the gourmet delicatessen, the giant redwood salad servers, the straw shopping bags, the puffed cereal seed and the Duchy Original organic ginger biscuits — is retro chic. Retro brings you back to an earlier age when only the leisured rich ate outside. It catapults you backwards to the last days of the old Hibernians. For those who dream, Avoca can transform suburban Shankill to a *fin de siècle* Lough Dan fishing lodge, full of wise gillies and grainy black and white photos of men who look like Tom Crean, holding up freshly caught out-sized river trout. Avoca is lifestyle. The rich, calm, refined lifestyle that is me. I am, like the distressed wood dresser in Avoca's entrance hall, elegantly understated.

Yummy flicks through the books which greet her on the way in. There are large, lovingly photographed volumes on the interiors of Hip Hotels, Houses on the Water or The Best Spa Hotels in Scandinavia. In HiCo-land, Scandinavia is always cool. Montenegro can come and go, so too can Tuscany, but Scandinavia and New England are timeless — all walnut timbers, boatyards and simple Shaker lines. Calvinist cool endures. It's funny how the full-on hedonistic Irish feel almost guiltily attracted to the furniture of the most mind-numbingly dull, sober people. It is as if we hope that having fallen, red-eyed drunk, into our handmade beds, the sober Shaker design will rub off on us and we will wake up with beautifully dilated clear blue Scandinavian eyes, no hangover, the sharp fjord air circulating, gently blowing the cobwebs out of the triple-glazed wood shutters into the silver birch forest beyond.

Everything here is nourishing and rustic, from the sea-salt and brown sugar face scrub and the rolls of chunky twine, to the hedgerow jam which conjures up images of those innocent, hazy August days and freckled children in country lanes, picking ripe blackberries from thorny brambles. Avoca is nostalgia squared.

'I PREFER THEIR EARLIER STUFF'
There are few better outlets for a HiCo to display his discerning good taste than via music. HiCo music snobbery is a particular affliction that can unfortunately strike the very young as well as the mature

adult. Picture the scene. A group arrives in your flat after the pub. The place is a bit raucous. That great Irish sound of bottles in bags clanking off each other echoes up the stairs. We are all in good form. One or two are a bit messy, but they'll be asleep on the sofa in no time. Life is good and there's a good three hours left in us before, one by one, we start to either slur or snore or both. Then you spot him — the HiCo music snob. He is the one forensically going through your CD collection. He picks out each CD and either approves or sneers. To the HiCo music snob your music collection reveals more about you than your job, friends or house. Music speaks volumes.

Music snobbery is an extreme HiCo affliction and it begins at an early age. By the time the HiCo music snob is in his thirties, the burden is so heavy it weighs on everything he does. So what you play is either given the thumbs down or if it hits the snob's radar screen, it is automatically de-legitimised by the immortal, 'I preferred their earlier stuff.' There are a couple of basic rules of HiCo music snobbery. The first is that all cheap, commercial music is disdained with a couple of notable exceptions that must be known. The second is that, like all HiCo appreciations, there has to be depth in your music knowledge. Therefore, no detail is too minute, all stories are valuable and above all, music is a function of knowledge and knowledge is a function of time, cultivation and taste.

Exceptions on the commercial music front could be a band like Abba who are uber-Deckland by virtue of being on the top of the office Christmas party play-list. In fact, anything played at the office party is Deckland by definition. Yet Abba are what the chin-strokers (HiCo musosnobs are frequently called chin-strokers even by other HiCo musosnobs) call perfect pop and are admired due to the 'complexity of their musical arrangements'. In the past year or so, Beyonce has been elevated into the perfect pop genre on the basis of the 'production values' — a music phrase which is both inclusive and exclusive at the same time. When you know what it means it is exacting, when you don't know what it means then, frankly, we shouldn't be having this conversation. Of the acts clogging up the airwaves these days, poor old Coldplay are the most despised by the HiCo musosnobs, perhaps because they try so hard. I suppose there are some things that even a Fair-trade wrist band can't protect you from.

Only a HiCo musosnob with an encyclopaedic knowledge of pop can sustain a 'perfect pop' assertion. It is a high-risk strategy which can either leave the HiCo on peerless ground or culminate in humiliation if the right references, associations and influences are not cited precisely. Precision is essential. A typical 'perfect pop' subject is Brian Wilson of the Beach Boys. Their album *Pet Sounds* is often cited as the best pop record of all time. His story, demons and influences, from his self-imposed exile to his corrosive relationship with his Dad and his years of mental control by his svengali Dr Eugene Landy, right through to his influence on the *Sgt Peppers* album, are taken as a given. To go one better, the HiCo musosnob must compare Abba's musical arrangements with those of the Beach Boys, make confident connections and move on.

Unlike Deckland, which is happy with whatever 98FM foists on it, the musosnob searches out the exotic. There's a lot of music so there's a lot to know. He must therefore major in something. And the more the record labels produce, the more obscure the HiCo musosnob's taste becomes. What about Brazilian post-punk? Sorry mate, just re-issued on Soul Jazz records. Surely 1960s Ethiopian Jazz music is exotic? Again apologies, mate, Donal Dineen bashes that out. And as the HiCo seeks out his discriminating high ground with a blizzard of facts, factoid and folklore, there is always the possibility of a gauche *faux-pas* such as volunteering a fact that is so well-known to the other HiCos as to make the speaker look foolish. This can knock an aspiring HiCo musosnob back years.

Speaking of back years, every generation of musonobs has their 'I saw U2 in the Dandelion Market' moment. This is a derivative of the 'I prefer their earlier stuff' approach. Seeing a band at their earliest incarnation infers leadership, independence and hipness. You are ahead of the crowd. It is a card-marking exercise, signalling how far ahead of the posse you are. For the Pope's Children, this is particularly acute in the area of dance music. HiCo dance snobs will be able to locate themselves in the Ormond printworks in the summer of '93, or the Asylum or Sides, or for the edgy lads the Slaughter House off Gardiner Street well before its gentrification. The mere utterance of these names is loosely translated as, 'Jesus, you're a real Johnny come lately to the scene, squire.'

For the HiCo musosnob, knowing at least a bit, and often a lot about genres considered alien by Decklanders is a given. In the areas of dance music they started having the same tastes, but they have diverged massively. No self-respecting HiCo musosnob would ever consider anything that would blare out of the back of a souped-up Nissan Micra.

Chapter 23

HiCos Dine In

THE FARMERS' MARKET

HiCos love farmers' markets. What could be more Hibernian than local, bulbous organic carrots, their roots still matted with treacly, gooey earth? If Patrick Kavanagh did groceries, he'd do farmers' markets. This is authentic and, like all good HiCo appreciations, farmers' markets tell a native story. And what could be more cosmopolitan than the world music duo playing the panpipes in the background or the fine selection of Moroccan tahini on show? Farmers' markets are the perfect HiCo fusion. The appreciation of the local Hibernian, melded with an intimate knowledge of the foreign, cosmopolitan and its sensibilities, trends and tastes, reveals your depth of culture, travel and learning as well as your rootedness.

The morning is sunny. The smell of real organic lamb sausage wafts in the air. There are children everywhere. Children are another HiCo giveaway. Deckland children are tethered to their young brother's uber-stroller as their mother negotiates the one-way escalator system of the Dundrum centre. HiCos kids on the other hand run around everywhere, freely expressing themselves. Deckland children are bribed, HiCo kids are consulted. (Indeed, a HiCo giveaway is loads of kids. As the size of the Deckland family has shrunk, the HiCo family has expanded. In the recent past, the poor had large families. Today, it is the opposite. The large HiCo family is a statement. It signals wealth spent in the right way. It signals coherence, continuity and solid traditional values in a disposable world.)

HiCo mummy and daughter, Naoise (sometimes in an effort to find the most esoteric Irish name to show their Hibernian colours they get the name gender wrong), are at the Sheridan's cheese counter in matching tie-dye T-shirts and sling-over bags. You can spot a HiCo mummy a mile off. She is the one who weighs less than her daughter. Mummy is a member of Sheridan's cheese club which Daddy bought for her, along with the weekend at Babbington House, for Mother's Day. It cost just €450 per year and for mummy it's an ideal way to try new cheeses and cheeses at their peak each month. Sheridan's choose three cheeses for their ripeness and seasonality and send them to her along with tasting notes on each of the cheeses. Mummy finds this excellent for dinner parties. There's such a glut of Gubeen these days, it's lovely to have something different. The tasting notes are so handy. She can just speed-read them when she pops into the kitchen to get more wine (ABC of course) and no-one at the table knows the difference when she announces nonchalantly, but exactly, that the finish is barkey, reminiscent of a young Gruyère. All they see is mummy effortlessly breezing through a twenty-guest dinner party, the HiCo hostess feeding, watering, entertaining and informing. You get extra points of course if you know the cheesemonger. As with bottled water, proximity to source is an indicator of HiCo purity.

In the Hico food hierarchy, nothing substitutes traceability. If you are close to the source, you are close to God. It reveals you to be connected. Process, or the journey, is so important for HiCos, particularly when the opposite of the wholesome organic process is barbarity and industrial farming which is devoid of any journey, story or narrative other than cruelty. By flippantly mentioning that Charlie the cheesemonger had dropped by that afternoon, mummy is ensuring that she is part of the inner sanctum. She is organic by association.

While the children are having their faces painted by a Crusty juggler on the make, HiCo mummy, who has been going through a Levantine period, loiters at the Lebanese food stall. Why not have a Lebanese starter tonight? Maybe some Bekaa Valley aubergine tahini, leavened bread from the Lebanese bakery with just a drop of Lebanese extra virgin olive oil? She will keep the bottle on the table so that her guests notice the rather exotic — and these days vaguely subversive — Arabic script. After all, anyone can have Andalusian extra virgin, but

Arabic, now that shows true inquiry. It will also allow her and her HiCo mates to naturally segue from palate to politics.

Every Levantine morsel will facilitate another educated point on Sunni versus Shia, Druze versus Maronite Christian, French versus Arabic, Crusaders versus Saladin, Sabra and Chatila, Muslim versus Jew, leading to round condemnation of Ariel Sharon with the 'no-one here is anti-semitic but' caveat. And like all good HiCos, the similarities with Ireland and the Hibernian angle could not be avoided for long. HiCos are infused with a sense of Irish exceptionalism. This allows them to wallow in the twilight world of victim equivalence and means that no other races' misfortunes are too awful not to be compared with something that happened here. Yes, you had your Srebrenica, we too had Balbriggan. You had the Holocaust, we had the Famine. You had your KGB, we had the B Specials. You had Sharpeville, we had Bloody Sunday, and so on. Empathy with the oppressed is very much part of the package. This is what parity of esteem really means.

Yet there are signs of change as HiCos are torn between our traditional post-colonial sympathy for the little guy and our new 'tell it like it is' booming economy convention which urges the downtrodden to 'get over it', safe in the knowledge that economics and property rights will solve everything. As a result of doing better out of globalisation than any other group in Ireland, the HiCos are more inclined than others to take the US line on the financial reality of geo-political problems, yet because they have immersed themselves in Hibernianism, they are more acutely aware of the overriding cultural Armageddon that comes with colonialism — even colonialism of the mind.

Mummy moves on deeper into the market, trying to avoid the legions of pregnant women gathered in huddles loudly discussing grape-seed perineum oil. She brushes past the proud, self-satisfied, camera-carrying young fathers with their expressive kids on their shoulders. She wishes she'd left her yoga mat in the car. It is difficult to carry it and her Lebanese booty around but to produce a plastic bag here would be akin to loading up a semi-automatic assault rifle at the children's birthday party. So she carries on uncomfortably. She passes the crêperie selling organic banana and fresh cream crêpes, past the Gallic kitchen with its gluten-free, free-range chicken pie. She is half-tempted to order in the entire dinner from a website, but that would be cheating. She sidesteps the double-heighted Jane stroller and moves on down towards the organic asparagus stand which is just beside the musicians who are perched on the old bandstand.

The musicians are a duet — a middle-aged Irish pair in full early 1970s mufti, sandals, kaftans, bangles, a pair of multi-coloured woolly hats. He has a fetchingly symmetrical full beard and pony-tail thing going on, while she simply has too many layers. He plays mandolin and Inca panpipes while she sings, rattles and shakes her tambourine. Their repertoire is exclusively Latin American folk songs. Despite being more Bolton Street than Bolivia, these Hibernian *hombres bolitas* are tapping into a deep Latin American fixation which often characterises HiCos. Our Saturday afternoon panpipers touch the HiCo sweet spot where magic realism meets Celtic mysticism, where liberation theology meets liberation struggle, where their bearded freedom fighters and our bearded freedom fighters hold their Kalashnikovs aloft, side by side, on the great global mural of the oppressed.

Mummy is now juggling organic asparagus and fennel in different individually wrapped, recycled, acid-free paper bags. The light drizzle is making these as useful as a cheap umbrella in a blizzard. As they begin to disintegrate, mummy seizes her opportunity to move up the organic shopper hierarchy. She commandeers a crate from the fit-looking mushroom seller. Nothing can be more authentic than walking around the farmers' market with a real wooden crate, overflowing with freshness, apples with carbuncles and carrots with soil clinging to roots. And speaking of roots, she has to have lots of root vegetables. She can almost feel her kids' eyesight getting better with all that untapped Vitamin A in front of her. Shopping has to be hard work, you must break sweat, flex your sinewy yogi-strengthened upper-body muscles. The closer you are physically to actually pulling the stuff out of the toiled earth the better. She could even be mistaken for a farmer restocking her stall from her Renault 5 van.

Other stall-holders smile benevolently at this picture of sized 8 maternal responsibility. Seeing this vision of petite pluckiness weighed down by a crate of goodness, the friendly pure-apple-juice seller from Lusk offers her a drop of his special Orchard Glow to fortify her on her journey as if she were Jesus at the 8th station. Mummy takes a free leaflet celebrating the end of oil. Organic farmers are messianic about the end of oil and are looking forward to it expectantly like Orthodox Jews waiting for the Messiah. When it arrives, they will be vindicated and their war against McDonald's, Tesco, cars, trucks, central heating, additives and tree fellers will be won. What they fail to appreciate is that the end of oil will give their sworn enemy, Sellafield, the biggest shot in the arm since Einstein split the atom.

Mummy gathers up Naoise and her friends, Lir and Setanta, and off they go, home to prepare dinner for twenty.

HiCos DINE IN

Walking into HiCo homes these days is like entering 'Doctor Who's Tardis. You open the unassuming door of a small Victorian terraced house in Portobello and you are greeted not by the pokey hall that was there twelve months ago, with a banister straight in front of you and a small room in on the right. Oh no. You step into a triple-heighted vaulted glass atrium, with a steel and aluminium suspended mezzanine. Giant Ivy hangs down from the mezzanine, making the place feel like a mini-Amazon or an ecologically friendly crèche in Rathmines. To your right where the Child of Prague used to be, there is a life-sized Samurai, shielding a tasteful (if there can be such a thing) water feature. The lights are on the floor rather than in the ceiling. All the brick is exposed and the expertly-varnished distressed hardwood floors are darkly stained. There is one enormous, intricately designed and suitably faded rug from somewhere in Rugistan that the hosts picked up on their silk trail trek last year. Apart from that there is just emptiness. There is no evidence of human habitation whatsoever. The music is mellow Groove Armada.

This is an altar to HiCo taste. All the materials are Hibernian, the Liscannor slate floor, the Monaghan brick and the Dublin Victorian reclaimed sash windows, but all the designs are cosmopolitan, from the New York-style entrance to the Asian theme. Although these people are well travelled, they appreciate the value of local material and tradition.

You pass the sandblasted glass loo on your right. It is divided into three zones. (Zonal peeing, now that's a new one to me.) The loo is enclosed, there are twin washbasins and a black slate 'Rainmaker' power shower which doubles as a stand-up steam cabin. Maybe you can get your fake tan sprayed on in there: by the look of it, the hostess has. Through the double-doors is a computer-controlled steam bath and multi-jet whirlpool shower, its discrete ergonomic shape masking more controls than the 'Starship Enterprise'. You half-expect to see Lieutenant Uhura manning it. 'It can massage' gushes the hostess. (For €8,000 I was expecting something more intimate.) The heated towel rails are polished chrome. Everything is sleek. There is no evidence of toothpaste stains, facial stubble or even shampoo for that matter. The soap is organic Provençal olive oil. There is one photo, original of course, a large and stunning angry sea at the Forty Foot, bringing you back to Dublin.

The kitchen is vast. The architect has pushed the house back about half a mile or so it seems. The only problem is that he was also obviously engaged by your neighbour directly behind who has done the same, so you are now eyeballing each other from over the wall like a pair of World War I trench snipers, both separated by two identical 'yours and mine' Japanese gardens replete with €3,000 bonsai plants that are ideally sized for stray Jack Russells to relieve themselves on.

You could land the government jet and a fully loaded Black Hawk in the kitchen. Like an airport, there are up-lighters everywhere, giving it a runway feel. Right down the central elevation there is a raised black Connemara marble 'island' which is both a workstation and the family HQ. It is the nerve centre of the HiCo house. This is where the relaxed, sophisticated HiCo family hang out, working, creating, stretching, chatting, gossiping and stuffing children's schoolbags with little advisory notes for the *múinteoir*.

Many years ago really posh people never went near the kitchens. Kitchens were for the help. In the 1970s the kitchen was seen as an instrument of oppression. Irish 1970s feminists were urging their sisters to get out of the kitchen, to break the chains to the kitchen sink. Back then, there was no more telling picture of female servitude than the suburban kitchen-bound Cork housewives in the 1975 margarine ad telling us that 'they'd never know it wasn't butter'. Yet in a stunning reversal, today's overqualified daughters of the liberation movement are kitchen devotees. So too are their husbands, or rather, partners. Their kitchens define them.

The better educated you are, the more time you spend in the kitchen. And the more time you spend in the kitchen, the skinnier you are. And the skinnier you are, the more you know about food. In fact, food is central to the HiCo experience and, crucially, they use local Hibernian products to make foreign cosmopolitan dishes.

When they are not eating it or talking about it, they are cooking it, roasting it, baking it, grilling it, frying it, poaching it, blanching it, flambéing it, marinating it, braising it, sautéing it, searing it, mashing it, whisking it, spit-roasting it, toasting it, coddling it, scrambling it, savouring it, tasting it, gobbling it, wolfing it, nibbling it, picking at it, and ultimately, of course, washing it down. For HiCos, food marks you out. It distinguishes the truly educated from the merely rich. Any Flash Harry can spend half the GDP of Ghana in Guilbauds, but to emulate and surpass Guilbaud himself in your own kitchen, now that's a sign of real cultivation. Slow cooking takes time. In HiCo Ireland, money is cheap, experience and achievement expensive, and you need both to sit twenty for dinner. The select twenty will be seated at an enormous teak table which is located just in front of the full-width, 60-ft, ceiling-to-floor, glass sliding door which leads out into a little bit of Kyoto in Dublin 8.

The kitchen wall has one or two original pieces of art. HiCos like to patronise and are keen to be seen as latter-day Medicis. It is not good enough to appreciate the art, knowing the artist puts you in a different league. It locates you close to the nexus of creativity. In this way, the HiCo can signal to all that although she might be number two at a multinational company selling loo cleaner, immersed in the spreadsheet twilight of listed corporations, she is at heart a Hibernian dreamer, an iconoclast, a Celtic soul rebel. Decklanders buy but HiCos commission. On long weekends Decklanders go to the Curragh, HiCos go to the Kerlin. Decklanders chip into a syndicate to buy racehorses, HiCos buy a friend's artwork.

Just under one of the oil paintings, to the left of the jar of artichoke hearts, is her system with its variable dual-zone temperature controls. Wine is central to the HiCo. She is the blind-wine-tasting champion of the group and, although keen to underplay her knowledge, she is a bit fussy until the end of the night when, like every Paddy, she will neck a bottle of paint thinners if she has to.

At the far end of the kitchen where the cooking plonk is kept is the super-sized fridge — the doors of which are wider than the front doors of most suburban semi-Ds. Have you noticed the size of these things? Irish families are getting smaller, yet our fridges are getting bigger. The double pull-out doors open up an entrance atrium which has a helpful map on the inside to tell you where you are and what you are looking for. You half expect a frozen mammoth to appear out of the chilly depths. This is a monument to frigidity — the *haute couture* of fridges. Replete with ice machine and adjustable control so that if just freezing isn't cold enough for you, you can do your bit for the environment and counteract the melting polar ice caps by setting it to minus 39. The mirrored glass is so thick it could stop a hail of bullets from another deranged, jealous HiCo. Don't scoff: fridge envy is alive and well in HiColand.

Fridge envy, Belfast-sink envy, garden feature envy, these are all characteristics of modern Ireland. In the past people used to marvel at someone's achievements, now it is their kitchens. More than ever before, people are judged by their houses. How many times have you heard stories of people saying they fell in love with the house? Well they did not; they fell in love with the image, the lifestyle and the dream that the house signifies. If the house is old they are sensitive restoration types, it speaks of bookshelves and Agas, terracotta-tiled kitchen floors and gravel driveways. If their dream is a modern Bauhaus structure full of sleek lines, angle and light, they are clean, scientific, rational, ecological, thoroughly modern types. They are future dreamers, rather than nostalgists. They are the type of people who use the word streetscape without blushing.

This a by-product of the housing boom. Nothing socially grades better than where you live. If you are a rich HiCo it is pretty straight-forward, you just trade-up until it is time to trade down. On the way up you act as patron, mentor and of course sucker. You are the image industry's walking ATM machine. Everyone loves your wallet, from glossy magazine editor, to gallery curator to bespoke furniture maker. You're invited to openings, private viewings and first nights. You are on the top table at charity dos. Your house is not just a place where you live, it is an entertaining space, it is a hotel, bar, boudoir and restaurant all in one. It radiates you and you reflect in it.

But if like many HiCos, for example academics, journalists and critics, you are not loaded, the condition rather than the size of your house is crucial. It allows you to distinguish yourself from the rest. For the HiCos who have fallen behind financially, small details allow them to balance the status scales against their richer university mates. So you will have financially strapped HiCos, living in little artisan cottages or former council houses in good areas that are a monument to good taste. They prefer the gritty authenticity of 1930s corporation estates to the sanitised blandness of bigger 1970s semi-Ds. They love their salt-of-the-earth neighbours but they won't send their children to the local national school, preferring the Educate Together school up the road. Their gardens pay homage to horticultural learning. Theirs is the front garden with the honeysuckle, foxgloves, hollyhocks, dahlias, alium, Cordylines, purple millet, ornamental grasses and gardeners' gloves lying by the gate. The rooms, though small, will display period rather than modern furniture. Sofas are frowned upon. Their book shelves (very important) will be overflowing. Book shelves are always on display, never hidden away. These are the adult version of a teenage record collection and reveal what the HiCo wants you to know about her. The poorer HiCo is neurotic about status. Her intelligence is always on display. Remember, being a HiCo is a state of mind more than anything else.

The guests sit down. The seating plan has been tricky. There are slightly too many architects and it's not for nothing that the collective noun for architects is a 'jealousy'. And as we are just days after the RIAI annual awards, the unsuccessful are bristling, the winners preening. The overall winner is seated innocuously down on the left beside the publisher. She is beautiful, sassy, successful and the subject of much back-biting and envy in this most notoriously bitchy profession. Those years in New York have given Zoë an unmistakable SoHo look, which she wears with ease.

She had converted to architecture following a highly successful period as an investment banker. Zoë was an uncompromising opportunist. When banking was booming she was at the centre of things. When building was buoyant she was again at the centre of it.

Zoë was Miss Lower West Side. She hung out in Alphabet City, in the hip bars of SoHo and the Village. She arrived back in 1992 and she managed to spoof a job on Wall Street, initially in the back office, sorting out trades, making sure that the traders were actually telling the bosses what they were up to. She knew the honours Maths would come in handy at some stage.

She was twenty, just out of UCG and life was good. The first time she strutted across the giant Lehman Brothers trading floor, the ticker tape signalling prices across the globe, analysts screeching stock recommendations down the 'hoot and holler' and traders roaring at green screens, she knew this is where she wanted to be — as far away from Athlone as possible and not another Irish person in sight.

Zoë rapidly moved up from back to front office and using her Leaving Cert Spanish she moved onto the Latin American distressed debt trading team in 1994.

If her uncle Brian, a Jesuit priest and liberation theologian working in the slums of Santiago in Chile, knew what she was doing he would kill her. He campaigned with Bono and Bob Geldof for Third-World debt relief and here was his favourite niece, making a fortune trading the very debts he wanted written off. After all, she became fluent in Spanish — the revolutionary language of Alliende, Borges, Benedetti, Castro and Guevara — by listening to her mother's brother when he came home during the summers in the early 1980s following his expulsion from Pinochet's Chile. He took a special teacher's interest in Zoë's Inter Cert Spanish, practised her pronunciation. He persuaded her to speak like a Latino, not Castilian. This casual fluency enabled her to negotiate with bankrupt holders of Latin American debt from Bogotá to Buenos Aires. She fast became one of the big swinging dicks of the trading floor, revered and feared in equal measure. Her bonus in 1996 was close to $1 million.

Zoë partied hard, staying up all night. In contrast to most of Wall Street who lived on the Upper East Side or in Rye, Connecticut, she lived in a small but very hip brownstone apartment on Charles Street in the West village. Zoë didn't come to New York to live in Foxrock. She was a regular in the local bars. She had a tab in Jerry's in Prince Street and SoHo and Fellinis come to think of it. Her aversion to the Irish in New York was uniform. So she avoided the trendy self-congratulatory Sin-é set on St Marks as much as the 'Ra heads in Sunnyside. On a good night, and she had many, she would helter-skelter towards the slummier bars — Max Fish and Milanos — and progress on to Save the Robots. Not only was Yamamoto on Spring Street her favourite boutique but she had a series of Japanese boyfriends. She began to get interested in art following a corporate opening at the Gagosian Gallery on Mercer Street.

Here she met Nestor, a beautiful Argentinean architect. Soon she decided that architecture was for her too and in the same way as her timing was impeccable in the Latin American bond boom, Zoë timed her move into architecture just as New York and Ireland were about to experience a property boom like no other. She returned to Ireland eight years later with a reputation for brilliant residential makeovers, lots of her own lolly and offices in New York and Dublin. Her RIAI award-winning design was for a multi-millionaire's summer house in Galway. In her acceptance speech she ascribed her main influences to be

Japanese cantilevered engineering and Connemara metamorphic rock.

Someone, I can't remember who, once said that the people who made the most money from the Gold Rush were not the speculators but the guys who supplied them with picks and shovels. Likewise in Ireland, the people who have made most money from the Land Rush are not so much the builders — although many have done very well — but those who have sold them services such as architects, designers and gardeners. These are the people at the top of the HiCo tree. We are living in the world of the celebrity architect and interiors guru. TV programmes are given over to bathroom makeovers, trading up and making the most of your outside spaces. This is not confined to HiCos. In fact, it is here that HiCos and Decklanders interact most. Deckland hires HiCo tastes and HiCos take Deckland's money.

In Deckland, the ultimate aim of the average worker is to turn the suburban home into an entertainment plaza. Our suburbs are on steroids, with massive extensions, huge decks, hyper-kitchens and super-sized bathrooms being grafted on to perfectly respectable houses every day.

Irish houses are experiencing the architectural equivalent of boob jobs, Botox, liposuction and collagen lips all at once — and are fast becoming bricks and mortar versions of Jackie Stallone. Interior design is the new plastic surgery and HiCo architects move from house to house wielding the taste scalpel, a little extension here, the annexation of a room there. What about knocking that wall down and opening up the space to the light? 'Nip/tuck' Irish style would be shot on a building site rather than a clinic. There is little point getting a boob job unless you are going to display your cleavage. Likewise, if you have just spent over €100,000 on a kitchen extension, you are going to have to show it off. Years ago, the difference between ordinary people and the really posh was that the posh entertained at home. Ordinary folk went out to meet friends on neutral territory — maybe a bar, maybe a hotel grill-room, but never at home. Home was designed to cope with the family and to function. It was where you could sleep, eat and watch TV; it wasn't in competition with the pub, restaurant or café.

Today, why go out to some communal trough with the rest of the neds when you can luxuriate in the refined privacy of your own home and show off your mosaic-tiled bathroom?

As the property market continues to roar, the stamp duty

implications of trading up mean that many people stay put and release the equity they would have spent on stamp duty on a compensatory mania for home improvement. This could be called DIY therapy. (This syndrome is particularly acute in suburban yummy-mummies, and explains why it is probably easier to pull in Woodies than Lillies.)

So we are seeing a huge increase in dinner parties and all the while the architect's star rises, while other HiCos such as academics, actors, critics and journalists see their status fall.

A recent survey by Spar reveals that 55% of Dubliners said that they were entertaining more at home in the past six months. The corresponding figures were 60% for Cork, 45% for Galway and a staggering 88% and 81% for those polled in Waterford and Limerick respectively.

After spiralling costs, the survey found that showing off their home was the main reason for the switch. Also, most people are doing their entertaining on a Friday — the traditional post-work night for going to the pub. A statistic that won't surprise us, but would shock most continentals, is that 87% of us admit to drinking a bottle or more of wine per person on a Friday night.

Who is benefiting? As in the Gold Rush, those who provide the high-end services are making out like bandits. As well as our good-taste gurus, wine sellers with their appreciation of Cosmopolitan tastes tailored for the Hibernian palate are doing a roaring trade. There has been a surge in wine buying. While pub sales of beer are falling, the wine market in Ireland has grown between 10% and 15% a year since 1999. Off-licences are thriving. In Britain, the split between on and off-trade sales of wine is 50:50. In Ireland, it is 15:85.

Back at the dinner table, the wine is flowing. On cue, the Lebanese tahini prompts informed discussions on the Middle East, Al Quaeda and our need to better understand Muslim culture. The HiCos are at home, on their own territory arguing the toss. They fuse their Cosmopolitan learning with their Hibernian sensibilities, part old Irish empathy with the colonised and downtrodden, part *Time* Magazine editorial with both eyes firmly on the global bottom line. Their view is a hybrid — half Seán MacBride, half Henry Kissinger. Their hearts are with the occupied Arabs, their heads with the price of oil and the global economy. They are the first Irish generation to see both sides of the international coin.

Chapter 24
The Returned HiCo

The maze of little streets wedged between Mountjoy prison, the canal and the North Circular Road are jammed by 2.30 pm — well before throw-in. Every time he thinks he sees a space up the road, HiCo man discovers, on pulling up, that the residents have erected a makeshift roadblock — usually a pair of beer crates with a plank suspended on them or an old 'Bargaintown' dresser and a few wrecked chairs. But the message is simple: 'Park here, mate, and your car will not be in the same condition when you come back.' This is 'neighbourhood watch' north-inner-city style. Can you blame the locals? They are penned in every Sunday in the summer as thousands pay homage at Hibernian Ireland's greatest and most glittering shrine — Croker.

Eventually, he manages to squeeze the Volvo in between two Fiat Ducados advertising McMahon's double-glazing of St Ignatius Road. A pair of Chinese teenagers are busy stuffing letterboxes with Domino's Pizzas fliers.

He gets the kids ready and snaps at the youngest who threatens to pee in the car. He is feeling a bit the worse for wear. He was entertaining Israeli property clients the night before at the atrocious two-all draw in Lansdowne. Luckily the corporate hospitality boxes in the East Stand are quite plush and the booze flowed. But all that talk about financing the merger and whether it should be bond or equity-driven began to drag. He wondered whether these blokes ever just chilled out and had a few scoops. The business blather was made all the more tedious by the result. By their own admission, Jews don't do sport, yet we managed to forfeit a two-nil lead. Anyway, the clients wanted to talk business and as his Irish consortium needed its block of shares, he had to make the running.

As usual the only buyers of property in central Europe are the Irish and the only sellers are the Israelis, who got in there first in the early 1990s when we were still working the sites in London — sites which we have subsequently bought. Indeed, the Irish are the biggest foreign investors in UK property. Back in mainland Europe, it feels like the Jews and the Paddies are the only two entrepreneurial races in Europe, book-ending a bureaucratic continent of nay-sayers. The foyer of the Marriott in Budapest any morning is a cross between the Wailing Wall and the Burlo on All-Ireland night — a sea of skull caps and GAA jerseys, hunkered down, talking yields, financing, covenants, speaking the language of property — the lexicon of corporate Ireland. At this stage he doesn't know whether it's better to be a buyer or a seller. But given that they are going to sell on to other Irish investors after they have taken their turn, he just wants the deal done.

As usual with HiCo man the conversation flows. He is a good talker and an even better listener, something he learned in London. He noticed how the English can negotiate without saying anything. Initially this used to make him nervous. We Irish don't like silences. But, when he realised that this was tactical, he quite enjoyed listening. People like others who listen to them and in his experience — despite all the talk about being hard-nosed, competitive and ball-breaking — negotiation is also about being liked. It helps if you realise most victories are pyrrhic and remember that the old Hibernian concept of the luck penny, leaving something on the table for the next fellow, is as valid on a Wall Street trading floor as it is at a West Kerry horse fair.

And this is the HiCo's secret — he puts everyone at ease. He is as comfortable on Hill 16 as in the boardroom of Goldman Sachs. He is cosmopolitan when he has to be and will happily discuss Alan Greenspan, the rise of religion in American politics and the dilemma for a Europe that wants to protect a 35-hour week when Indian engineers are prepared to work a 35-hour day!

But as a true Hibernian he has a deep understanding of what Dublin versus Meath means. Sport may be the common denominator of the corporate world, but the Augusta Masters, the Australian Open and corporate softball can never make him feel like this. He fuses the local with the international effortlessly. His is the first Irish professional elite to celebrate the Hibernian culture from which the GAA springs as well as the international business culture which pays for the corporate boxes at the new Hogan Stand. Traditionally a love of GAA went hand in hand with a suite of other much greener, narrower views including support for economic isolationism. It is not that these have gone away, but they have simply changed to reflect the facts on the ground.

For example, years ago a regular at a bar called Fallon's in the Coombe went by the name of R.E.M. This did not stand for rapid eye movement nor was he a devotee of Michael Stipe. R.E.M. referred to his three pet hates — Rangers, England and Meath. This is no longer an essential combination. These days you are more likely to have an English navvy on an Irish site, Italian or Spanish Catholics lining out for Rangers and the distinction between where Meath starts and Dublin ends at Croke Park has blurred.

Likewise, the GAA has mutated and many now feel extremely confident about our Hibernian culture without having to define it by what it is not. As a result, at some stage over the past ten years, GAA became chic. It is bankrolled by the biggest brands in the country, Guinness, Bank of Ireland and Vodafone. Even the *Financial Times* — the bastion of Anglo-Saxon financial haughtiness and the world's most globalised newspaper — now carries articles on Gaelic football which it terms 'Europe's most successful indigenous sport'. Its influence is spreading far out from its natural hinterland. Blackrock College, the bastion of south Dublin's rugby-playing elite, fielded a senior Gaelic football team in 2003 for the first time since the 1930s. GAA has had a Hollywood-style makeover and nothing represents the Hibernian revival more than the new Croke Park — the third biggest stadium in Europe.

Compared to Croker, Lansdowne Road is a tip, although the two Swiss cottages in the corners are nicely idiosyncratic. It is rather ironic that the cosmopolitan sports of rugby and soccer are using an old, 1940s stadium and passing off its dilapidation as old Hibernian charm existing only in fairytale Ireland where nothing works, nothing is on time, nothing is urgent and sport is Corinthian rather than professional. This conceit is yet more ludicrous when you realise that some of the journeymen togging out in green, who could barely trap a bag of cement, take home €20,000 a week. In contrast, the quintessentially Hibernian GAA has the ultimate cosmopolitan stadium with a capacity of 80,000 — yet the players are amateurs.

With 800,000 members in the country, the GAA is arguably one of the most important organisations in the state and for years it was pure Hibernian — the polar opposite of cosmopolitan Ireland. Its gradual change in recent years, no longer banning foreign sports but opening up Croke Park, not from a position of weakness but from strength, could be the script for the Hibernian/Cosmopolitan fusion of the recent past. A financially much fitter GAA — the richest sporting organisation in the country — is giving its downtrodden cosmopolitan cousins a helping hand in their time of need. Such generosity comes from self-confidence.

On his way to the ground, HiCo man passes young lads drinking on the banks of the canal and on towards the legions of Dubs outside Quinns on the top of Clonliffe Road, poured into their Arnott's strips, kissing the three castles for the RTÉ cameras. The atmosphere is electric and unthreatening. This is a family affair. There are as many little girls in Meath jerseys as lads in the blue of the city.

In the old days, before the spread of the BabyBelt, Dubs and Culchies knew who was who. But in recent years that has blurred. I noticed this recently playing a soccer match in Ratoath, Co. Meath. The accents of those on the Ratoath team perplexed me. Half the lads had the pure Meath *patois*, dropping the 'r's everywhere. The other half were unadulterated Cabra. I was in the BabyBelt — home of the Kells Angels — where Dubs become Culchies and Culchies become Dubs. I was playing against the new breed, the first generation commuters, the Dulchies.

Dulchies and their kids were very much in evidence as they walked down to the Canal End. A father in neutral colours with a daughter in full Dubs rig-out was holding hands with her younger brother who was head to toe in the green and yellow of the Royal County. The family's divided loyalties reflect the bad planning, traffic, ten-hour crèches and multinationals that symbolise the Dulchies, or Royal Blues as they are called in Navan.

When HiCo man reaches the vertiginous upper echelons of the Canal End, the true feat of engineering becomes evident. The stadium is magnificent, but as impressive as the view and the pitch are the loos. There are loads of them and they are spotless. You see, the HiCo is a very practical dreamer which probably comes from reading all those design magazines. He learned the value of organisation, planning and bathroom sensibilities while in the US. He is part of the first generation of Irishmen who worries about the length of queues in women's loos. The GAA's concern about women's loos places them on a higher evolutionary plane than their soccer and rugby alickadoo counterparts. However, despite being at the top of their game, the GAA still cannot prevent the great new Irish speculation craze from infecting the Holy Grail. Companies that bought the corporate boxes for a song in the 1990s are now taking advantage of the huge upsurge in corporate entertainment in the full-on nation and are flogging them off to the highest bidder for the All-Ireland finals. This is the sporting equivalent of the property auctions page.

Looking down at his two children, Eamonn and Niamh, he never really thought he would be here. For all those years in London and New York he had avoided the Tayto-crisps shillelagh-ism of Setanta Sports, Irish bars and Kilburn High Road. There were of course some notable exceptions to this rule, Giant's stadium, any Pogues gig and 'The Crying Game' to name a few. But his Irishness had been ambiguous. Like all his peers he left here more than he was pushed. He wanted a brownstone in New York, a roof-terrace in Primrose Hill, an apartment in the Marais. He wanted a lifestyle commensurate with his education. He got out to imbibe possibilities, to embrace cosmopolitanism and to achieve a career that Ireland could never offer. In fact, for most of the 1990s he was a self-loathing Irishman and the last thing he was going to do was create a home-from-home in London, New York or Paris. Like many of our 200,000 returned emigrants he is much better educated than those who stayed behind. A recent study[1] which looked at the oldest of the Pope's Children, who were born in 1970 and who did their Leaving Cert in 1987, reveals that only 5% of those who left school without a qualification went abroad; 15% of those with Junior or Leaving Cert emigrated, while one in every four who had a degree emigrated between 1986 and 1992. This was an extraordinary brain drain. More than any other class, Ireland exported a professional elite. This was an emigrant aristocracy.

The new 'wild geese' embraced the cosmopolitan rules of the world's mega-cities and many have put this ease down to being Irish — but crucially being Irish in the mind and not in the ghetto. These were Hibernian individuals rather than part of the Irish tribe. In the past the Irish succeeded in the US by being one united ethnic bloc. The

HiCo emigrant eschewed all this; in fact he avoided it like the plague. He regarded Irishness as a personality trait and in this world of cosmopolitan meritocracies, office politics, promotions and head-hunters, this personal edge was much more valuable than any security the ethnic tribe could offer. Being Irish was an attribute, like being a two-footed footballer.[2]

The recent emigrant combines Irish charm and American drive. But as well as that he still maintains a European perspective. He was much more cynical about corporate life than the typical American or English corporate NCO. And throughout the 1990s, many thousands invented a romantic, surreal Ireland without the squinting windows, lack of opportunities and begrudgery — almost an Ireland without the Irish!

The HiCo migrant accredited to his invented Ireland everything that was the opposite of London or New York. Where the metropolitans were busy, Ireland was slow; where they were greedy, Ireland was generous; where New Yorkers were unfriendly, Dubliners were salt of the earth; where London was polluted, Ireland was clean, and so on. Ireland became for him and many others an invented place which offered an idyllic lifestyle. It was jammed with wholesome things like communities, families and schools with dedicated teachers, houses with gardens and sagacious savants who knew how to put life before work. It was their escape valve from the obsessive compulsive behaviour of corporate America.

So although the HiCo individuals avoided being part of the Irish gang — no Fields of Athenry or pints of Harp on 3rd Avenue for them — they created an Irish nirvana in their heads to which they would escape when the time to settle down came. Theirs was an imagined Ireland: what Seamus Heaney describes 'as a mythologically grounded and emotionally contoured island that belongs in art time, in story time, in the continuous presence of a common unthinking, memory life'.[3] They were codding themselves. Ireland was home and home meant nostalgia. They were *à la carte* Irishmen, Hibernian dreamers and cosmopolitan realists.

The game begins. The Dubs start badly and immediately are four points down. Gradually they claw themselves back. The stadium is an explosion of colour. The Hill is a sea of blue — flags, hats, fliers and San Siro-esque flares. The stands are green and yellow, banners are unfurled, and children hurl unspeakable abuse at the ref who is a dot on the horizon. The noise builds. Every challenge is replayed, recounted and reworked by the aficionados. The Dubs win well in the end.

Out on the street, in the looming shade of the enormous stand, a huge Guinness poster symbolically obscures the entrance to Holy Cross College and the Archbishop's Palace. There was a time when the Bishop himself threw the ball in. No longer. The GAA has ditched the Bishop and brought back the pagans. The scene is dark and menacing, a muscular young Setanta faces a half dog/half wolf — the Cú of Chulainn. The skies blacken over. The scene is the Bog of Allen in winter. But we know the script: the youthful hero tosses the *sliotar* high, draws back, muscles bulging, pulls, makes perfect full-on contact. The ash almost smashes on impact, the *sliotar* bullets through the air straight down the throat of the snarling hound, who keels over. The legend of Cuchulainn is born. 'Guinness, live the legend' states the ad. In the words of historian Roy Foster, there we go again, 'telling tales and making it up in Ireland'.[4]

The returned emigrant heads for home, the legend still alive. He and his tribe have come home — these Hibernian Cosmopolitan nomads, the elite of the Pope's Children, with their own ideas of how things should be done and how the country should be run.

Notes

Chapter 1 (pages 3–13)

1. (a) 'The World in 2005', *The Economist* Intelligence Unit's 'Quality of Life Index', found at *http://www.economist.com/media/pdf/QUALITY_OF _LIFE.pdf*

   (b) World Database of Happiness, Happiness in Nations, Rank Report 2004, *Average happiness in 90 nations 1990–2000*, found at *http://www2.eur.nl/fsw/research/happiness/index.htm*. The Irish link is *http://www2.eur.nl/fsw/research/happiness/hap_nat/reports/Nreport/ NA21.HTM*.

2. *Obesity: the policy challenges*, Report of the National Taskforce on Obesity, 2005.

3. R. Mahony and C. O'Herlihy, *Thirty Year Trends in a Large Irish Obstetric Cohort* http://www.imj.ie/news_detail.php?nNewsId=2612&nVolId=100)

4. Household Budget Survey 2003, Central Statistics Office.

5. Durex Global Sex Survey 2004, available at *http://www.durex.com/cm/gss2004result.pdf*.

6. Ibid.

7. *http://www.finfacts.com/Private/bestprice/alcoholdrinkconsumptionprices europe.htm*.

8. Submission to Commission on Liquor Licensing prepared by ASTI, February 2001: 'There is much concern about underage drinking and its associated problems. Recent research in Ireland indicated that underage drinking is a serious problem. A survey of 15–16 year olds reveals that 33% are drinking alcohol and of these under the legal age of 18 years almost 44% were current drinkers' (Health Promotion Unit, Southern Health Board). 'A study among a sample of 14–15 year olds in Dublin revealed that 59% drink sometimes, 16% drink regularly and 20% engage in binge drinking (Brinkly, Fitzgerald & Greene 1999). Studies in the 80s showed that alcohol use among young people in Ireland was moderate compared to other countries (Morgan & Gimble 1989). However, international research indicates that young people in Ireland have the highest rates of alcohol use in Europe and the highest rates of binge drinking. The average

age at which young people start drinking is 11.6 years. Recent research in Ireland among members of the Teachers Union of Ireland regarding their attitudes to underage drinking confirms that underage drinking is a serious problem. Teachers believe that over 60% of 13 to 18 year olds have tried alcohol, 80% of 16 to 17 year old and 60% of 16 to 17 year olds drink regularly, at least on a weekly basis.'

9. The UN Office on Drugs and Crime (UNODC), 'Ecstasy and Amphetamines Global Survey 2003'. Source: 'UK and Ireland in top three of Ecstasy use', *DrugScope*, 29–30 September 2003: 'A new study released by the UN shows that Australia, the UK and Ireland lead the figures in ecstasy usage. The first ever UN global survey on ecstasy and amphetamines reveals increased production, trafficking and use of synthetic drugs worldwide. Numbers using these drugs now exceed the numbers of cocaine and heroin users combined. In the last decade, seizures of amphetamine-type stimulants (ATS) have risen from about 4 tons to almost 40 tons. Estimated production has reached more than 500 tons a year. More than 40 million people have used ATS in the past year. The UNODC survey points to the global nature of the ATS problem. Unlike cocaine and heroin, whose production is limited by geography and climate, ATS can be produced anywhere. Currently, production is mainly in Europe and North America. Tables showing the annual prevalence of ATS use in selected countries reveal that Australia has the highest percentage of its population using ecstasy (2.9%), followed by Ireland (2.4%) and the UK (2.2).' The full UN report can be downloaded at:

　　www.unodc.org/unodc/publications/report_ats_2003-09-23_1.html.

10. *Quality of Life in Ireland: A Study for Guinness UDV Ireland*, Amárach Consulting, March 2002.

11. Working Long Hours and Taking Work Home in Evening and Weekends. A survey by O2, published 13 April 2005: *www.o2.ie*.

12. Various CSO documents back up this assertion. For example, see *http://www.cso.ie/newsevents/documents/vstats.pdf*.

13. From *http://www.checkout.ie/MarketProfile.asp?ID=106*

As consumers become more aware of ingredients in soft drinks, Red Bull maintains that it is supplementing these traditional sugary sodas with more beneficial drinks for a 'pick-me-up' product such as Red Bull. According to the company, the product has been scientifically developed for times of increased concentration or mental and physical strain. Being aware of a growing demand by weight-conscious consumers, it successfully launched a sugar-free option into the market in 2003, Red Bull

Sugarfree, which it says offers the same great energy boost with only eight calories. Energy and water are the only growth categories in the soft drinks sector, which reflects this shift in consumer lifestyles. Combined, they now equate to 28% of the total soft drink market. Red Bull believes it is the global market leader with a worldwide share of 60% of the energy drink category.

14. Central Statistics Office, National Income Statistics, 2005.
15. J. Kelly and A. Reilly, 'Credit card debt in Ireland: recent trends', in *Quarterly Bulletin 1*, Irish Central Bank, 2005.
16. 17.18% of all food consumed in the United States is done so in a car. Estimates for Ireland suggest that we are not far behind as evidenced by the explosive growth in convenience food shopping, hot food counters and the emergence of Breakfast Roll Man. According to David Whelan, Musgrave Group national sales manager for the food service sector, Ireland is following the US in its food consumption habits; he expects that by 2010, 50% of all food consumed in Ireland will be done away from the home, which will double the food service market. The food-on-the-run culture has been labelled 'dashboard dining'; 27% of all food consumed in Ireland is eaten away from the home, compared to just over 30% in the UK. *www.checkout.ie* 2004.

Chapter 2 (pages 14–27)

1. *Geographical perspective on outputs from Census 2002*, National Institute for Regional and Statistical Analysis, NUI Maynooth, 2005.
2. As above, based on 2002 Census.
3. R. Florida, 'Global Creative Class Index', in *The Fight of the Creative Class: The New Global Competition for Talent*.
4. European Commission, *The Social Situation in Europe*, Eurostat 2004, p. 69.
5. Ibid, p. 35.
6. *Quality of Life in Ireland: A Study for Guinness UDV Ireland*, Amárach Consulting, March 2002.
7. 'Society and Political Culture', in J. Coakley and M. Gallagher, eds, *Politics in the Republic of Ireland*, 3rd ed., London, Routledge.
8. 'The World in 2005', *The Economist* Intelligence Unit's 'Quality of Life Index'.
9. University of Michigan, *World Values Survey*, statistics generated on *www.nationmaster.com*.
10. European Commission, *The Social Situation in Europe*, Eurostat 2004.

11. European Commission, *The Social Situation in Europe*, Eurostat 2004, p. 147.

12. University of Michigan, *World Values Survey*, statistics generated on *www.nationmaster.com*.

13. *Quality of Life in Ireland: A Study for Guinness UDV Ireland*, Amárach Consulting, 2002.

14. European Commission, *The Social Situation in Europe*, Eurostat 2004, p. 69.

15. Ibid, p. 127.

16. Ibid, p. 69.

17. Ibid, p. 128.

18. European Foundation for the Improvement of Living and Working Conditions, *Quality of Life in Europe*, May 2004.

19. Ibid.

20. *Consumer Trendwatch Wave 2*, Amárach Consulting 2005.

Chapter 3 (pages 28–35)

1. Author's calculations from CSO population statistics 1970–80, *www.cso.ie*.

2. T. Fahey: 'Trends in Irish Fertility Rates in Comparative Perspective', *Economic and Social Review*, vol. 32, no. 2, July 2001.

3. Ibid, p. 159.

4. Ibid, p. 164.

5. Ibid, p. 174.

6. Birth, Death and Marriage statistics, CSO 2005, *www.cso.ie*.

7. *www.euroactive.com*.

8. *www.nationmaster.com*.

Chapter 4 (pages 36–51)

1. R. Mahony and C. O'Herlihy, *Thirty Year Trends in a Large Irish Obstetric Cohort*, http://www.imj.ie/news_detail.php?nNewsId=2612&nVolId=100)

2. *Obesity: the policy challenges*, Report of the National Taskforce on Obesity, 2005.

3. *National Perinatal Statistics*, Report compiled by the Economic and Social Research Institute, 2005.

4. J. Walsh, R. Foley and M. Charlton, 'Travel to Work Patterns', in *Geographical Perspectives on Census 2002*, National Institute for Regional and Statistical Analysis, NUI Maynooth, 2005.

5. *Geographical Perspectives on Census 2002*. National Institute for Regional and Statistical Analysis, NUI Maynooth, 2005.

6. R. Mahony and C. O'Herlihy, *Thirty Year Trends in a Large Irish Obstetric Cohort*, http://www.imj.ie/news_detail.php?nNewsId=2612&nVolId=100).

7. *Geographical Perspectives on Census 2002*, National Institute for Regional and Statistical Analysis, NUI Maynooth, 2005.

8. *National Perinatal Statistics*, Report compiled by the Economic and Social Research Institute, 2005.

9. Ibid.

10. Ibid.

11. 'Irish Babies' Names', Central Statistics Office, 2004.

12. Steven D. Levitt and Stephen J. Dubner, *Freakonomics: A Rogue Economist Explores the Hidden Side of Nearly Everything*.

13. Ibid.

Chapter 5 (pages 52–67)

1. AC Nielsen Ratings for 2004 and 2005. See *www.medialive.ie*.

2. *The Irish Times*, 15 November 2003.

3. Central Statistics Office, 2005, Irish Labour Force Office.

4. For more on this device, see the Achieveatron in David Brookes, *On Paradise Drive: How We Live Now (And Always Have) in the Future Tense*.

Chapter 6 (pages 68–76)

1. *The Economist*, June 2005.

Chapter 7 (pages 77–96)

1. For those interested in the historical role of religion in economics, see David S. Landes, *The Wealth and Poverty of Nations: Why Some are So Rich and Some So Poor*.

Chapter 8 (pages 97–114)

1. C. Kindleberger, *Manias, Panics and Crashes: A History of Financial Crises*, John Wiley & Sons, 4th ed., 2001.

2. Central Bank, Dublin, various reports 1992–2005.

3. Central Bank, Dublin, *Summer 2005 Economic Commentary*.

4. JP Morgan, *Study of Bank Profitability*, 2004, JP Morgan Bank.

5. *The Phoenix*, 20 June 2003.

6. *The Irish Times*, 6 December 2003.

7. *The Irish Times*, 1 October 2003.

8. For an expert discussion on trophy shopping by Japanese developers in

the late 1980s, see Edward Chancellor, *Devil Take the Hindmost: A History of Financial Speculation*.

9. *Geographical Perspectives on Census 2002*, National Institute for Regional and Statistical Analysis, NUI Maynooth, 2005.

Chapter 9 (pages 115–127)

1. For a more rigorous treatment of this historical topic, see Declan Kiberd, *Inventing Ireland: The Literature of the Modern Nation*.

2. Small Firms Association annual report, quoted in 'The Business', RTÉ 29 September 2005.

3. Keanonomics is an Irish version of certain parts of the American labour market, explored in Robert H. Frank and Philip J. Cook, *The Winner-Take-All Society: Why the Few at the Top Get So Much More Than the Rest of Us*.

4. Robert H. Frank and Philip J. Cook, *The Winner-Take-All Society*.

Chapter 10 (pages 128–142)

1. Figures from Central Statistics Office.

2. For more on excessive consumer spending and its impacts on society, see Robert H. Frank, *Luxury Fever: Money and Happiness in an Era of Success*.

3. Woodies Stores.

4. US Department of Transportation Bureau of Travel statistics.

5. Central Statistics Office.

6. Some of the excesses in the *Irish Times* engagement column are small beer in comparison with the *New York Times* Weddings Announcement. For more on the latter, see David Brookes, *Bobos in Paradise: The New Upper Class and How They Got There*.

Chapter 12 (pages 148–155)

1. DIY Declan is an Irish version of a David Brookes character, Patio Man, who features in *On Paradise Drive: How We Live Now (And Always Have) in the Future Tense*.

Chapter 13 (pages 156–164)

1. EU Commission, 'Drivers of productivity growth: an economy-wide and industry level perspective', *EU Economy 2003 Review*, Brussels, November 2003.

Chapter 14 (165–180)

1. Eurobarometer, *Urban Audit Perception Survey*, July 2005, p. 4.

Chapter 15 (pages 181–188)

1. *Obesity: the policy challenges*, Report of the National Taskforce on Obesity, 2005.
2. Amárach Consulting.
3. *Obesity: the policy challenges*, Report of the National Taskforce on Obesity, 2005.
4. Sky Ireland sources.

Chapter 17 (pages 200–214)

1. European Foundation for the Improvement of Living and Working Conditions, *Quality of Life in Europe*, May 2004.
2. *Quality of Life in Ireland: A Study for Guinness UDV Ireland*, Amárach Consulting, 2002.
3. To read more about rejectionists in a global context, see Charles Leadbetter, *Up the Down Escalator: Why the Global Pessimists are Wrong*.
4. For an interesting examination of types like Trade-off Triona, see Desmond Fennell, *Cutting to the Point: Essays and Objections, 1994–2003*.

Chapter 19 (pages 222–231)

1. The idea for the HiCo, although a uniquely Irish character in terms of our own history, culture, language etc., was sparked by David Brookes' Bobos. For a superb treatment of this tribe in the USA — its buying habits, cultural values and foibles — read *Bobos in Paradise: The New Upper Class and How They Got There*.
2. Author's calculation based on Table C of Principal Demographic Results Census 2002 and annual CSO data on estimated returned migrants.

Chapter 24 (pages 269–275)

1. Alan Barrett, 'The Labour Market Characteristics and Labour Market Impacts of Immigrants in Ireland', ESRI, *www.esri.ie*.
2. Mary Corcoran, Department of Sociology, NUI Maynooth: 'Issues of Self Identity and Collective Identity among the Transnational Irish Elite', *Etudes Irlandaises*, Special issue on Ireland/America in the twentieth century, vol. 28, no. 2, Fall 2003.
3. S. Heaney, 'Correspondences: emigrants and inner exiles', in R. Kearney (ed.), *The Irish at Home and Abroad*, Dublin, Wolfhound Press, 1990, p. 23.
4. R.F. Foster, *The Irish Story – Telling Tales and Making It Up in Ireland*, Penguin, 2001.

Bibliography

— Bernstein, Peter L., *Against the Gods: The Remarkable Story of Risk*, Wiley 1998.
— Brookes, David, *Bobos in Paradise: The New Upper Class and How They Got There*, Simon & Schuster 2002.
— Brookes, David, *On Paradise Drive: How We Live Now (And Always Have) in the Future Tense*, Simon & Schuster 2004.
— Cairncross, Frances, *The Death of Distance: How the Communications Revolution Will Change Our Lives*, Harvard Business School Press 1997.
— Chancellor, Edward, *Devil Take the Hindmost: A History of Financial Speculation*, Plume 2000.
— de Boton, Alan, *Status Anxiety*, Penguin 2005.
— Fennell, Desmond, *Cutting to the Point: Essays and Objections, 1994–2003*, The Liffey Press 2003.
— Florida, Richard, *The Rise of the Creative Class: And How It's Transforming Work, Leisure, Community and Everyday Life*, Basic Books 2002.
— Florida, Richard, *The Flight of the Creative Class: The New Global Competition for Talent*, HarperCollins Publishers Inc., New York 2005.
— Foster, Roy, *The Irish Story: Telling Tales and Making It Up in Ireland*, Oxford University Press USA 2004.
— Frank, Robert H., *Luxury Fever: Money and Happiness in an Era of Success*, Princeton University Press 2000.
— Frank, Robert H. and Philip J. Cook, *The Winner-Take-All Society: Why the Few at the Top Get So Much More Than the Rest of Us*, Penguin USA 1996.
— Galbraith, John Kenneth, *The Affluent Society*, Mariner Books 1998.
— Hutton, Will, *The State We're In*, Vintage 1996.
— Kiberd, Declan, *Inventing Ireland: The Literature of the Modern Nation*, Jonathan Cape 1995.
— Krugman, Paul, *The Accidental Theorist: And Other Dispatches from the Dismal Science*, W. W. Norton 1998.
— Krugman, Paul, *The Return of Depression Economics*, W. W. Norton 2000.
— Krugman, Paul, *The Great Unravelling: Losing Our Way in the New Century*, W. W. Norton 2003.

— Landes, David S., *The Wealth and Poverty of Nations: Why Some Are So Rich and Some So Poor*, W. W. Norton 1998.
— Leadbetter, Charles, *Up the Down Escalator: Why the Global Pessimists are Wrong*, Penguin 2002.
— Levitt, Steven D. and Stephen J. Dubner, *Freakonomics: A Rogue Economist Explores the Hidden Side of Nearly Everything*, William Morrow 2005.
— McDonald, Frank, *The Construction of Dublin*, Eblana Editions 2000.

Index

St Patrick's Day, 32, 248
Sallins, Co. Kildare, 157, 162
San Andreas Fault, 91
Sandycove, Co. Dublin, 114
satellite dishes, 182, 187–8
Scandinavia, 97, 169, 220, 253
Schmidt, Conrad, 133
school transport, 11
Schull, Co. Cork, 223
Scoil Bhríde, 233, 237, 239
Scott, Ridley, 150
SDLP, 207
security workers, 183–4
self-employment, 10, 19
Sellafield, 261
Seoige, Gráinne, 224
Serbia, 22–3, 215
Seven Deadly Sins, 200–202, 205
Seven Notion Army, 60
'Sex and the City', 141
sexuality, 4, 5–6
Soft Peppers album, 255
Shamrock Rovers, 117
Shannon airport, 90
shareholder value, 84
Sharon, Ariel, 259
Shaw, George Bernard, 26
Shaw, Robert, 59
Sheridan, Jim, 194
Sheridan's cheese club, 258
shiftwork, 160
Shining Emerald, 197
shopkeepers, 243–5
shoplifting, 199
shopping
    habits, 251–3
    hierarchical, 130–33
Shrek, 235
'shut door panic', 99–100
Sides, 255
Singapore, 90, 95
single parents, 8, 30, 46–7
Sinn Féin, 178, 188, 202, 203, 207, 212
SIPTU, 102
Skelly, Jackie, 248
Skinner, Mike, 26
Sky TV, 187, 213, 215
    dishes, 153, 182, 187–8
Skyland, 177
Slaughter House, 255

Sligo, County, 158
Smith, Adam, 126
Smith, Noel, 109
Smurfit, Michael, 109
snobbery, 19, 109, 241–2
social class, 28, 62, 202–3
    blurring distinctions, 15–18, 54
    HiCos, 241–2
    inequality, 19–27
    middle-class nation, 15–18, 19
    Respectocracy, 117–18
    slipping status, 123–5
social mobility, 14–18, 19, 20–21, 54, 126–7
social policy, 92
Social Situation in Europe, The, 20
Socialist Workers Party, 204
soft drink consumption, 168, 210
Solpadeine, 7
Sony Playstations, 186
South America, 260, 266
South County Dublin Golf Club, 109
sovereignty, 203
Spain, 20, 85, 95, 182, 242
    investment in, 104, 106
Spar, 65, 160, 161, 162, 193, 194, 197, 199, 268
Spears, Britney, 140, 183
speed bumps, 169–71
spending patterns, 11–13
spiritual quest, 246–9
Stakhanov, Aleksei, 156
Stalin, Josef, 79, 166, 221
stamp duty, 267–8
Starmakers, 58–61
Statoil, 161, 162
Stradbally, Co. Laois, 162
Strauss, Franz Joseph, 80
strawberry stalls, 14
Streets, The, 183
Sunday Independent, 23
superstars, 121–2
Sutter, Johann, 211
SUVs, 65, 67, 133–5, 169–70
Swayze, Patrick, 55
Sweden, 92
sweets, 31–2
Switzerland, 78
Swords, Co. Dublin, 177

Visit **www.panmacmillan.com** to read more about all our books and to buy them. You will also find features, author interviews and news of any author events, and you can sign up for e-newsletters so that you're always first to hear about our new releases.